Uncommonly Savage

UNIVERSITY PRESS OF FLORIDA

Florida A&M University, Tallahassee
Florida Atlantic University, Boca Raton
Florida Gulf Coast University, Ft. Myers
Florida International University, Miami
Florida State University, Tallahassee
New College of Florida, Sarasota
University of Central Florida, Orlando
University of Florida, Gainesville
University of North Florida, Jacksonville
University of South Florida, Tampa
University of West Florida, Pensacola

Uncommonly Savage

Civil War and Remembrance in Spain
and the United States

PAUL D. ESCOTT

University Press of Florida
Gainesville · Tallahassee · Tampa · Boca Raton
Pensacola · Orlando · Miami · Jacksonville · Ft. Myers · Sarasota

Copyright 2014 by Paul D. Escott
All rights reserved
Printed in the United States of America on acid-free paper

This book may be available in an electronic edition.

First cloth printing, 2014
First paperback printing, 2019

24 23 22 21 20 19   6 5 4 3 2 1

Library of Congress Cataloging-in-Publication Data
Escott, Paul D., 1947– author.
Uncommonly savage : civil war and remembrance in Spain and the United States / Paul D. Escott.
pages cm
Includes bibliographical references and index.
ISBN 978-0-8130-4941-0 (cloth)
ISBN 978-0-8130-6433-8 (pbk.)
1. Spain—History—Civil War, 1936-1939. 2. United States—History—Civil War, 1861–1865. I. Title.
DP269.E723 2014
946.081—dc23   2013038963

University Press of Florida
2046 NE Waldo Road
Suite 2100
Gainesville, FL 32609
http://upress.ufl.edu

Para Candelas, el gozo de mi vida

Contents

Acknowledgments ix

Introduction 1

1. Background 7

2. Ideology and Memory: The Continuing Battles 44

3. The Past and Political Evolution 107

4. Reconciliation: An End to Civil War? 163

5. Economic Change and the Transformation of Cultural Landscapes 194

Notes 217

Bibliography 247

Index 259

Acknowledgments

I gratefully acknowledge the support and assistance of Wake Forest University for a Reynolds Research Leave and thank the Department of History and the Graduate School Publication Fund for supporting a portion of the costs of publication. In addition, thanks go to the very helpful staff of the Hemeroteca of the Santa María de los Ángeles library of the University of Salamanca, and to Jeffrey Crow, Javier Garrido, Fernando Luis Corral, Simone Caron, and Meredith Babb. Any errors or shortcomings remain my sole responsibility.

Introduction

> The tradition of all the dead generations weighs like a nightmare on the brain of the living.
>
> Karl Marx, *The Eighteenth Brumaire of Louis Napoleon*

All wars leave a legacy of bitterness and hatred, but internecine conflicts create the deepest scars. There is something different about such intrafamilial conflicts. People who once were part of one national family divide, define each other as the hateful enemy, and aim for the jugular. On both sides of an internecine conflict there is a feeling of betrayal, a sense that those who were brothers or sisters have been traitorous to their commitments or to the nation. The resentments fueled by national division often give such wars a particularly ferocious quality. Then the war comes to an end, and, in many cases, the deeply alienated antagonists have to find some way to reunite, to live with each other and the bitter memories of division.

This book is about the problems left by such wars—the historical wounds—and how nations deal with them. Its focus is on the legacy of internecine conflicts, and it explores that subject by comparing two nations that are not often lumped together. Spain and the United States both fought extremely bitter and hugely destructive civil wars. The wars themselves were different in many ways—in causes, timing, geographical patterns, and many other particulars—but the legacies of these conflicts were similar. Both Spain and the United States bore historical wounds that were very deep and whose disfigurement and pain lasted long after the fighting stopped.

What was the nature of the divisive legacies common to both countries?

First to be remembered were the human costs. For both Spain and the United States these were so enormous that they produced pain and grief in vast numbers of families. Until the latter days of the Vietnam War, the number killed in all the United States' wars did not exceed the deaths of the Civil War. Spain likewise experienced a daunting number of fatalities during the war itself, and approximately fifty thousand executions swelled the death toll after the victory of the Nationalist forces led by Generalísimo Francisco Franco.[1] These dead would be mourned and remembered through the lifetimes of more than one generation. The loss of loved ones was a bitter legacy, a fundamental wound.

Augmenting that pain through later years were resentment and outrage over the way combatants met their death or the manner in which armies fought. Unconscionably overcrowded prison camps and Sherman's destructive March to the Sea implanted lasting rancor in the United States. In Spain, attacks on churches, summary trials by military tribunals, and executions that consigned enemies to *fosas*—common, unmarked graves—intensified feelings of injustice. Thus how soldiers fought and met their deaths was an added cause of bitterness.

Civilians also died in significant numbers during each country's war, and even more suffered greatly in numerous ways. Hunger was widespread in the Confederate States of America, and state governments directed insufficient relief efforts at more than a quarter of the white population. An estimated two hundred thousand people had to leave their homes, become refugees, and flee to safety. A consequence of the war in Spain was the creation of hundreds of thousands of exiles, many of whom never were able to return to their homes.[2] Severe wartime privations there gave way to a decade of hunger in the 1940s. Few people, despite being lucky to survive, would forget these kinds of dislocation and suffering.

Even more significant for future hostility was the moral or ideological dimension of past conflict. Deeply held beliefs caused persistent and potent division. Professor Harry Stout points out that even ordinary people had to find some way to "justify a level of killing that reached one million casualties" in the United States.[3] Northerners believed that the Union was a sacred cause, and a portion of them viewed the destruction of slavery as holy work. Southerners had their own ideology. They insisted that slavery elevated Africans and was ordained by God. Their leaders, far from apologizing for racial slavery, declared that it was the ideal labor system and the foundation of freedom and equality for whites. Warring Spaniards believed at least as deeply that their fight had transcendent importance. Republicans fought for democracy, social equality and justice, freedom of thought, and a secular, progressive state. Nationalists believed they were participating in a holy crusade for God and country (*Dios y patria*). They saw Spain as Christian civilization's last bulwark against atheism, communism, the Masons, and international Jewry.

Devotion to such beliefs would not evaporate when the fighting stopped. Defeated Southerners stubbornly resisted every social consequence of emancipation and denounced the "horrors" of Reconstruction. Franco's regime imprisoned or crowded into concentration camps three hundred thousand to four hundred thousand Republicans and purged fifty thousand primary school teachers suspected of holding Republican views.[4] These events did more than sow the seeds of future division; they created powerful new animosities that extended the internecine conflict. Add to these things the contribution that human ego—the humiliation of defeat or the pride of conquest—makes to such searing experiences, and the enormous challenges that war's legacies pose for society are clear.

This book will compare the ways in which Spain and the United States have dealt with their legacies of bitter division. To put it another way, it will examine how these two societies have remembered, debated, and argued about their civil wars and how those past loyalties and divisions have affected later generations. Through a comparative lens it will consider the nature and sources of historical memory; the battles over memory in ideology, commemorations, and politics; the effect of past divisions on subsequent political evolution; the meanings of reconciliation; and the long-term relevance of economic and social change.

Comparing the legacies of internecine conflict in Spain and the United States involves more than enumerating similarities and differences. Comparison also opens the possibility of comprehending the history of two societies in a common framework of analysis. In that sense comparison can show the way toward common, underlying patterns, which are rooted in social structures, social processes, and, ultimately, human nature. This connection leads us from events to processes and forces and thus it takes us closer to the dominant influences on history and on the behavior of individuals and groups. Spain and the United States have separate stories but common themes.

Their history also is part of a larger drama of historical wounds, of how various societies confront legacies of hatred and division. How can once-divided nations resolve their conflicts, reconcile enemies, or move beyond a troubled past? What is required or wise? Is it necessary to achieve justice—to right all past wrongs, punish the guilty, and compensate the innocent? Or is it better to close the door on a bloody history—to declare amnesty and look resolutely to the future? What can a recently invented third option—a Truth and Reconciliation Commission (TRC)—contribute? Every situation is different, and these questions are only part of the agenda of this book, but perhaps the experiences of Spain and the United States can shed some light on these larger questions.

* * *

Examining postwar struggles to determine right and wrong, or to create dominant ideologies and interpretations of the war, takes us into the realm of remembrance. Memory must be understood both as a personal experience and as a social force that unites people and influences the present. Individuals can choose to guard or discard their personal memories, as Friedrich Nietzsche pointed out; a person can choose to build an identity around memories or define herself in a new direction, breaking with the past. "Collective" or "social" memories, on the other hand, serve to influence or motivate groups varying in size from a family to a nation. Voluntary organizations, institutions, and governments all have a stake in the content of "collective" or "social" memory, for it can be a powerful tool in the competition for power. It is vital to remember, however, that when we speak of "collective," "social," or "historical memory," as Paloma Aguilar Fernández aptly defines it, we are always referring to an interpretation of the past, an interpretation shared by members of some group who have a common identity and seek common goals. This type of memory becomes part of the struggle between social forces fighting for supremacy. In "collective memory" or "historical memory," the contending narratives are rival versions of the past that differ because of their implications for the present and future.[5]

This book will try to ask useful questions about these alternate interpretations of the past. Who created the differing interpretations of a common, bloody history? What purposes do these historical memories serve, and what explains why some interpretations become salient and have staying power through time while others come to be ignored? How are the origin and persistence of historical memories related not only to the past but also to the social groups and evolution of the present? How does the argument over the past affect the way a society defines itself through historical memory? What is the relationship between history, as practiced by historians, and the historical memories that jostle for influence and power in society?

Spain and the United States have wrestled with similar challenges but under different circumstances and through dissimilar periods of time. The similarities and the differences in their experiences are revealing for the processes that unfolded in both countries—processes related to ideology and memory, the meaning of reconciliation both immediately and in the longer term, and the power of the past to affect politics. The interplay of continuity and change is especially interesting. Both histories show, in the political and cultural realm, the strong grip of past conflicts on the present, but in the economic sphere, they document the erosive and creative power of economic change.

* * *

This study is divided into five parts. Because Spain and the United States have rarely if ever been studied together, and because readers with a detailed knowledge of both countries are few, it has seemed absolutely necessary to begin with a background chapter. This offers a very condensed overview, in two brief parts, of the relevant history of Spain and the United States. These historical summaries are not intended to be exhaustive, complete, or original. In fact, as very brief accounts, they cannot be entirely satisfactory. Their purpose is merely to give the reader who is not familiar with one nation or the other sufficient information to inform later comparisons. The second chapter focuses on memories, commemorations, and ideologies. It analyzes first Spain and then the United States while drawing comparisons between them. Chapter 3 examines the role of the past in politics, where the legacy of conflict has shaped party identities and policies despite the necessity of adjusting to change and new challenges. Chapter 4 looks at the concept, methods, and reality of reconciliation, which is the unavoidable end point for nations that remain unitary after a civil war. A final chapter assesses the impact of economic change and similar forces that can affect the transformation of cultural landscapes.

There is a dialogue between the sections on each country within every chapter. By giving sufficient attention to each country's history, it is hoped that the processes of historical memory, argument, and adjustment will be clear. Through cross-references between the two national histories, every effort is made to highlight the similarities and differences that exist and to analyze their significance.

1

Background

Despite widespread beliefs that both Spain and the United States are exceptional, both have shared in the modern struggles of national integration. Their paths to becoming modern democratic nations embracing diverse populations have not been easy.[1] Local or regional loyalties have interfered with the building of a strong national identity or hindered the construction of a powerful state. Tensions between industrial development and agricultural wealth have brought economic elites into conflict. Religious convictions have produced at least as much division as unity. Powerfully entrenched forces that looked toward the past have contended with dynamic groups oriented toward the future. Ideologies that claimed supreme importance have collided. These various internal stresses contributed in each case to a highly destructive civil war, and in each nation the legacies of that conflict have been long lasting.

In brief sections on first Spain and then the United States, this chapter attempts to provide a minimal amount of background information—enough to make later comparisons intelligible and useful.

Spain's Torturous Path to Modern European Democracy

We consider ourselves, in the cultural and ideological plane, as the heirs of the historical-religious spirit of Trent, of the Counter-Reformation, of the Syllabus, of the battle of the Catholic Church against the grave rationalist errors . . . the "false modern civilization."

José Pemartín Sanjuán, *Accion Española: Antología*, volume XVIII, number 89 (Burgos: 1937): 377–78

History can deceive us greatly by showing us not the native aptitudes of a people, but rather only those that have been allowed to develop.

Miguel de Unamuno, *Collected Works* 3:716

> We are much better off than 30 years ago.
> King Juan Carlos de Borbón, February 24, 2011

Throughout its long history, Spain developed both within and apart from Europe. By the sixteenth century it had become Europe's greatest imperial power with extensive New World possessions blessed by the papacy. But its rise to power came after centuries of Arab occupation, the wars of the Reconquest, and the slow and partial extension of monarchical power over various independent regions and cultures. Before Columbus sailed to the Americas, the Catholic monarchs, Ferdinand and Isabella, installed the Holy Office of the Inquisition, which pursued heretics and nonbelievers as Spain expelled the Jews and the Moors. Then, as the Reformation caught fire in much of Europe, Felipe II embraced the Counter-Reformation and made his kingdom the chief defender of the Catholic faith. Thus Spain's period of greatness was closely tied to orthodox Catholicism in Europe and in its New World empire, and as Spain's imperial power declined, its distance from European currents of change increased. Orthodox Catholic Spain remained isolated from and hostile to Protestantism, the Enlightenment, and substantial elements of economic development.

The Napoleonic wars and the events of the nineteenth century introduced modern ideas of constitutionalism, economic liberalism, and widespread suffrage, as well as the beginnings of industrialization. But Spain entered the twentieth century as a society that was only beginning to modernize and still deeply influenced by strong conservative elements that fought against such changes. Thus thinking observers often embraced the idea of "the two Spains"—one that was inspired by the Enlightenment, that was modernizing, attracted to liberalism and democracy, and oriented to Europe, and another centered on the Catholic Church, social and religious orthodoxy, and resistance to all secular and modern thought.[2] By the end of the nineteenth century a traditional, hierarchical, and less-advanced country had developed within itself conflicting elements of modern thought and change.

On the one hand, patriots opposed to Napoleon's invasion had written a constitution in 1812 in Cadiz that became "the model for advanced democrats from St. Petersburg to Naples." Liberal governments in the 1830s had sold church lands in hopes of opening up the economy and creating a class of substantial peasant farmers. After 1890 universal suffrage was the basis of supposedly democratic institutions. On the other hand, those institutions had been "perverted by a selfish oligarchy" and election returns were "manipulated and falsified at will." The sale of church lands ended up benefiting existing landowners and other powerful groups, while "rural misery" increased among landless laborers and small proprietors. Most rural dwellers were uneducated and strongly influenced by the local priest. The power of the church, in alliance with large landowners and local notables, remained great, and a standard text for seminaries and Catholic schools taught that the "Holy Office [of the Inquisition] is the most faithful portrait of our character."[3]

Meanwhile, economic change was adding another layer of difference to the two Spains. Industry, especially in textiles and metals, was developing in the northeast, in Catalonia and the Basque Country. There the emerging bourgeoisie clung to its own version of conservative social ideas; in Barcelona employers hired thugs and unleashed violence against workers, who in turn organized to protect their interests, frequently as Anarchists. Yet in 1900 "almost two-thirds of the population worked in agriculture" and illiteracy reached 60 percent. There was a sharp contrast between volatile and growing towns of commerce and industry and a Spain of "rural poverty, ignorance, and illiteracy." In the rural countryside, prominent and wealthy families, closely allied with the church, formed a social hierarchy vigilant against deviations from conservative thought. As a result, "profoundly religious" villages often stood in opposition to liberal towns where, the clergy warned, attacks on the church would originate. There tended to be more small farms and modest landholdings in the north, but in the south, especially, a large class of desperately impoverished day laborers was growing. The development of a strong Anarchist movement in rural areas, notably Andalusia and the Levant, was unusual in Europe and "is perhaps most simply explained by the hostility of employers and landowners to any form of labour organization, leaving violence as the only alternative."[4]

Every aspect of a modern, secular society was considered dangerous, even heretical, by the Catholic Church of nineteenth-century Spain and Rome. Church leaders viewed the Enlightenment, rationalism, the advance of scientific thought, and tolerance of new ideas as threatening. Because these challenged an ancient worldview centered on God alone, they reacted harshly. In 1864 Pope Pius IX published the Syllabus of Errors, which specified and condemned many increasingly common modern ideas. Among these "errors" were the following assumptions or ideas: that human reason "is the sole arbiter of truth and falsehood," that religious truths could "proceed from the innate strength of human reason," that "divine revelation is imperfect," that prophecies and miracles "are the fiction of poets," and that true philosophy can dispense with "supernatural revelation." In the sphere of social and political action, the Syllabus denounced freedom of religion, Protestantism, socialism, communism, secret societies, divorce, and any limitation by civil government of the power and influence of the true church. Secular state-supported education for all children was not only inferior to the education of the church, but Catholics were not to give approval to such a system. Allowing a variety of religions and freedom of thought, the pope warned, tends to "corrupt the morals and minds of the people." The Catholic Church should be "the only religion of the State."[5]

This reactionary church was a dominant influence on the social thought of nineteenth-century Spain. Priests and religious orders played the major role in education, and the church habitually concentrated its educational efforts on the children of the elite or the emerging bourgeoisie in cities and towns. The sale of church lands had merely strengthened the rich or certain favored individuals while cementing their close relationship with the church, and under an 1851 agreement with the Vatican the Spanish state paid the clergy. Such close ties between the church and society's social, political, and military elites reinforced the power of the church but also stimulated a tradition of anticlericalism. Conservative thought warned of impious secularists "who persecuted and despoiled the Church." Major political changes fanned fears of "the Church in danger," and Catholic leaders denounced freedom of religion as "heresy." Some anticlericals, on the other hand, burned convents and attacked priests. During a week of violence in Barcelona in 1909, there was "an orgy of convent burnings."[6]

Weak governments at the beginning of the twentieth century were unable to cope with these volatile forces—or with defeat in the Spanish-American War of 1898. The loss of Cuba, Puerto Rico, and the Philippines was a shock to society, and a brutal war in Morocco soon intensified its effects. Thirty-four governments quickly succeeded each other in twenty-one years. Then, after a defeat in Morocco, General Primo de Rivera delivered a *pronunciamiento* in 1923. As they had done before, the military, the church, and the conservative elite acted together to exercise power, as King Alfonso XIII decided to accept a military dictatorship. In the process he broke his oath to defend the Spanish constitution, thus undermining his own legitimacy. Initially Primo de Rivera benefited from economic recovery in Europe and invested in infrastructure such as dams, irrigation, and roads, but the Great Depression weakened his already problematic position. After eight years of dictatorship, Primo de Rivera resigned and went into exile. Soon after his fall, King Alfonso XIII saw in the results of municipal elections a widespread rejection of his leadership, and he too went into exile. To the secular, anticlerical, progressive elements in society, a new day seemed to be dawning. Enthusiastic Republicans filled the streets of Madrid and proclaimed the Second Republic.[7] The stage was set for a combustible clash of ideologies—from bolshevism to fascism and national socialism—that soon would engulf all of Europe.

From 1931 to 1936 the fledgling Second Republic struggled against extremist forces of both the Right and Left. There were attacks on priests, nuns, and church property, labor insurrections, military plots against the government, violent street protests by the right, and escalating rhetoric from all sides. Power shifted with elections from the Left to the Right and back again to the Left, as the forces of the two Spains struggled for ascendency. At first reformers took charge, drawing up a progressive constitution that guaranteed liberties, permitted divorce, and established the state's neutrality toward religion. The government suppressed the Jesuits, prohibited the orders from teaching, made religious instruction in the public schools voluntary, ended financial support for the clergy, secularized cemeteries, and barred government officials from religious ceremonies. The Catalans receive a statute of autonomy.[8] After these initial steps the government of Manuel Azaña went farther. It sought to reform agriculture, aid industrial workers, establish public schools, and modernize and trim a bloated military. Its reforms were partial and less than effective; for example, the government ordered priests to continue teaching because there was a shortage of teachers—and the limited nature of its success led to a briefly successful communist insurrection in Catalonia in 1932. But all these measures energized the Right, which gained power in elections at the end of 1933. In 1934 desperate farm workers seized land in the south, industrial workers struck in the northeast, and miners rebelled in Asturias. The conservative government crushed these uprisings, reversed Republican legislation, and placed army officers hostile to the republic, such as General Francisco Franco, in key positions.[9]

The pro-Republican groups were always far more varied and disunited than the forces of the right (which included traditional monarchists, conservatives, Fascists, the military, landowners, and other groups that favored authoritarian and corporatist approaches). But in 1936, after protracted negotiations, the elements of the Left formed the Popular Front to contest elections marked by apocalyptic predictions. There was rhetoric from some leaders on the Left about the need for "civil war" if the right prevailed, whereas right-wing propaganda urged support for "God and Country; to conquer or to die." The Republican forces won, drawing support from intellectuals, urban and industrial areas, the south and southwest, Galicia, the Basque Country, and Catalonia. The strength of the Right remained overwhelming, however, in central regions, small towns, and among economic and religious elites who shared with many rural Spaniards a profound fear of communism and reform. Fascist organizations and demonstrations increased, as a new government under Azaña proved powerless to stop industrial workers from striking or farm workers in the south from seizing large swaths of land. On July 17, after the assassination of a right-wing leader, significant parts of the army attempted to seize power. The failure of this uprising to control all of Spain resulted in three years of odious, cruel, and sanguinary conflict.[10]

The Catholic Church played a highly visible role in all the controversies of the 1930s. Spain's most important archbishop, the archbishop of Toledo, Cardinal Segura y Sáenz, reacted to the establishment of the Republic by immediately condemning the constitution. That document's statement that authority derived from the people was "a postulate of official atheism" and the first of many "wrongs" inflicted on the church. Quoting the current pope and past holy fathers, he denounced secularism as the "plague of our time," labeled ideas of modern rights stemming from the French Revolution as "craziness" and "libertinism," and predicted "disastrous consequences." This, writes one scholar, was a church "fundamentalist, militant, and combative . . . with an ideology of a monopolistic character." Laicism, wrote a respected Spanish Augustinian educator, was "the great modern social error" because it rejected a world totally subject to God and the church. Pope Pius XI soon issued an encyclical on "oppression of the Church in Spain" which condemned "the apostasy of society that today feigns to alienate itself from God and therefore from the Church." In the actions of the Republican government the pope saw "malice," "a hatred against the Lord and his Christ nourished by groups subversive to any religious and social order," and "a soul deeply hostile to God and the Catholic Religion."[11]

Thus it was not surprising that church leaders quickly bestowed their blessing and imprimatur on the military's uprising. They viewed Spain as the only remaining bulwark of Catholicism against the corrosive, spiritually dissolving, godless secular trends of the modern world. The army's revolt seemed to them to be an opportunity—perhaps the last opportunity—to save Western civilization from spiritual disaster. Spain's glorious destiny would be to defend the true religion against what one ecclesiastical publicist called the "unbelief and modern rationalism" that led inevitably toward "Bolshevism." Democratic and radical movements were the work of the devil, whom another priest described as "the first socialist in the world." With this "frozen ideology incapable of adapting to new political and social realities," church leaders hoped through the military's revolt to build "a dike" against the world's corruption.[12]

If the stakes were high in the eyes of Catholic leaders, so was the price Spain paid in human lives, physical destruction, and social embitterment. The war lasted for three years and became a rehearsal for World War II. In a battle of ideologies, Nazi Germany and Fascist Italy aided the Nationalist army, which soon was led by Francisco Franco, while Soviet Russia and Mexico proved to be the only supporters of the Republicans. Thousands of individuals from various nations came to support the Republican cause, but otherwise the Western democracies remained on the sidelines.[13] Franco's army expanded its control from areas of strength in the north and west and then the south, making steady gains against Republican forces that were less professional and often less well coordinated. The Nationalists battered at Madrid and Catalonia and by the spring of 1938 had cut the remaining Republican-held territories in two. In May 1938 the Republicans tried to sue for peace, but Franco continued fighting in an effort, as many historians believe, to eliminate more of his enemies.[14] At the beginning of April 1939 the last Republican forces surrendered.

The toll in human lives was great and soon grew higher. Since battles took place in many parts of the country, the physical destruction was on a grand scale, and in addition to the roughly 325,000 lives lost, one must consider the wounded and disabled as well as the hunger, suffering, and emotional losses of civilians. Also, as was the case in the U.S. Civil War, both sides committed outrages that sowed seeds of bitterness for future generations. "By the end of the Civil War, 13 bishops, 4,184 diocesan priests, 2,365 men in religious orders, and 283 nuns had perished as a result of anticlerical violence," especially in the first six months of the conflict, and many churches and religious buildings were sacked or burned. Both sides executed their enemies, but the Nationalists were more aggressive in this respect. Franco's forces executed 150,000 during the war, usually without judicial process or after a drum-head military trial. Republicans of obscure background or well-known figures like the poet Federico García Lorca were rounded up and shot, their bodies dumped into hastily made graves, or *fosas*, beside the road. Another fifty thousand were executed in the years right after the war and three hundred thousand to four hundred thousand imprisoned or crowded into concentration camps. Fifty thousand primary school teachers were purged on suspicion of Republican sympathies, and hundreds of thousands fled the country. Many of these people remained in exile for the rest of their lives, while millions more in Spain witnessed the end of their hopes for the future.[15]

General Franco, who took the title *caudillo*, or leader, aligned himself with the Fascist governments of Germany and Italy during World War II but to Hitler's disgust avoided contributing troops or resources, aside from eighteen thousand volunteers who formed the Blue Division and fought in Russia. As the victory of the Allies grew near, Franco began to distance himself more from the losing side, but the democratic nations of Europe shunned his dictatorial government throughout the 1940s. Looking inward, Franco pursued a policy of economic autarky, trying unsuccessfully to make Spain self-sufficient.

The decade of the 1940s was a time of terrible hunger and suffering for many Spaniards, and also a period of tight control over the social and private lives of citizens. Those suspected of Republican sympathies, or even of "grave passivity," lost public jobs, and authorities opened three hundred thousand dossiers on citizens who for any reason fell under suspicion. The regime praised "denunciation" as a "patriotic virtue" and worked to preserve a sharp line between supporters and those who, as General Emilio Mola Vidal had put it, "do not think like us." Censors kept watch over publications and the dangerous cinema, which a prominent Jesuit called "the greatest calamity that has befallen the world since Adam." Spaniards knew that they had best attend mass, and church and state viewed human nature, especially sexuality, "in the darkest terms." Women were to be entirely subordinate to their husbands and fulfill only domestic, maternal, and religious roles. Cardinal Segura warned that unless a "breeze could pass" between a couple, dancing was "the satanic work of moral corruption, public scandal and sin, a school of degrading orgies of concupiscence."[16]

Franco was deeply conservative and religious, but he was always more interested in power than in any form of ideological purity. He maintained his supremacy by playing different groups of supporters—the Falange, the church, army leaders, technocrats of the influential Catholic organization Opus Dei[17]—off against each other. Meanwhile, he provided Spaniards with a steady stream of propaganda about the virtues of his government. Through the years he also changed his arguments and emphasized different parts of his ideology. At all times, however, he used an iron fist against opponents and subversive groups, imprisoning or executing enemies and critics. Whenever and wherever opposition arose—among leftists, university students, workers who were organizing clandestinely—Franco used the Guardia Civil, army troops, or prisons. Nationalist groups in Catalonia and the Basque Country, especially, fought against his centralizing efforts and the suppression of their different languages and cultures. Their resistance, particularly among the Basques, became increasingly violent, though it won them considerable sympathy while the dictatorship continued.

In the 1950s the Cold War brought important benefits to Spain's repressive dictatorship. Franco had deemphasized the Fascist Falange in his anti-Communist regime, and U.S. president Dwight Eisenhower decided to obtain military bases in Spain by making Franco an ally. The agreement with the United States meant a massive infusion of foreign aid to the backward and struggling Spanish economy. Even though much of the aid was tied directly to military bases and arrangements, its effects spread through the domestic economy. It also brought Spain closer to Europe and to NATO and bestowed a new degree of respectability on a regime that began to boast domestically not just of anticommunism but also of economic progress. Some voices began to speak of reconciliation, both outside and inside the regime. Notably, leaders of Spain's Communist Party, most of whom were in exile, decided to work for change within the system and began to organize workers inside Franco's official trade unions. Students also began to protest, another sign that the iron façade of the regime might eventually crack.

In the 1960s an important Franquista minister, Manuel Fraga Iribarne, had great success promoting tourism. As hundreds of thousands of sun-seeking Europeans began to travel to Spain's beaches, Franco even permitted bikinis; for the conservative *caudillo* the glow of monetary infusions had obscured the sinful spectacle of female flesh. Fraga began to talk of an "opening" in society and took steps to moderate censorship in the press and in movies. (A popular saying went, "With Fraga you even can see the panties.") Another important event in the economic sphere was the ascendency for several years of technocrats associated with Opus Dei. Modeling their ideas on French policies of development, and benefiting from the other changes, they achieved some success. Franco's propagandists began to emphasize themes of peace, stability, and progress bestowed by the *caudillo* on his people. But the social conflicts and internal tensions between his regime and a changing society were not diminishing. Instead, they were increasing.

The attempt to open a repressive dictatorship to the economic boom of the West without encountering liberal currents of thought or democratic aspirations was doomed to failure. Economic growth took place, but it also brought fundamental changes to a society already chafing under Franco's decades-long denial of liberty. Some of the *caudillo*'s supporters were restive, and even the church began to criticize and distance itself from the regime. Vatican II had as great an impact on Spanish Catholicism, especially among many younger priests, as economic and social change had on the citizenry. Spaniards were eager for an end to the dictatorship's repression, and they were increasingly connected to the world of European democracy. Whereas only 1 percent of Spanish households owned a television at the beginning of the 1960s, 62 percent were owners before the end of the decade.[18]

Democratic currents of feeling flowed within the labor movement and especially in the universities, where persistent student strikes led to the declaration of a national state of emergency in 1969. Because students were overwhelmingly middle class and came from the marrow of society, the violent repression of striking students provoked widespread alienation. Moreover, the character of nationalist protests from Catalonia and the Basque Country had become much more acute. Catalonian nationalism often appeared modern and progressive; from the Basque Country, however, the terrorist organization Euskadi Ta Askatasuna, or Basque Homeland and Freedom (ETA), began assassinations of members of the regime. A strong indicator of the popular resentment of Franco's government was the fact that, despite its violent campaign of terror, ETA enjoyed a substantial measure of approval as a symbol of resistance. Moreover, the advanced age of the *caudillo* clearly indicated that change was on the horizon. Franco announced that Juan Carlos, the grandson of Alfonso XIII, would become king in the future, and Admiral Carrero Blanco, a rigid hard-liner determined to continue the dictatorship, became prime minister. But in 1973 ETA killed Carrero Blanco with a powerful bomb that sent his automobile flying over tall buildings in Madrid. Then, after a long illness, Franco died in November 1975.

There followed a Spanish "miracle" that later evoked much pride: the peaceful Transition from dictatorship to democracy. Members of the regime, perhaps using some hindsight, have later testified that they knew a substantial change was inevitable; some conservatives claim now that the Right, through its active cooperation, gave democracy to Spain. "The regime did not take notice of the radical change that had occurred in Spanish society in the [']70s," said Eduardo Navarro, a well-educated social progressive within Franco's government. "The society wanted to be like the rest, it wanted to make itself like France, Italy, England." Navarro added, "All the university youth had a sense that it could not continue as before," and Oscar Álzaga, a conservative lawyer active in rightist politics during the years of the Transition agreed that "all the young people of the regime wanted to abandon a ship that was sinking." Manuel Fraga Iribarne seemed to many a likely candidate to lead the change to democracy, but at critical moments he undercut his position with some strongly right-wing decisions. Nevertheless, Fraga's analysis of the crisis point in Franco's dictatorship was accurate: "It was a society of middle classes, urbanized, and any person of common sense saw that a different political system had to come into being."[19]

Despite the importance of these underlying and potent forces, the successful creation of a democratic government was far from certain. Rightwing partisans of Franco opposed any liberalization, and many elements of the army's high command were extremely conservative. Leftists were suspicious of virtually all the existing leadership class, tainted by its collaboration with Franco, and the escalating violence of ETA troubled the entire society. Enormous credit was due to the youthful king, Juan Carlos de Borbón, to Adolfo Suárez, who soon became prime minister, and to the active participation through elections of an overwhelming, pro-democratic majority of the Spanish people. The king, Suárez, and others managed to convince the existing, undemocratic officeholders of the dictatorship to vote themselves and their institutions out of office, to extinguish the system in which they enjoyed power.

There is little doubt that King Juan Carlos envisioned a democratic future. Gabriel Cisneros, a conservative and one of the coauthors of the Constitution of 1978, recalls that Juan Carlos, before his coronation, "could not have a clear view of the route, could not see clearly the how, but had very clearly the will and [knowledge of] the goal he would reach. He was extremely clear that the Monarchy either would be democratic and parliamentary or it would not be." Alfonso Osorio, who served under both the king and Suárez, has noted that "the King had one very clear idea: no politician who had been a minister under Franco would be the president who directed the political transition. I heard him say that many times." The politician he chose, Adolfo Suárez, had never been a minister under Franco, but he had served as secretary general of the *caudillo's* party, the Movimiento. Nevertheless, Suárez saw democracy as both desirable and inevitable, and had even affirmed that belief in a conversation with the aging Franco.[20] Suárez used his influence within the Movimiento and shrewdly appealed to expressions of the popular will in order to advance his project, first of passing the Law of Political Reform and then electing a new Cortes,[21] or legislative body, that would draw up a democratic constitution.[22]

The measure of Suárez's success is that he obtained from Franco's Cortes 425 votes in favor of the Law of Political Reform, as opposed to only 59 against and 13 abstentions, and at the end of 1976 almost 78 percent of the Spanish electorate went to the polls to vote overwhelmingly, by 94 percent, in favor of the changes. Two years later the constitution—drawn to include a system of autonomies, or extensive local self-government, for Catalonia and the Basque Country, especially, but also for the rest of the nation—would similarly win approval.[23]

The construction of an open, democratic system of political competition required additional crucial decisions, even before the constitution was ratified. The Cortes approved a law of amnesty in July 1976 that covered political actions that did not endanger or damage the life of people; this amnesty, therefore, covered most of the dictatorship's functionaries but did not include ETA. After the first referendum, in March 1977, a general pardon applying to prisoners was added, and two months later the Council of Ministers approved the release of the majority of Basques accused of terrorism. In the fall of 1977 the new parliament approved a wider amnesty. It amnestied all actions, whatever their result, motivated by political views and occurring prior to December 15, 1976; allowed a more conditional amnesty for acts between December 15, 1976, and October 6, 1977; and restored rights to those imprisoned for political activities, including members of ETA and other violent groups, such as right-wing squads. In the spring of 1977 the government also legalized the right to strike and gave legal status to the Communist Party, despite powerful opposition from the army.[24]

Suárez's minister of foreign affairs, Marcelino Oreja, has stated that "Adolfo Suárez was not thinking of a democracy of parties. He wanted to make the change to democracy and the democracy of parties was the result of what he did." Nevertheless, Suárez led his newly formed Union of the Democratic Center, or Unión del Centro Democratico (UDC) to victory by a plurality in 1977 and 1979. But he found himself increasingly beset by problems. The constitutional provisions and laws allowing autonomies did not satisfy Basque terrorists, as the violence of ETA reached new and disturbing heights. The conservative military, already outraged over legalization of the Communist Party, complained loudly about the anarchy threatening the country. Dissension developed within Suárez's party, and its more conservative elements were deeply offended by a law allowing divorce. By late 1980 discontent with the government was widespread, and this dissatisfaction included even the king. In January 1981, Adolfo Suárez announced his resignation.[25]

A sudden, frightening military challenge to Spain's fledgling democracy occurred the next month, as the legislature was meeting to install Suárez's successor, Leopoldo Calvo Sotelo. On February 23, Lieutenant Colonel Antonio Tejero, accompanied by two hundred members of the Guardia Civil,[26] went to the Congress of Deputies building and stormed into the legislative chamber. Shots were fired into the air, and Tejero threatened the deputies, ordering them to obey and be silent, while he took charge and awaited the arrival of higher military authorities. All the while, Spanish television was recording this event, and the news quickly spread. Through an anxious night the population nervously waited to learn the outcome. A number of high-ranking generals was involved in this plot, and tanks rolled onto the streets of Valencia. But King Juan Carlos worked with advisers to contact other commands throughout the country, ascertain their loyalty, and make clear his will as commander in chief that they respect the constitution. Early the next morning, when the king went on television to announce his firm support for democracy and constitutionalism, the failure of the plot was becoming evident. Eventually Tejero and his armed forces left the Congress of Deputies without blood being shed. Tejero and twenty-nine others, after trials by the Supreme Council of Military Justice and the Supreme Tribunal, were found guilty of a military rebellion; those most responsible received prison sentences of up to thirty years, while others served only a year or a few years. The new president, Calvo Sotelo, called for elections in the fall of 1982.[27]

When the Socialist Party, Partido Socialista Obrero Español (PSOE), won an absolute majority, a new era in Spain's modern democracy began. The victory of the Socialists had a double significance. Spain's young democracy had proved that it could change the party in power, and it had done so after the long years of a reactionary dictatorship by giving a leftist party an absolute majority. In 1977 and 1979 the Socialists had secured the second largest number of votes. Now they would control the government for what turned out to be the next fourteen years. In 1986 they again won an absolute majority in the Congress of Deputies, and in the elections of 1989 they controlled exactly half the seats and thus were not obliged to govern from a coalition.

The leader of the Socialists was a charismatic young figure named Felipe González. The party's success rested in significant measure on his attractive personality and on the kind of policy directions he chose. The Socialist Party made a transition from doctrinaire Marxism to being a reformist, democratic, market-oriented but left-leaning organization, and González played a major role in that transformation. He was part of the younger Spanish Socialists who early in the 1970s wrested leadership away from the party's exiled, longtime secretary general. As a deputy in the Cortes between 1977 and 1979, González pushed his party in a reformist, non-Marxist direction and showed a willingness to work with and give consideration to leaders of more conservative or moderate opinion. He chose not to pursue punishment for those who had carried out Franco's repression and showed a willingness to accept the economic liberalism of the market. These positions provoked a serious challenge to his leadership in 1979, but González recovered from an initial defeat within the party and imposed his policy directions.

González's reformist, moderate orientation undoubtedly responded to the situation of Spain at the time and the possibilities of a society containing strong conservative or reactionary elements. But it also was a reflection of his background and personal experience. In an extensive interview granted to the newspaper *El País* in 2010, González recalled that his family had not been closely attentive to public affairs or deeply concerned with politics. "I did not get into politics from a political indoctrination or a family political tradition, but from the repugnance that was produced in me to live in a dictatorship and not have liberty," explained González. He felt that the "militant communists were admirable for their sacrifice," but he took note of the fact that dictatorship was part of their international movement. "My position was not ideological, I repeat, it was anti-dictatorship. By exclusion I arrived at the socialist option." In these feelings González reflected the reality of many talented young Spaniards. Alfredo Pérez Rubalcaba, the leader of the Socialist Party of today, recalled in similar fashion that he "arrived on the left from anti-Franco-ism. If there had not been Franco-ism I believe that I would have been a good professor."[28]

While pursuing left-leaning socialist values of concern for individual rights, equality, and solidarity, González led Spain into closer relationship with democratic, capitalist Europe during his fourteen years as president of the government. One of his main goals was to align Spain with the European Community (EC), and this his government accomplished. Spain had applied for membership in the EC in 1977, but the less-developed state of the Spanish economy led member states to demand changes. González undertook these, at some cost to farmers, to industry, and to his popularity, and in 1986 Spain became a full member of the EC. NATO was a thornier issue for the Socialists and the left. They had vigorously opposed the decision, taken at the end of 1981, to join NATO, and González had pledged to hold a referendum on withdrawal from the western military alliance. Once in office, however, he began to see more advantages to Spain's membership and discerned that it was linked in some degree to full membership in the European Community. When he finally scheduled the referendum, in 1986, he argued for continuing in NATO and triumphed by a narrow margin.

Domestically, González's governments consolidated the institutions of democracy by giving Spain a number of years of governance that proved popular with the people but also through instituting some reforms. Adolfo Suárez had first tackled the difficult challenge of taming an extremely conservative, antidemocratic army and reducing its excessive number of higher officers. González worked with a small, progressive faction in the army, the Democratic Military Union, to liberalize the armed forces and change their culture. He knew that the instruction given within the military to officers and the values conveyed were of great importance. Accordingly, González asked these progressive officers how long it would take—assuming that the military academies then were teaching "the values of the Constitution and the role of the Armed Forces in a constitutional framework"—for a rising officer to become chief of staff. "Well, until 2015" was the answer. With an expletive, González replied that "we don't have time, we will have to do some things before then. And we did them."[29]

His governments also implemented the constitution's provisions for establishment of *autonomías*, or autonomous communities, a type of provincial or local government, similar in some ways to a federal system but with unique Spanish characteristics. Under the constitution several *autonomías* in the northeast and northwest of Spain—Catalonia, the Basque Country, Galicia, and Navarre—were entitled to a greater degree of self-government than other regions due to their history, which included non-Castilian languages, unique cultures, and the existence in past centuries of special rights or privileges. But other, new autonomies also were created throughout Spain, which now has nineteen in total. Spaniards and their political leaders embraced the idea of assuming certain public responsibilities through the autonomies, and over time a kind of competition for privileges and recognition has developed. The result has been greater regional pride, greater attention to local culture and treasures, but also an expensive duplication in administration and—more seriously—rising demands for independence, stimulated in part by the politics of coalition-building in the Congress of Deputies.

Economic growth was often strong during González's years in office, and membership in the European Community brought economic benefits to Spain. The Socialists increased public spending from 25 to 49 percent of gross domestic product (GDP) in ten years, gave more support to universities and cultural institutions, and made some progress in the level of employment. But unemployment remained high, probably due to a lack of competitiveness in the economy as well as governmental regulations to protect workers that increased the costs of hiring on other than a temporary basis. The problem of unemployment, or *paro*, remains a significant challenge for Spain (and has increased to crisis proportions during 2011–13). Yet it was corruption, rather than unemployment, that did the most damage to the political fortunes of the Socialists. A variety of scandals began to come to light toward the end of Felipe González's presidency, including the apparent funding through the interior ministry of Grupos Antiterroristas de Liberación, or Antiterrorist Liberation Groups (GAL), a paramilitary organization that assassinated members of ETA as well as some innocent victims. The Socialist Party lost the elections of 1996, and the leading conservative party, the Partido Popular, or "People's Party" (PP), formed a coalition government.[30]

José María Aznar, the new president, had campaigned against the devolution of power to the autonomies, as a threat to national integrity, but ironically the realities of governing through a coalition resulted in greater concessions to them. In domestic policy the PP proved to be socially conservative and economically liberal in the classical sense. Aznar's government showed respect for traditional values and for the church and pursued privatization in the economy and the reduction of government regulations. It advocated reform of the welfare state and smaller government, but Aznar was careful to present the party as free from Franco's type of repressive conservatism. Years of economic growth and sound budgeting aided the PP,

In 2000 Aznar and his party won an outright majority, thus giving evidence again that Spain's democratic system was mature enough to change power and direction through the ballot box.

By 2004, however, criticism had developed, especially over Aznar's support for American intervention in Iraq and his increasing disregard for public opinion. Three days before balloting was to take place, Spain suffered its version of the United States' 9/11. On March 11, known in Spain as 11-M, terrorist bombs ripped open trains in Madrid's metro system, killing 191 people and maiming many others. As evidence began to come to light that Al Qaeda was behind this act of terrorism, Aznar personally and his ministries repeatedly insisted that ETA was to blame. The government's tendentious response caused many voters to doubt its veracity. Suspicion grew that officials wanted to avoid any connection with the unpopular war in Iraq and a possible reprisal by Al Qaeda. When the ballots were counted, PSOE, the Socialist Party, emerged victorious behind its leader José Luis Rodríguez Zapatero. PSOE repeated its victory in 2008 but was defeated by the PP, now led by Mariano Rajoy, in 2012.[31]

Spain's democracy today is far from perfect, but most of its deficiencies are not unique. Surveys of public opinion reveal widespread discontent with the character of political life, which seems to be dominated by two phenomena: constant attacks and counterattacks by the major parties, often in a rancorous, personal, or exaggerated style; and revelations of greed, venality, and financial corruption by officeholders.[32] Neither the United States nor European democracies have been immune from such problems. The terrorism of ETA is different and has remained a serious and frustrating problem for modern Spain. In addition to taking strong security measures, governments led by the PP or PSOE have, on occasion, engaged in careful talks with the terrorists in hopes of convincing them to abandon their murderous tactics and acts of violence. In 1997 the people of the Basque Country, as well as Spaniards elsewhere, staged a massive protest against ETA's violence, and in 1998 the peaceful political parties of the Basque region entered into the Pact of Estella with ETA. Their purpose was to point the way toward a nonviolent reintegration of ETA into political life, but they failed to receive the hoped for support of the terrorists. By 2012 ETA's band seemed to be much weaker, and Bildu, a newly organized Basque party that sympathizes with ETA's demands for independence, had won both legal recognition as a legitimate political party and control of a number of towns and cities. A definitive end to Basque terrorism seems close but not yet attained, and as long as it remains unresolved, it will continue to be an important item on Spain's political agenda. Given the Franco dictatorship's hostility to the peripheral nationalisms and its insistence on both centralization and the Castilian language, the problem of ETA can be considered one of the longest lasting legacies of Spain's civil war.

Victory Deferred: The United States' Long Journey toward Equality

> We hold these truths to be self-evident, that all men are created equal, that they are endowed by their Creator with certain unalienable Rights, that among these are Life, Liberty, and the Pursuit of Happiness.
>
> Declaration of Independence, 1776

> The new Constitution has put at rest, *forever*, all the agitating questions relating to ... the proper *status* of the negro in our Form of civilization. ... *its cornerstone rests, upon the great truth that the negro is not equal to the white man; that slavery, subordination to the superior race, is his natural and moral condition."*
>
> Alexander H. Stephens, vice president of the Confederacy, 1861

> We have already waited 100 years and more and the time for waiting is gone. ... It's not just Negroes, but really it's all of us, who must overcome the crippling legacy of bigotry and injustice. And we shall overcome.
>
> President Lyndon Johnson to Congress, 1965

Rarely or never does one hear conversation in the United States about "the two United States." Yet there is good reason to apply this concept in a manner similar to Spain, for in both countries there was a deep division in the society and culture that led to civil war. In addition, there were two United States in the sense of two regions moving in profoundly different directions with different and conflicting social systems. The slaveholding South, like the conservative alliance of church, wealth, and army in Spain, formed a social system whose leaders believed in inequality, hierarchy, privilege, and values of the past. Consciously out of step with the direction of modern development, the South's planter elite feared change and was increasingly committed to reactionary, antidemocratic ideas. Like the conservative Spanish elite, it saw itself as threatened, on the defensive, yet in possession of timeless truths about human societies. To protect its reactionary values and social power, this elite rose in the rebellion of secession, breaking the Union in anticipation of future aggressions by the newly elected Republican president, Abraham Lincoln.

The clash between North and South existed as a potentiality from the founding of the Republic, for the taproot of later conflict was a moral inconsistency in the new nation's fundamental documents. American colonists had rebelled against Great Britain in the name of freedom and human equality. They were motivated by a newly realized conviction that *all* men had political rights, rights that no government could justly deny. Proudly they expressed these beliefs in the Declaration of Independence, their ringing affirmation of liberty and indictment of tyranny. Yet racial slavery was a reality in their midst. Slaveholding constituted a denial of those unalienable rights for which they fought and the arbitrary oppression of some due to their race. It was most common in the southern colonies, and before 1808 the importation of additional slaves from Africa was actually increasing in South Carolina and Georgia. But slavery also existed in the North, where deeply ingrained racial prejudice bolstered economic interests.

The founding fathers did not regard this inconsistency as a fatal flaw, for leaders from all parts of the country generally were in agreement that slavery was undesirable, inconsistent with American values, and a political and social evil. And in the years immediately after independence, there was notable progress toward eliminating the institution. By 1800 northern states had decreed the end of slavery either by law or by court decision, in what has been called the First Emancipation. In Virginia, the largest slaveholding state, planters of troubled conscience freed approximately ten thousand slaves. The institution still had a large presence in the United States, but few disputed that it was a "necessary evil," something that could not be eradicated at that moment but that ought to pass away with time.[33]

Events exploded such wishful thinking shortly after 1800. The invention of the cotton gin by Eli Whitney made it possible to sell short-staple cotton to the burgeoning British textile industry. Previously a few southerners had made rich profits from long-staple cotton, a specialty crop that could thrive only in a small area along the Atlantic Coast and Sea Islands. Short-staple cotton was a much hardier plant. It could be grown in almost all parts of the South, but its sticky seeds had made it commercially worthless until Whitney developed an inexpensive machine to separate the seeds from the fiber. Now this crop could become a profitable export. The cultivation of short-staple cotton took off like a rocket, and white southerners looked to slave labor to make their fortunes through cotton. As the population grew and expanded into fertile new lands across the Appalachian Mountains and along the Gulf Coast, cotton production soared, and the number of slaves soared with it. By 1860 there were almost four million slaves in the South, and the two regions of the country were moving in decidedly different directions.[34]

In the North a transportation revolution—accomplished through canals, steamboats, improved roads, and then the railroad—had created a large, unified market and boosted commerce. Producers specialized in what they could do best and sold their products to consumers who were hundreds of miles away. Court decisions cleared the way for corporations and entrepreneurs. Cities were growing rapidly, and industry began to develop. Machines that saved time and labor increased output, not only in factories but also, by the 1850s, on midwestern farms that used the mechanical reaper. Along with a belief in the value of incentives and free labor, northern society developed a vigorous reform impulse, and religiously inspired criticism of slavery intensified after 1830. Racist attitudes remained deeply entrenched in the North, but public disapproval of slavery was growing, along with an unwillingness to allow southern planters to block or stand in the way of northern progress.[35]

The South, on the other hand, was an economically semideveloped region, whose large plantations produced three-quarters of the world's cotton while a multitude of small farms engaged in mainly subsistence agriculture. Socially and politically, the antebellum South bore a number of similarities to rural Spain before 1930. A minority of slave owners accumulated great wealth while exploited slaves provided the vital agricultural labor. Nonslaveholding white families strove for independence and a social status that was racially superior to the slaves and therefore, they were told, equal to the richest planters. Transportation was poor, cities were few, and the middle class of merchants or professionals was small and dependent on the planters. Moreover, this slave-owning elite dominated political institutions and propelled social thought in increasingly reactionary, hierarchical directions. Except for Missouri and Arkansas, slaveholders were the majority in every southern state legislature in 1860. In the lower South they controlled 62 percent of all legislative seats and as much as 82 percent of the seats in South Carolina. After 1830 southern politicians and intellectuals had abandoned the "necessary evil" argument in favor of an insistence that slavery was a "positive good." On religious grounds they argued that it was ordained by God; on political grounds they asserted that it eliminated conflicts among whites and united the racially superior class; for sociological reasons they claimed that it produced a sounder and more stable society, even one whose treatment of aged slaves was morally superior to free labor's practice of discarding the injured factory worker.[36]

Like the conservative elite and church in Spain, the South's elite felt threatened by change and deplored new social ideas or philosophies. Planters and politicians in the South condemned northern reform movements as dangerous "isms," denouncing Fourierism, communism, free love, women's rights, utopian communities, and of course abolitionism. As early as 1835 South Carolina condemned abolition societies as "incendiary" and called on northern states to "promptly and effectually suppress" them by making it "highly penal to print, publish, and distribute" any materials that might "excite the slaves" to revolt.[37] Their deep sense of being on the defensive sprang from two sources: international developments and national politics. Southern slaveholders were aware that humanitarian sentiments in Britain, France, and the West steadily had triumphed, as these countries rejected and circumscribed slavery. Now they saw the abolition movement growing on their doorstep. The unprecedented popularity in the North of Harriet Beecher Stowe's novel, *Uncle Tom's Cabin*, documented growing sympathy for the slave, if not for abolitionism. Even more serious was the imminent loss of political means to defend slavery against the rising tide of disapproval and criticism that might someday sweep away the foundations of their society.

The political threat to slavery centered on two areas: the U.S. Senate and the nation's territories. When the Constitution was written, the South was the most populous part of the nation, and southern leaders had expected it to stay that way. Instead, immigration and population growth in northern farms, towns, and cities soon outstripped the South, with the result that northern interests dominated the House of Representatives. The Senate thus became the only branch of the legislature where southern states, enjoying equal representation with any other state, could protect their interests. As long as the South had at least half of the seats, its leaders could block unfriendly legislation. From 1820 onward, protecting that equality of representation in the Senate was a top priority for southern politicians, but they lost the battle in 1850, when the Compromise of 1850 permitted California to enter the Union as a free state. Even more threatening for the future of slavery and the South was the status of the territories. If a rapidly multiplying northern population filled up the territories, their votes and their free labor ideas could overwhelm southern interests. Moreover, southern leaders believed that slavery needed room to expand, not only to secure new lands for southern energy and ambition but also to save racist southern whites from drowning in the black sea of a pent-up slave population.[38]

In 1846 John C. Calhoun, followed by other southern leaders, claimed new constitutional rights for white southerners in the territories. His theory asserted that southerners were entitled to take their slaves into all the territories without restriction. Arguing that the territories belonged to all the states, and asserting that states alone had the sovereign power to reject slavery as a social institution, Calhoun insisted that slaveholders were free to populate the territories and try to make them into slave states without restrictions by Congress. The Supreme Court endorsed Calhoun's views in 1857. Its decision in the *Dred Scott* case revealed regional divisions among the justices and proved highly controversial. Even before that point, southern politicians had been putting every effort into preserving or expanding their influence in the courts and the executive branch, with enough success to convince many northerners that a slave power conspiracy was on the road to taking over the nation's government. Surrounded by threats, yet encouraged and emboldened by large and seemingly continuous profits from cotton, the South's aristocratic politicians became increasingly belligerent. They warned that their honor depended on full acknowledgment of their rights, exactly as they interpreted them.[39]

When northern votes gave the 1860 presidential election to Abraham Lincoln, who viewed slavery as a "monstrous injustice" that enjoyed constitutional protection but should not be allowed to expand, seven states of the lower South seceded and organized a new government. Unwilling to wait and see if the new administration would prove hostile or dangerous to their interests, they launched the Confederate States of America in Montgomery, Alabama, and later moved their capital to Richmond, Virginia. Southern leaders justified secession as needed to defend slavery and racial superiority against future threats and as a response to what they described as past insults and wrongs. In a gesture recalling the Declaration of Independence, these states published to the world formal expositions of their reasons for breaking the Union. But in opposition to the Declaration of Independence's moral principles, they rejected and defied the humanitarian direction of Western thought. Slavery, they insisted, was more than a constitutional right. It was "the revealed will of the Almighty Creator," as Texas put it, or the basis of "a properly ordered, conservative society," as one prominent minister explained. The South's Protestant churchmen insisted that "authority and obedience" were God's plan for society and slavery "an organizing element in that family order which lies at the very foundation of Church and State." The enslavement of black southerners, said the seceding states, was both a preponderant economic interest and a sacred social principle.[40]

Like the initial uprising of the army in Spain, secession did not fully accomplish its aim, for eight slave states remained in the Union. With 40 percent of the slave population, 37 percent of the South's white population, a third of the South's horses and mules, and half of its urbanization and industrial capacity, the loyalty of these other slaveholding states would be highly significant in war. After shots were fired and Lincoln called for troops to suppress a rebellion, four of the eight states joined the Confederacy. These additions proved to be too little to bring victory but enough to guarantee that the ensuing war would be protracted, costly, bloody, and destructive. When Northern opinion rallied behind opposition to the South's rebellion, the likelihood of a vast and destructive bloodletting became a virtual certainty.[41]

The position of the North, as the war began, was crucially important. It revealed what would prove to be a major difference in comparison with the Spanish civil war: the North was *not* determined to settle completely all outstanding issues, as were Franco's Nationalists. The conflict between North and South was over the future of America's racial arrangements. But the North went to war merely to preserve the Union, not to free the slaves or establish racial justice. When subduing the rebellion proved difficult, a worried Abraham Lincoln issued the Emancipation Proclamation as a war measure, a necessary military step designed to weaken the South and strengthen the North. He feared that this war measure would fatally divide the racist population of the North, and although his concerns proved excessive, there was abundant and harsh criticism of his action on the grounds that it would elevate the status of African Americans. Never at any time was the Northern majority interested in making the war a crusade for racial equality. This fact set strict limits on what a Northern victory would accomplish, on how the North would interpret its victory, and on how much interest Northerners would have in dealing with racism.[42]

Fundamentally, the American Civil War was not about Union or slavery alone, for these issues were indissolubly connected to race. Did the United States believe that all men were created equal, that all people had unalienable rights, or did its founding values apply only to white people? As Alexander Stephens, vice president of the Confederacy, put it just before the war began, the fundamental question was "the *status* of the negro in our form of civilization." Southern leaders aimed to create an aristocratic republic for white men only, and the South seceded to ensure that slavery would remain the status of African Americans. To block secession, the North went to war and later decided that it must attack slavery in order to win. But the "*status* of the negro" in a democratic society was not resolved by the North during the war. That question remained a basic issue for a nation born from the ideals of the Declaration of Independence.

As in Spain, the Civil War in the United States proved to have enormous costs and to produce great bitterness. Roughly 625,000 men died, both from wounds on the battlefield and from disease, which ravaged both armies in an era before modern medicine. The damage inflicted by lead projectiles was usually great, shattering bones and requiring amputations done with dirty saws and scalpels and without anesthetic. There was great physical destruction in the Confederacy, where most battles were fought. The South's fledgling railroad system was torn up by invading forces and worn down from heavy use. Military operations destroyed bridges and factories, while soldiers of both sides trampled crops underfoot and killed livestock to gain a better meal. In South Carolina, for example, the number of hogs—the animals that furnished meat for most families—plummeted from 965,000 to only 150,000.[43] The Confederate South lost two-thirds of its wealth, reckoned both in physical property and slaves, and its share of national wealth dropped from 30 percent to only 12 percent. Such statistics do not touch the disruption of people's lives and the destruction of their plans and dreams.

The war also created feelings of rancor and rage that would last for generations and penetrate as deeply as those in Spain. Beyond the deaths of 30 percent of Confederate soldiers, the South's prideful planter class was appalled by General William Tecumseh Sherman's march through Georgia to the sea. The length and scope of the war had hardened Sherman's views. "We are not fighting armies but a hostile people," he concluded, "and must make old and young, rich and poor, feel the hard hand of war." He resolved "to make Georgia howl," and when he captured Atlanta and ordered its evacuation, he responded to complaints of the city's leaders by telling them bluntly, "War is cruelty, and you cannot refine it; and those who brought war into our country deserve all the curses and maledictions a people can pour out." As his army marched from Atlanta to Savannah, he discarded the doctrine that war should be made against armies not civilians. Instead his troops tried to destroy everything that might be industrially or agriculturally useful to the Confederacy, creating a vast "Burnt District" where the stench of slaughtered animals was almost unbearable. Later his soldiers left the capital of South Carolina smoldering in ashes. General Benjamin Butler also had enraged the Southern elite during his administration of occupied New Orleans. Frustrated by the hostile attitude of Southern ladies, one of whom leaned from her window to pour a chamber pot on the head of Admiral David Farragut, Butler issued an order that any woman who engaged in future contemptuous behavior would be treated as a "woman of the town playing her avocation"—a prostitute.[44]

Jefferson Davis, president of the Confederacy, stoked these fires of resentment and sectional hatred. To stiffen Southern resistance and combat discouragement, he repeatedly denounced Northern soldiers and civilians in extreme terms. Northerners were "the most depraved and intolerant and tyrannical and hated people upon earth," he asserted. They were guilty of "every crime conceivable," including the burning of "defenceless towns" and the "pillag[ing]" of people's homes by a "brutal soldiery." Davis charged that the purpose of the Emancipation Proclamation was to "incite servile insurrection" and unleash "a general assassination" of masters by their slaves. Lincoln thus was responsible for "the most execrable measure recorded in the history of guilty man." In one speech Davis even declared that "hyenas" were preferable to Yankees. On the Northern side, war also turned people against their former fellow citizens. Many felt outrage over the treatment of captured Union soldiers at Andersonville prison, where thirteen thousand men died, and the record of Confederate troops was morally culpable. On more than one occasion, vengeful Confederate troops slaughtered defenseless or captured black Union soldiers. The presence of black men in the Union army's ranks confirmed Southerners' mistaken fears that the United States aimed to make African Americans equal to whites.[45]

When the war ended, however, the victorious North had to deal with race. No longer could it avoid a question that its newspapers and magazines had often asked: "What shall we do with the Negro?" The task of Reconstruction—bringing the southern states back into the Union in some fashion—forced consideration of that question. In 1865 the answer seemed clear: leaders in the North had little interest in improving the status of the freed slave, now economically dependent on hostile former slaveholders. President Andrew Johnson decided to reconstitute Southern states through the participation and voting of white men only. In fact, he soon allowed influential leaders of the Confederacy to join in that process. Only when the violent racism and rigid intransigence of the defeated South became painfully evident did a different branch of government, the northern Congress, decide that something more was needed. Yet almost three years elapsed before events forced Congress to make a limited and temporary commitment to the political equality of African Americans.

The events from 1865 to 1868 underscored how serious the problem of racism was in American democracy. During Reconstruction under Johnson, violence against the former slaves was a part of daily life in the South. Large-scale riots by whites and police broke out in Memphis and New Orleans, and the whites-only southern legislatures enacted black codes that reduced freedom for African Americans to something much like slavery. Congress, after deciding not to admit southerners elected under Johnson's plan (including the Confederacy's vice president, Alexander Stephens), passed a civil rights act designed to safeguard some basic legal rights and block racially discriminatory penalties in the law. President Johnson vetoed this measure, and southern whites continued their adamant resistance. Forced to go further, northern lawmakers overturned Johnson's veto. Next they proposed the Fourteenth Amendment, which would constitutionally make blacks citizens, prohibit states from violating citizens' rights, and create the possibility of reducing southern representation in Congress if black men were excluded from the ballot box. The response of southern state governments was to reject the amendment overwhelmingly, thus defeating its ratification. At this point Congress saw that the only path to a different result was to reconstitute the South's electorate and form new southern governments. In the Reconstruction Act of 1867 northern legislators required voting for black men, new elections, and approval of the Fourteenth Amendment as a condition for southern reentry into Congress.[46]

With this law and the Fifteenth Amendment in 1870 (which forbade denial of the right to vote "*on account of* race, color, or previous condition of servitude"),[47] the North's Republican Party hoped that it had finished with the race issue. Unlike the victors in Spain, northern Republicans did not want to see the conflict over race through to a final resolution. In 1939 General Franco and his Nationalist supporters acted differently; not merely happy to have won the war, they were determined to impose their will on the peace. They proceeded to purge enemies, dominate their defeated opponents, and insist upon their vision for Spanish society on the nation. Thus Franco's efforts to control the future did not end with victory. Instead he renewed those efforts with the advantages gained through victory and continued them with consistency, determination, and cruelty for thirty-six more years.

Nothing of the kind occurred in the United States, where the will to apply the Declaration of Independence quickly evaporated. The victorious North had never been committed to a thorough restructuring of southern society or to the eradication of racism. The preservation of the Union had been its major goal, with emancipation an added war measure. Reforming society to establish racial equality was never contemplated by more than a few, while significant parts of northern opinion deplored any interference with state rights and condemned the central government for interfering too much in southern social arrangements. As early as 1865 there were prominent Republicans who desired a prompt return to normal conditions, and only a minority believed that the basic problem demanded stronger measures.[48] After three years of conflict with President Johnson and southern whites, the majority of Republican lawmakers were even more ready to put racial issues aside.

The dismaying and violent story that unfolded in the South under Congress' 1867 Reconstruction Act soon redoubled northern attitudes of indifference and futility in regard to the race issue. The Ku Klux Klan appeared throughout the South, acting as the terroristic arm of former white leaders. Its hooded riders threatened, beat, stabbed, shot, and killed black men and white Republicans who tried to bring about change in the South. The North's response was tepid and ineffective, but even the dispatch of a small number of troops, shackled by restrictive orders, added another deep grievance to the white South's list of perceived wrongs. If legal action seemed likely to imperil the Klan, it simply went underground but continued its work, and whites on southern juries blocked many federal prosecutions. Faced with these events, the North pulled back further from any strong policies. The Supreme Court joined the retreat in 1873 and 1883, when it issued rulings, in the Slaughterhouse Cases and Civil Rights Cases respectively, that narrowed the scope of the Fourteenth Amendment and overturned or weakened what laws were on the books.[49]

By 1872 southern whites had regained control of most state governments; by the end of 1876, they controlled them all. Black southerners were again in dependent positions, lacking education, wealth, influence, allies, or political power. Moreover, northern Republicans had signaled with the election of Rutherford Hayes in 1876 that their interference in the South was essentially over. During the remaining decades of the nineteenth-century, northern Republicans occasionally discussed fairness in federal elections or the idea of federal aid to education, but they did nothing. The South had lost the war, but in terms of the underlying issue of race, it had won the peace. The defeated party in the United States' civil war failed to gain independence and had to reenter the Union, but in contrast to Spain, it emerged with significant elements of victory. The white South was allowed to impose its will on African Americans with determination, consistency, and cruelty for one hundred years.

That victory by the conquered came at a high price, however. The South moved even more clearly into a separate, disadvantageous path of development. It became the poorest part of the country, locked into a declining agricultural economy, isolated from the richest currents of economic progress, and ignored by a northern society caught up in new events and new directions. Southern whites forced blacks to remain subservient, working in the fields, growing cotton. But now cotton was a problem crop, a deadweight pulling the region down instead of the key to wealth. The world's demand for cotton had ceased to grow rapidly during the Civil War. Because the war caused southerners to lose their position as dominant suppliers of cotton, they worked hard to regain that leadership only to find, by the end of Reconstruction, that they now produced too much of the crop. Prices began to fall. Growing indebtedness caused many white small farmers to lose their farms. Black laborers, trapped by sharecropping contracts, made no money or fell into debt and could only hope to better their situation by growing more cotton. The landowners and merchants who supplied basic commodities to black labor—and charged high interest in the process—were able to retain their relatively wealthy, privileged, and powerful position in the society. But the South as a region was poor and backward. It continued to be the unprogressive, hierarchical, conservative, and elite-dominated part of the "two United States."[50]

Some advocates of a "New South" tried to change that late in the nineteenth century. Henry Grady, a journalist and one of their most eloquent spokesmen, declared, "There was a South of slavery and secession—that South is dead." The Confederate soldier may have returned from battle to find "his house in ruins, his farm devastated, his stock killed, his barns empty, his trade destroyed, his money worthless, his social system, feudal in its magnificence, swept away," but, said Grady, he promptly began to rebuild. While trying to assure northerners that the South was treating its black citizens fairly, Grady insisted that southerners had "put business above politics," "fallen in love with work," and raised up cities, schools, and factories. "We have challenged your spinners in Massachusetts and your iron-makers in Pennsylvania." It was true that some industry developed in the postwar South, but it was predominantly low-wage, low-skill industry, and its leaders allied themselves with the regressive political elite to resist social change and sometimes to benefit from convict labor.[51]

By the 1890s the economic distress of southern farmers had reached such heights that many whites broke away from the Democratic Party, which prided itself in having "redeemed" the region from the racial horrors of Reconstruction. These desperate, dissident whites, by voting for the new Populist Party and cooperating with black Republicans, threatened to change the economic and financial structure of the South. At this point the leaders of the Democratic Party intensified their rhetoric of white supremacy and turned to fraud, intimidation, and violence to beat back the Populist challenge. Then, to secure their power thereafter, they passed a variety of laws to deny the ballot to blacks, as well as to many poorer whites. This assured the Democrats of consistent victories, and to consolidate white support through virulent racism they also enacted an ever-growing number of Jim Crow laws, which segregated black people in public places and marked their status as inferior and degraded. A complaisant Supreme Court in 1896 gave its stamp of approval in *Plessy v. Ferguson* to the fiction of "separate but equal" treatment, judging it to be consistent with the Fourteenth Amendment.[52]

The two United States became more firmly established with the new southern political system. Patently unequal and undemocratic, it created a regional politics starkly different from the rest of the nation. Disfranchisement was the foundational element of this political system. Discrimination against African Americans also eliminated competition; one party now dominated politics in the South completely. In general elections there was no meaningful contest for offices. The only opportunity for competition came in the Democratic Party's primaries or nominating processes, for nomination as a Democrat was tantamount to election. With one party controlling politics so completely, there was hardly any reason to go to the polls and vote because the result was certain. In little more than a decade political participation in the South plummeted to abysmal levels. And to solidify this system and tamp down any objections to it, southern Democrats perennially stressed the race issue, inventing dangers to white supremacy and in the process encouraging lynching, racial hatred, and discrimination.[53]

Meanwhile, the North followed a different path, immersed in economic growth and social and economic change. Industrialization rapidly spawned new factories, railroads, urban slums, and urban amenities. Agriculture specialized and mechanized further in order to feed the industrial and commercial population. Before 1900 the nation had become one of the world's industrial powers, and the Census Bureau reported that a majority of the population was urban rather than rural. That population grew rapidly as a result of an enormous wave of immigration that resumed in the 1880s and brought millions of poor but eager workers into northern factories. Along with greater wealth and soaring production came recessions, pollution, labor conflicts, anger over railroad rates, and attempts (usually foiled) to regulate the powerful new industrial interests. As the twentieth century began, the United States, led by the North, went to war with Spain over Cuba and become an imperial power through the acquisition of Cuba, Puerto Rico, and the Philippines.

These changes were rife with implications for the nation's Civil War legacy. Their most important effect was simply that they dominated the attention of northerners, causing them to think less about the past and its enduring issues and infusing the population with a large body of newly arrived citizens for whom the Civil War was completely irrelevant. Very important as well was the fact that immigration, imperialism, and popular ideas of social Darwinism all reinforced the North's inclination to ignore racial oppression in the South. The North's new immigrants were rarely from the British Isles or Northern Europe. Overwhelmingly they came from Southern and Eastern Europe or from Russia and were Catholic or Jewish or Eastern Orthodox. Often their skin was olive-toned, their hair dark, and their features and language different. Some brought ideas or political views deemed dangerous. Old-stock, Protestant northerners reacted with disapproval, hostility, and prejudice against these new Americans. Scholars and writers published books warning of their racial inferiority and criminality. When imperialism placed conquered darker-skinned populations in distant lands under the nation's authority, racist attitudes gained still more acceptance and respectability. The unfinished agenda from the Civil War grew longer.

After the Populist Party met with defeat, a more urban, middle- and upper-class movement called Progressivism gained enough power in the nation to enact some economic reforms.[54] Progressives tried to rein in industrial trusts and monopolies, regulate the railroads, reform the banking system, and improve the conditions of labor with workers' compensation laws and an eight-hour workday. But Progressivism was a "lily-white" movement. It developed within an environment of racist thought and did virtually nothing to end discrimination or challenge racial injustice. In fact,

Woodrow Wilson, one of Progressivism's most successful presidents in domestic reform, extended segregation into the federal bureaucracy and praised the blatantly racist film *Birth of a Nation*. As historian Rayford Logan points out, at the turn of the twentieth century, the United States reached "the nadir period" of its racial attitudes. Racism was widely accepted and solidly respectable, both North and South. The founding ideals of equal and inalienable rights had been submerged through time and social change and almost forgotten.[55]

The long road traveled by thousands in the civil rights movement eventually put equality back on the national agenda, but it was a difficult and often dangerous process.[56] During many decades idealistic individuals, both known and little noticed, struggled against discrimination and the majority's indifference. Risking retaliation, economic loss, or violence, they worked to resist and publicize injustice. The black community overcame disadvantages to strengthen itself, gradually producing more teachers and leaders, more professionals and educated citizens, who would bring pressure to bear on institutions and decision makers. In various fields black artists, singers, writers, or sports figures proved that talent was not restricted by race. Organizations like the Urban League and the NAACP chipped away at the structures of discrimination. The Legal Defense Fund of the NAACP, staffed with many graduates from predominantly black Howard University Law School, began to achieve some important court victories during the 1930s and 1940s.

As in Spain, however, it seems clear that structural changes in the economy and society did even more to erode the underpinnings of the racist, Jim Crow system and make a frontal attack possible. African Americans began to migrate from the South, where opportunity was virtually nonexistent. During World War I and World War II, better paying factory jobs opened up in many northern cities, and the wave of immigration from the South increased markedly. Although blacks met widespread discrimination in the North, there they could organize their own churches, voluntary associations, and newspapers, and ... they could vote. The new concentration of black voters in some northern cities began to create a political force. When they voted together, African Americans could be the deciding factor in close elections, a fact that gave them influence. In 1929 Chicago elected a black congressman, Oscar Stanton De Priest, and black voices began to gain some weight in the northern Democratic Party and awaken long-ignored ideals. Southern whites retained great power in the party nationally and in Congress, but a new crop of northern Democrats began to insist that civil rights must be on the party's agenda.

Another similarity with Spain was the power that foreign affairs had to promote internal changes. Spain's economy benefited greatly from President Eisenhower's decision to make Franco's government a military ally. World events forced the United States to face and address some of its racial failures and social problems. First the climate of opinion within the United States felt the impact of World War II. The Allied democracies frequently declared that they were fighting against the tyranny, racism, and genocidal policies of Hitler and the Axis powers; the Allies' goal for all peoples was self-determination and "freedom from fear and want."[57] It became embarrassing and difficult for American leaders to discuss such ideals while the nation subjected black Americans to discrimination at home. African American soldiers did their full part to win the war, and they returned from battle less willing to accept a second-class citizenship. When the Cold War began in earnest, the United States and the Soviet Union became rivals for the support of a host of new darker-skinned nations emerging from colonization. Over and over again United States leaders proclaimed the superiority of their social system over the Soviet Union's. But in the battle for world opinion and in the effort to influence Africa, Asia, and non-aligned countries, the Soviets seized every opportunity to publicize America's discrimination and injustice. Jim Crow had become a liability to national interests in the Cold War.

The ideals of World War II and the pressures of the Cold War quietly influenced domestic policy in various respects and were at least a small factor in the Supreme Court's decision in *Brown v. Board of Education* in 1954.[58] The propaganda advantage that Russia exploited by playing up racial incidents and segregation was a backdrop to the thinking of all the nation's leaders. Overturning its 1896 precedent, the Court ruled that "separate educational facilities are inherently unequal." It was a watershed decision that shocked many southern politicians and galvanized a variety of forces working for justice. Over the next several years, as southern white leaders organized a campaign of "massive resistance," the forces of change grew: Rosa Parks refused to move to the back of a bus in Montgomery,

Alabama; black children tried to go to school in Little Rock, Arkansas; the federal government ultimately used troops to enforce a court order; and Martin Luther King Jr. emerged as an eloquent and morally inspiring leader. Nonviolent protests multiplied in cities and towns across the South, and the northern public began to pay attention to scenes of harsh repression of peaceful demonstrators who were demanding basic rights or the chance to use a restroom in downtown stores. The civil rights movement organized and fueled by black Americans became a mass democratic movement, with considerable white support.

The federal government, where southern whites had great power in Congress, was slow to act. But peaceful protests amid ugly, rising violence forced the government's hand. Weak civil rights laws of the 1950s gave way to a strong proposal by John F. Kennedy in 1963. Noting that "we are confronted primarily with a moral issue," Kennedy told the nation in a televised speech that "the time has come for this Nation to fulfill its promise." The question of racial justice, which was the crux of conflicts over slavery and the Civil War, at last moved to the top of America's agenda. A massive but peaceful and emotionally moving March on Washington that summer demonstrated widespread support for change. After Kennedy's assassination, his successor, Texan Lyndon Johnson, embraced the proposed legislation and employed skills that he had honed through long years in the Senate to win passage of two important laws.[59] The Civil Rights Act of 1964 outlawed segregation in hotels, restaurants, theatres, and other places of public accommodation and barred governmental discrimination. The Voting Rights Act of 1965 dismantled the legal apparatus that kept blacks from voting and dynamited the foundations of the South's peculiar political system. As federal registrars put African Americans' names on the voting rolls, a new political era dawned.

Prejudice did not easily disappear, and even though other laws and court decisions followed, many more battles had to be fought. But these changes created new ground rules for society, all of whose members experienced a different social environment. Ironically, the South may have been the region that benefited most. With segregation and a reputation for unsavory repression and violence removed, national and international businesses began to invest in the region. Prosperity began to shine in unprecedented measure on the Sunbelt, and indices of southern wealth and income approached national norms for the first time since the Civil War. In the 1970s the tide of migration by African Americans out of the South actually reversed, as large numbers of black people began to return to the region of their birth and to its new opportunities. In that same decade a new wave of governors took office in the South, proclaiming that the days of segregation and racial discrimination were over.

Lyndon Johnson had foreseen, however, that other political changes were in store. After signing the Civil Rights Act, he observed to an aide, "I think we just delivered the South to the Republican Party for a long time to come."[60] Republican presidential nominees began pursuing a "southern strategy," offering conservative ideas on social policy to southern whites, who were increasingly oriented to business and profits and living in suburbs, where the party often found strong support. Before the century was out, in some southern states the core of voting strength for Democrats was little more than the black population and small liberal groups, such as college professors. Modern Democratic politicians often gained most of their support in areas where slavery had been most concentrated, because many African Americans still lived in those regions. The South has been almost solidly Republican in the past several presidential elections.[61]

The long history of segregation, like southern resistance to racial equality and the changing patterns in politics, illustrates a notable difference between United States and Spanish history. In Spain most leaders and ordinary citizens seized the Transition from dictatorship to democracy as an opportunity to overlook, look beyond, or supersede the past. It is common for Spaniards to talk of *olvido*, or the forgetting of the past. In the United States, however, southern whites resolved never to forget the Civil War. If it soon meant little to a large portion of Northerners, the majority of southern whites nourished resentments about the war and supposed wrongs they had suffered well into the twentieth century. The massive political, economic, and social changes after 1965 replaced many old ideas with new ones, but often the theme of regional resentment survived. The exclamation "Forget, Hell!" which characterized the anger of uneducated, rural "good old boys," gave way to words of challenge from prosperous businessmen. When North Carolina's NationsBank purchased Bank of America, a vice president in Charlotte crowed that the takeover would prove "to the damn carpetbaggers that there was something intrinsically worthwhile about the

South." This southerner's comment is different from the old attitudes of Confederate patriotism, but it is an attenuated legacy of past events that had created two United States—the changing, forward-looking North and its different, backward-looking counterpart, the South.[62] Later chapters will explore more fully the influence and legacy of civil war in the United States and in Spain.

2

Ideology and Memory

The Continuing Battles

> The pain of the great historical wounds flows on, taking advantage of whatever occasion.
>
> Francisco Nieva, member of the Spanish Royal Academy, 2006

The bloody conflicts in Spain and the United States would not be forgotten. As costly internecine conflicts they demanded postwar justification and explanation. The death toll produced psychic pain. The scale of destruction challenged national pride. What had gone wrong to produce such conflict?

Before their civil wars, both Spain and the United States were proud nations in an era of nationalism. Spain, once Europe's dominant imperial power, entered the twentieth century mindful of its great heritage and troubled by its precipitous decline. Long before the disaster of 1898, when Spain lost virtually all that was left of its once vast empire, leaders had been debating the causes of national weakness. The conservative and reactionary elements in Spanish culture blamed departures from tradition and changes in the nation's character. They saw the Enlightenment, and even before it the influence of humanists such as Erasmus, as insidious cultural forces that had undermined Spain's strength. More forward-looking and secular forces in Spanish culture felt a need to modernize the nation and align its life more closely to that of Western European nations that were gaining in power. The chasm between these opposed diagnoses of Spain's decline as a world power reflected the forces that led to civil war.

The United States, though a newcomer to the world of nations, had yielded nothing to ancient Spain in respect to national pride. The colonists had wrested their independence from England, then the greatest of European powers, and citizens and leaders of the new nation took enormous pride in their ideology of political liberty and representative government. A bumptious conviction that the nation was the new model for human progress expressed itself among southern planters, northern businessmen, and small farmers of both sections. Although the divergent social systems of North and South were on a path that would lead to war, national pride was potent and growing even in the 1850s. With striking casualness, leaders of the South could talk of extending the virtuous American system to Mexico and the Caribbean, while their counterparts in the North could mention the annexation of Canada as a likely future event.

When such deep-seated attitudes had to confront the reality of fratricidal slaughter and division, national pride collided with national failure of an essential kind. The contrast demanded both explanation and expiation, for the hugely destructive civil wars were an offense against the national ideal. At the level of national culture efforts would have to be made to explain and justify what had taken place. To rescue the national narrative, civil war would have to be reinterpreted as something positive both for Spain and for the United States.

For individuals, too, a challenge of reorientation lay ahead. Deep and bitter conflicts like these do not resolve themselves cleanly or with finality. Although military battles identify the victor and the vanquished, long-lasting and painful emotions remain. No matter how severe the ramifications of victory or defeat may be, the arguments about who was right and who was wrong, who should be honored and who should be condemned, continue. Quickly or eventually, the contest moves to another plane—that of morality—where for many combatants and their descendants consensus becomes extremely difficult to reach.

Ideology magnified the bloodshed and destruction of internecine conflict. For Spain the ideological conflicts between bolshevism and fascism that soon engulfed all of Europe obviously were of great importance, but across the Atlantic the racial issue had a similar intensifying impact. A set of beliefs was necessary to justify the extent of slaughter, and each side relied on an ideology to explain its cause and sustain its mounting sacrifices.

In both countries it identified each side with some transcendent good. As a result, the men and women who sacrificed but survived, who fought and absorbed losses, were not likely to abandon their ideology lightly. It made sense of their commitment and justified their descent into violence. Once the shooting stopped, their wartime ideologies would be transformed into historical memories and commemorations. These collective acts of memory and commemoration would elevate individual acts to the plane of virtue and explain away vast societal failure.

Divisive experiences and emotions extend also to the children, grandchildren, or great-grandchildren of those who fought the war. Victory and defeat had ramifications for them that were both personal and familial. They felt the war directly, for changes to society affected them personally, often in painful or disadvantageous ways. They also felt the war indirectly but strongly, for they were socialized by their families into beliefs that linked personal identity with their ancestors' role in the war. Thus for succeeding generations the war continued as well, although the passage of time created some differences. Because later generations lived under different conditions, they naturally thought and acted in ways appropriate to *their* time and circumstances. But ideology, memory, and commemoration continued to be important.

These patterns—national and personal—characterized both countries, although some notable differences in their histories created significant variation as well. What was common was the underlying process by which people carried their beliefs into postwar reality, creating historical memories and commemorations. After both civil wars the persisting arguments about who was right and who was wrong followed the same logic. The victors sought to elaborate, or stand by, their original justification for beginning and continuing a war. As time passed and conditions changed, they adapted their arguments to serve new purposes. Those on the losing side, on the other hand, needed to reduce or expunge the stigma of being in the "wrong" and having history's verdict pronounced against them. They could approach this task in different ways. Insistence on the original justifications was common, but some efforts involved a new or creative argument that might make the losers' case more convincingly or effectively. Other defenses had a reactive character—responses designed to counter the criticisms of the victors. As the argument continued, the victors then would respond to their opponents, leading to a sequence of charge and countercharge with repetitious elements.

In both countries certain points became central pillars of justification or core grievances against the other side. In the United States, for example, southerners modified their defense of slavery to insist repeatedly that slavery was only the occasion for war, not its cause, while they lovingly crafted an attractive myth about the lost glories of a plantation society where black and white had lived in harmony. As key grievances, southerners cited the destruction and damage to civilians of Sherman's March to the Sea or complained of the "horrors" of Reconstruction. In Spain, Republicans emphasized that Franco's uprising had destroyed a democratically elected government, while Nationalists stressed their defense of church and nation and then evolved a number of arguments over time to stress the benefits of Franco's dictatorship. To counter criticism of his attack on a democratically elected government, they emphasized the disorder and dangers of prewar society. As repetition made these elements familiar, the passage of time and the arrival of new generations brought novel points into the discussion. For example, the *nietos*, or grandchildren, in Spain have raised issues that their parents and grandparents chose to leave unaddressed, while the mythology about Lincoln has evolved away from historical reality to serve society's changing needs.

The main differences between Spain and the United States in these areas are the product of contrasting experiences during the immediate postwar decades and contrasting governmental structures. In Spain General Franco imposed a harsh, repressive dictatorship that lasted more than thirty-five years. Throughout this period he insisted on controlling the argument and imposing his interpretation, using the cause of National Catholicism as justification for warfare and postwar rule. The Republican side of the debate was silenced. Only exiles living abroad were able to write or speak about their beliefs. After Franco's death circumstances further delayed the surfacing of internal debate over the rights and wrongs of the war. The agenda of the Transition—shaped by widespread desires for democracy and fears of another military uprising—put a premium on consensus rather than debate.

Defeated Confederates, on the other hand, rapidly seized the high ground in establishing their interpretation of the war. There were racial and structural reasons for this somewhat surprising result. The victorious North shrank from addressing the most fundamental issue of the war—race. Controlled by prejudice and unwilling to insist on racial equality, the North allowed the defeated South to win the peace, at least in regard to race. In addition, the post–Civil War United States remained a large country with a small central government. In the federal system, states retained a great deal of power, and diverse local loyalties and beliefs shaped the culture. Unlike Franco's Spain, leaders of the victorious North lacked the power to impose uniform values or practices on a pluralistic society.

Clearly, the level of human determination made a difference in regard to the victors, just as strength of will or lack of opportunity affected the actions of the vanquished. Southerners in the United States energetically began to develop and modify their ideology soon after the last shot was fired, whereas the defeated Republicans in Spain were unable to enter a real debate for decades. The two nations had a symmetrical experience, but it was mirror-image symmetry, with the loudest voices coming from the defeated side in one country and from the victors in the other. This difference naturally changed the timing of emerging controversies and predictable developments. This mirror-image symmetry applied also to the recrudescence in later generations of beliefs that had been suppressed or ignored. In Spain, of course, it was the Republican values that came to the fore in later years, whereas in the United States the repressed ideal of racial equality finally gained power in the civil rights movement.

Another important difference stems from the deep and continuous involvement of two institutions in Franco's uprising and subsequent dictatorship: the Catholic Church and the Spanish army. These institutions were critical in causing, defining, and maintaining Franco's conquest of power and his government. In comparison, the American Civil War arose far more from the clash of politicians and political forces. The armies of both North and South were composed of volunteers or draftees, who quickly returned to civilian life. Although evangelical American churches had played a large role in bringing on the war through their uncompromising and contrary teachings in the North and South, they soon moved toward consonant, aligned postures after the war.[1] New voluntary organizations and politicians took the lead in debating the war, whereas in Spain key institutions remained highly visible and bore significant responsibility. Those roles for Spain's church and the army meant power and influence during the dictatorship, but they also entailed serious implications for the Transition and after, when social realities changed. This chapter will explore the continuing battles over ideology and memory in both countries and analyze the similarities and differences in their experiences, beginning with Spain.

Ideology and Memory: Spain under and after Franco

It has not been a matter of a civil war, but of a *Crusade* for religion, for patria and for civilization. . . . For God and for Spain.

Bishop Plá y Deniel, 1936

With the democratic change, [the church] is seen as the right hand of the dictator.

Bishop Xavier Novell, 2011

If memory is not opened definitively and completely to know the truth . . . captive and disarmed memory will cause the nationalist troops to have gained their ultimate objectives.

Emilio Silva and Santiago Macías, *La Fosas de Franco*

Let us hope that the grandchildren of my grand-daughter will finally forget.

A seventy-two-year-old visitor to the Valley of the Fallen, quoted in *ABC*, July 30, 2006

Spain's Catholic Church played a key role in creating the victor's ideology in the civil war. Like the United States' slaveholders, it had been developing an ideology and a litany of grievances before the war. Its leaders, like the "fire-eaters" of America's antebellum South, took the lead in spreading alarm and demanding action against the government.

The church had reacted to the establishment of the Second Republic with disapproval and fear, and long before General Franco and the army launched their uprising, religious leaders denounced the Republicans. Pope Pius XI's encyclical in 1933 against the republic and its "deplorable laws" reinforced a sense of grave crisis among Spanish bishops and priests. They saw in society's conflicts a "frightening ideological confusion," a struggle between the Right and Left for "the *new reconquest of Spain*," and "an abyss that was opening under" Spaniards' feet. In 1935 Augustinian educator Teodoro

Rodriguez published a book calling on Spanish Catholics to awaken to the nation's "nightmare" of "religion persecuted, the *Patria* insulted and humiliated, the home undone." Warning of "Masonic Judaism," he declared that Bolsheviks, following "the Jew Marx, are trying to make Spain the second nation, where may be developed all the horrors of anarchic communism." The next year, Zacharías García Vallada, a Jesuit, published *The Destiny of Spain in Universal History*, which argued that "God has signaled his purpose"—"the providential mission of Spain was the defense of Catholicism." Spain could choose to be "the City of God" or "the City of the Devil."[2]

Once the army attempted its coup on July 17, 1936, leaders of the church seized the opportunity to define the uprising as a religious crusade. Although General Franco was both religious and reactionary, his first radio broadcasts emphasized the idea of a political struggle between Spain and Russia or between Spain and revolutionaries following foreign directions; the radical and incompetent republic, he argued, had been delivering the nation to Marxist revolutionaries. Quickly, however, bishops and other high clerics grafted a religious ideology onto the Nationalist cause. Within three weeks the bishops of Pamplona and Vitoria had issued a joint pastoral letter praising Franco's fallen soldiers as martyrs. Shortly thereafter Monsignor Olaechea of Pamplona declared that the conflict was "not a war" but "a Crusade . . . the most holy that the centuries have seen." At the end of August Salamanca's Bishop Plá y Daniel issued his pastoral letter, "The Two Cities," which described Franco's forces from God's celestial city fighting against the "earthly city embodied by Communists and anarchists, the sons of Cain." The military's attempted coup was a "Crusade for religion, for *patria* and for civilization." Thus it was as one with the church's stands "in favor of *order* against *anarchy*, in favor of the installation of a *hierarchical government* against a dissolving *communism*, in favor of the defense of *Christian civilization* and its foundations, *religion, patria, and family* against those *without God and against God.*" The archbishop of Toledo, Cardinal Isidro Gomá, reported to Rome that the republic had brought Spain to the brink of a "Marxist and communist abyss" and that the battle was between "religion and atheism, Christian civilization and barbarism."[3]

In July 1937 Spain's Episcopal Conference issued to bishops throughout the world a report defending Franco's Nationalists and framing the civil war in an apocalyptic perspective. God had made Spain the testing ground for "ideas and events that aspire to conquer the world." The war was a "battle of irreconcilable ideologies," a struggle "between bolshevism and the Christian civilization." At stake was "order, social peace, traditional civilization, the patria, and . . . the defense of religion." The Republican side desired "the elimination of the Catholic religion in Spain" and "the implantation of communism," whereas Franco's patriotic army was the force that could stop "the enemies of God" and be "the guarantee" of religion. After denouncing the republic's Popular Front government for allowing anarchy and promoting Communist ideas, the bishops made wildly inflated estimates of the violence that had, in fact, occurred against priests and churches. Christians in other lands needed to understand, argued the bishops, that the army's uprising was for the defense not just of Spain but also of Christian civilization.[4]

With this background, Franco defined his movement and, initially, his dictatorship as a crusade for National Catholicism. He was saving the nation and Catholicism from grave dangers, including communism, atheism, Judaism, and Free Masonry. His National Department of Propaganda treated the civil war in Manichean terms, preaching a spirit of vengeance to exterminate the enemy "without compassion." This extreme ideology obviously appealed to church leaders, with their apocalyptic perspective, but to the rigidly conservative elites in the economy and the army, as well.

After Franco achieved victory in 1939, compromise with the evils threatening Spain was not permissible.[5] Without pity, his forces executed fifty thousand soon after the war ended, imprisoned hundreds of thousands, and imposed tight controls on the society. Authorities opened three hundred thousand dossiers on people under suspicion and urged citizens to show "patriotic virtue" by denouncing neighbors suspected of being "reds." With Fascist salutes citizens had to declaim that Spain was "one, great, and free," while the government centralized administration and suppressed languages other than Castilian.[6] The church gave its full support and ceremonial imprimatur to the regime, managing through its organizational presence and prestige to relegate Fascist ideology to a subordinate role. Church leaders dominated and took over the annual celebrations that Franco scheduled to recall "the Glorious uprising, the Victory, and the Fallen." His commemorations became "a strictly religious ceremony always presided over by the Church and its clergy."[7]

By establishing a dictatorship, Franco took full advantage of the opportunity to impose his interpretation of history and prohibit all others. In contrast to the situation in America, one side from the Spanish Civil War was forced to be silent, or largely silent, for decades. The Republican half of the "two Spains" had not disappeared, but its surviving adherents were silenced and suppressed. In addition to those killed or imprisoned, thousands of talented and well-educated Spaniards fled the country, forced into an exile from which many never returned. Deprived of the life they had known, these people also lost their country, even if they eventually returned, for time changed the Spain they had known. Thousands of others had to escape hunger and suffering at home by immigrating to other nations in Europe or South America. Families were torn apart or divided either by the regime's repression or by political differences.

Meanwhile, with the church's support, Franco wrapped his dictatorship in a fundamentalist, antisecular, backward-looking Catholicism. Schoolbooks praised the fusion in sixteenth-century Spain of the "Catholic ideal" with the "military monarchy," a fusion that the twentieth-century *caudillo* obviously was continuing. Students learned that in modern times his National Movement had saved the traditional essence of Spain from liberalism, socialism, democracy, the Masons, and the Communists. Crucifixes, prayer, and religious ceremonies were all part of a religiously structured public education, where a widely used text listed these "principal errors condemned by the Church . . . materialism, Marxism, atheism, pantheism, deism, rationalism, Protestantism, socialism, communism, trade unionism, liberalism, modernism, and Freemasonry." All blame for the outbreak of a bloody, fratricidal war fell on Republicans, who, Franco's regime insisted, had allowed or encouraged radicalism, the burning of churches and convents, the weakening of the army, social disorder, and secessionist impulses from Catalonia. With the defeat of the Fascist Axis powers in World War II, the church backed Franco in giving new emphasis to the threat of international communism and calling for internal unity.[8]

Throughout the dictatorship the influence of the church and its social values remained strong, despite competition from the Falangists or other elements backing Franco, and despite the inevitable changes brought by time. Censorship by the church regulated social and private life as tightly as Franco's government scrutinized political activity. Clothing, recreation, books, movies, and music all had to conform to church standards, as did attitudes supporting woman's traditional, subordinate role in the home. Franco literally turned back the clock on women's rights, restoring the 1889 civil code in addition to backing the church's restrictive vision of women's place in society. Censorship of literature included even the works of such famous Spaniards as Miguel de Unamuno and José Ortega y Gasset. The government and the church aimed to control belief and action, and Franco readily used force and violence to enforce conformity.[9] Although the segregated South in the United States would insist on adherence to the ideology of discrimination, it fell short of the surface uniformity imposed by the dictatorship.

This attempt to make Spain "permeated by Catholic values in every aspect of its life" was too harsh to be completely successful. One scholar has described the 1940s as a time of fear, with silence deployed as a defense against suspicion. Social organizations withered as people isolated themselves, and "the result was a claustrophobic society that made daily life very difficult. Although Spaniards knew that it was wise to attend mass, one Catholic historian has noted that compulsion is different from sincere belief and expressed his doubt that the "religious reconquest" desired by the church ever "took place."[10]

Franco's ideology never abandoned the ideas of national Catholicism, but it changed its emphases and evolved over time to adapt to changing circumstances. As the decades advanced—pushing the war further into the past and ushering into society a new generation that had not experienced its battles—attitudes changed and the regime sought additional justifications for its hold on power. By the 1950s the regime was downplaying its previous Fascist character as it pursued military agreements and financial aid with the United States and Western institutions. Many Spaniards, especially students in the universities, were inclined to view the civil war not as a glorious crusade but as "a useless fratricidal slaughter." Rather than solving the nation's problems, it had been an immense tragedy. Textbooks now blamed the war on Spaniards' inability to reconcile their differences or spoke of a "national tragedy." In turn, the dictatorship began to speak about peace rather than victory, and prosperity rather than a crusade against evil. Some individuals who had been part of the Nationalist cause, including the disillusioned Falangist writer Dionisio Ridruejo, began to consider some type of social reconciliation. In 1964, on the twenty-fifth anniversary of the Nationalists' victory, the government chose to publicize "the Peace of Franco" rather than his victory in war. From the Ministry of Information and Tourism came historical works by Ricardo de la Cierva that dropped the word "crusade" in favor of "the War of Spain." Publicity increasingly linked the person of Franco with stability and economic progress and suggested that without him Spaniards would fall back into conflict.[11]

Another important aspect of ideology under Franco, and one that was prominent in the United States was well, was the effort to honor Nationalist soldiers who died in battle. The emotional compulsion to bear witness to loved ones killed in war is older than Sophocles' *Antigone*, and it became a vital part of public commemorations organized by the regime and the church. In 1940 Franco chose an austere but impressive site to bear the name Valley of the Fallen and house a basilica. Located near the Escorial, the imposing sixteenth-century palace and monastery built by Felipe II, Franco's project required eighteen years to build. Under compulsion, thousands of Republican prisoners dug into a mountainside and hewed out of solid rock an enormous church. Above it rises a huge cross visible from a distance of forty kilometers. Franco's intent was to honor through burial the Falangist leader, José Antonio Primo de Rivera, and thousands of Nationalist troops who died in battle during "our glorious Crusade." Eventually, some Republican dead were buried there as well, without permission from their families, so that Franco could say that the Valley of the Fallen honored all who died in the Civil War. But in the public mind the complex always remained identified with the Nationalists, their army, and the church.

In addition to a vast space for religious observance within the rock, the site houses a Benedictine abbey and, on nearby hillsides, numerous smaller shrines representing the stations of the cross. A couple of years after construction was complete, the Catholic Church gave significant sanction to the project; Pope John XXIII elevated the church to the status of a basilica. Thereafter, Nationalists celebrated commemorative masses on important dates and honored both fallen soldiers and leaders like the Falangists' José Antonio. After Franco's death, the *caudillo*'s body was buried there as well, near the altar. Both the site's history and its Fascist style of architecture made it a physical and spiritual tribute to National Catholicism, a colossal monument designed to perpetuate the victor's ideology.

Although the church was central to Franquista remembrance, secular commemorations were another part of the efforts of Franco's regime to impose its ideology on society. That goal guided his designation of national holidays. July 18, when Franco arrived in Morocco from the Canary Islands to join the uprising, became perhaps the most important national holiday, since it officially elevated both the Nationalist military campaign and its *caudillo*. April 1, the date on which the Nationalists declared their victory, was another major holiday, and the government suspended work for all on both dates. Other important holidays on which all public offices closed honored José Antonio Primo de Rivera or linked the regime to key dates in Spanish history, such as the outbreak of resistance against Napoleon in 1808. For more than a decade Franco staged a giant "Victory Parade" on April 1, until he later moved the parade to May. These public celebrations demonstrated the regime's power while offering the Spanish public a reason for relaxation and entertainment, courtesy of the regime. The government rewarded loyalty while extracting at least the appearance of support from its foes.[12]

Through the decades of Franco's rule, it was impossible for Republicans to debate the war openly or advocate for their interpretation of events, as defeated southerners did in the United States. There, ironically, the losing side in the civil war proved more outspoken and insistent than the victors. Such was impossible in Spain's repressive dictatorship, but the war itself had identified the essential elements of Republican ideology. Key beliefs and values of the Republicans survived, though silenced, in the minds of all those who had fought against the Nationalists. Wartime Republican slogans had spoken of "the people against the privileged" and of "democrats, republicans, and anti-fascists against the reactionaries, monarchists, and fascists." The republic had represented for its partisans democracy, equality, freedom of thought, and social change against aristocracy, reaction, and stifling religious control. United to the idea of a struggle against fascism and forces of the past was the basic point that the Second Republic was a legal, constitutional government overthrown by a military uprising. These core ideas were not erased by the decision of Spain's Communist Party in

1956 to pursue a policy of national reconciliation that would involve pulling down the dictatorship "peacefully." The means had changed but not the goals.[13]

With Franco's death and the dramatic but tense transition to democracy, a new era—and ultimately a revival of ideological arguments—began. The Transition has been a great source of pride for Spaniards, but for part of the population today it is also problematic. Freedom to examine the past led first to a growing stream of historical studies or movies and then to reconsideration of the Transition itself. A common criticism of the way democracy arrived in Spain is that it involved or imposed a process of *olvido*. In this view the transition to democracy was incomplete and inadequate, because the crimes of the dictatorship and a full recognition of the reality of Spain's repressive past were swept under the rug and ignored. Not all Spaniards are in agreement with this criticism, however. The simmering debate over the adequacy of the Transition masks two types of division: a divergence of attitudes within the population that survey data have consistently documented and an evolution of perspective that is rooted in generational change.[14]

A difficult and unforgiving reality imposed itself on the generation that made the Transition. On the one hand, the problems of maintaining the aging dictatorship in the face of social change and growing opposition were increasingly obvious. On the other hand, the forces of reaction remained strong and nervously vigilant. There were hard-liners within the regime (referred to as the "Bunker") who were determined to continue a repressive government. The army's high command was filled with arch-conservatives who saw resistance to change as their duty, a sacred responsibility to the army and the nation. Although the highest ranking official in Spain's Catholic Church, Cardinal Vicente Enrique y Tarancón, was in those years giving voice and influence to younger priests inspired by Vatican II and ideals of social justice, most of the church hierarchy remained staunchly conservative. The hostility toward democratic and social change was apparent in the reaction to Cardinal Tarancón's liberal attitudes. Officials of Franco's regime snubbed and insulted him, and during the funeral in 1973 of Carrero Blanco, Franco's president, ultra-rightists shouted "Tarancón, al paredón," or "Tarancón, up against the wall." In such conditions the creation of a democracy was highly uncertain and surrounded by risks, as the attempted coup in 1981 amply confirmed.

Thus, in the period of Transition, democratic leaders, including those of the far Left, put aside any desire for vengeance or long-delayed justice and opted to cooperate with all those on the Right who would accept change. The Socialists under Felipe González moved sharply toward the center. Santiago Carrillo, the leader of Spain's Communist Party, or Partido Communista de España (PCE), similarly chose cooperation over confrontation, taking controversial steps in order to cooperate with and support the new democratic regime. Recalling this period, Carrillo has written that the people feared a return to conflict, were "avid as much for liberty as for peace," and were hungry for social change. Given the strength of conservative elements, even the Communists accepted the fact that capitalism would have hegemonic power in Spain's future. But "the renunciation of physical revenge by the conquered over the conquerors" was "indispensable to achieve a reconciliation on democratic bases." Although putting aside a moral rendering of accounts could be "very painful," Carrillo's party recognized and credited "the good faith of those who, having been part of the regime, had decided to collaborate with the anti-Franco opposition in the construction of a new democratic system." In that process Spaniards would work together to establish "among all [groups] new civilized relations."[15]

In this spirit and facing these realities, the leaders of the Transition approved first, in July 1976, a law of amnesty that covered officials of Franco's regime whose actions had not endangered or damaged people's lives. Not until almost a year later did the Council of Ministers approve the release of most Basque prisoners accused of terrorism, and the government waited until October 1977 to pass a law of amnesty that covered political actions involving bloodshed, by Franquistas or the ETA.[16] The delay in giving legal recognition to the Communist Party was another product of the need to move carefully toward democracy. What Santiago Carrillo called "the factor of fear" hung over the Transition, with the population understandably afraid after "forty years of war and terror ... that the generals would make a coup if the country inclined too much to the left." But to Carrillo and the leaders of the Transition, their decisions were never a matter of forgetting: "The PCE never thought or spoke of forgetting Spain's past or even less the

Civil War, but of *overcoming* the past—of considering it as a moment of our history." The measures of amnesty in the Transition were a means to move into the future, to open a new democratic path for Spain and its citizens.[17]

And indeed, as historians have shown, the past never was forgotten in Spanish literature, cinema, or academic works. Although politics in the Transition omitted a rendering of accounts, the nation's culture gave steady and ample attention to the Spanish Civil War and, to a lesser extent, Franco's regime. From the 1970s forward there has been an outpouring of books, articles, essays, and documentaries about the civil war. Scholars as well as popular writers have examined the war and the dictatorship. Even during the 1950s, under Franco's repressive regime, film directors such as Juan Antonio Bardem and Pedro Lazaga had treated the war and themes of reconciliation, though with care and protective symbolism. José María Gironella's novel, *Los Cipreses Creen en Dios* (The Cypresses Believe in God), was an early example of a literary work that treated some Republicans as decent and well-intentioned people, and the war has continued to be a fascinating setting for novelists and their readers, as demonstrated by the great success in 2011 of María Dueñas's *El Tiempo entre Costuras* (The Time between Seams).[18] What has encouraged judgments about "forgetting" is the fact that this widespread interest never translated, until quite recently, into any type of political action.

A sizable majority of Spaniards, as shown repeatedly in surveys of public opinion, have not wanted to revisit a bloody past or try to reopen and settle its controversies. Immediately after Franco's death, polls showed that Spaniards valued peace, stability, and order even more highly than they did justice, liberty, and democracy—results that surely reflected the uncertainty of the time and the dangers surrounding the transition to democracy. But surveys also have documented a desire for gradual, peaceful change and a reluctance to make divisive judgments. The percentage of the population that viewed Franco's dictatorship favorably fell steadily to around 10 percent by 2000, while the percentage of the population that viewed it negatively rose to almost 40 percent. But a large plurality—still 46.4 percent in 2000—persistently described the dictatorship as a time that would be viewed both positively and negatively. Memories of order and economic progress have combined, at least for much of the population, with fear of renewed conflict to produce these results. Spanish commentators also see the influence of collective guilt over the violent past and the dictatorship, as well as painfully personal conflicts that lie just below the surface in small towns and rural areas.[19]

Scholars and intellectuals have been an important source of dissent from these widespread attitudes, with most of the critical views coming from the Left. In both the United States and Spain, those on the defeated side have wanted to argue their case before history's tribunal and have their day, at least, before the court of public opinion. Franco's repression, which prohibited that argument for so long, made its ultimate reappearance inevitable. Therefore, in recent years the case is being made, from various disciplines or perspectives, that those guilty of crimes and human rights abuses under Franco should be punished, or at least that their actions should be investigated and the truth made known. These arguments will be examined more fully in a later chapter.[20] Here we examine the fact that their appearance is connected to a process of political change and generational succession in Spain.

With the passage of time, change has affected sentiments on the Right as well as the Left. Partisans of the dictatorship and its values did not disappear, but their numbers thinned and their energy diminished as the democratic system functioned and gave satisfaction to most Spaniards. One year after Franco's death a large crowd, but less than 150,000, assembled in Madrid. The following year between 500,000 and 1.5 million loyalists turned out in the Plaza de Oriente to praise the dictator and the values of the past. But thereafter the dictator's followers and the proponents of fascism became a walled-off, shrinking band. Democratic elections had revealed the desire for change of the overwhelming majority. After five years, attention to the dictator faded and the king became more prominent, especially after his role in squelching the attempted coup of February 1981. Splits in Franco's support appeared, and demonstrations in his memory became smaller. In 1984 the government enacted a ban on the sale of Francoist symbols. By the 1990s only small groups of rightists celebrated the memory of Franco or José Antonio Primo de Rivera. A sure sign of changing opinion was the fact that legislators from the Right and Left insulted each other on the dictator's birthday with charges of being pro-Franco. In 1992 *El Mundo* reported that only five thousand turned out to honor Franco's death, and the group included many "ladies of advanced age . . . *Franquistas* adorned with medals ... 'skin heads,' German neo-Nazis, and French and Italian fascists." Twenty years after the Transition, ten million Spaniards—more than a quarter of the population—were born after Franco's death, and another eleven million barely retained any memories of the dictatorship.[21]

A renewed impulse to debate the civil war came less from the extreme Right than from generational change that injected old debates into later politics. As historians such as Santos Juliá and Josefina Cuesta Bustillo have pointed out, the generation of the *nietos*, the grandchildren of civil war antagonists, has forced onto the public agenda issues that their parents avoided.[22] What governs the timing of such a development is not a matter of consensus among scholars. According to the French historian Henry Rousso, the perception of the past, especially a traumatic past, modifies itself every twenty or twenty-five years, and for the case of Germany, Andreas Huyssen argues that more than forty years were required to confront and debate the Nazi era. The American case, however, suggests that while perceptions definitely change over time, circumstances can delay debate or allow it to begin promptly. Defeated southerners renewed arguments about their role in the American Civil War within a decade; widespread racism, on the other hand, precluded effective arguments by African Americans for one hundred years. For Spain the reality of dictatorship, followed by a perilous process of transition, imposed a delay which generational change required twenty years or so to overcome. By the 1990s the world was different and Spain had moved far beyond the dictatorship, so it was natural for a younger generation to see the past in a new way. "Memory," observes Michael Richards, "is shaped by our changing surroundings and the way we interpret them."[23]

One consequence of the maturation of the *nietos* in Spain was a revival in politics and popular culture of the old debates about the civil war. Among Spain's population, this younger generation was, by far, the segment most inclined to view the dictatorship in negative terms and most interested in revisiting the war's issues or identifying its victims.[24] In previous years such interests had prompted consideration in the Congress of Deputies of various, limited measures related to exiles or to the Republican victims of the war and postwar repression. The victory in 1996 of the PP, the Partido Popular, seemed to raise the stakes and stimulate Republican sympathies.

The PP, after all, counted among its supporters the most conservative, pro-Franco elements of the population. In reaction, calls for recognition of the war's vanquished side intensified.[25] Soon concern with these questions had spilled over into popular literature and the press, and the moral debates over right and wrong in the 1930s revived.

What is striking about the renewed controversy in Spain—just as in the United States—was the fact that the basic terms of debate changed little. The fundamental points that were contested in the 1930s became contested once again. Human nature and human emotions kept old arguments at the forefront of debate. New elements could appear as additions to the list of arguments, but the original charges and countercharges did not disappear.

This pattern derives in part from the moral power of the original conflict, the deeply held beliefs and deeply felt emotions that caused people to go to war still retain much of their relevance. Such convictions and visceral motives have staying power. Moreover, after the war is over there is a need, in the moral sense, to counter criticism or explain one's action. As controversies revive, that need continues to be strong, whether for participants or for descendants who have been socialized into their families' political perspectives. Also, in both civil wars there was at least a grain of truth within each side's perspective, and that fact seems to justify to later generations the defense of their ancestors' words and actions. As long as the circumstances of the present still tie grandchildren to the interests of their grandparents' class or group, those *nietos* will rise in defense of the past, using the arguments of the past.

Descendants of the defeated Republicans felt that their ancestors had died or been punished for defending a legally elected, democratic government whose policies looked toward the kind of future society that became the norm in Spain. Their sense of the injustice done to Republicans soon provoked a vigorous right-wing defense in the popular press. Best-selling books appeared by César Vidal and Pio Moa. Moa, who earlier had belonged to a violent left-wing group, now gave staunch support to views that had been part of Franco's justifications and propaganda. In *The Myths of the Civil War*, he challenged Republican claims of legitimacy and progress and painted the Nationalists as defensive and responsible. He argued, among other points, that if the Second Republic came into being peacefully, it was because monarchists had *allowed* elections; that the Second Republic immediately embarked on hostile policies, including the burning of churches, convents, and culturally important buildings; that it allowed leftist revolutionary violence in 1934; that disorder and crime had become insupportable by 1936; that fascism was not a real danger; and that the real and imminent danger was a radical leftist revolution. Franco's uprising was a response by "the conservative mass of the country." César Vidal attacked the Republicans by stressing the anti-Semitism of Basques in the republic, the violence of anarchists, divisions within the Left, and Stalinist influence over that era's Communists. He claimed that the workers' uprisings in 1934 were part of the Socialist Party's plans for "an armed uprising to tear down the [more conservative] Government elected legitimately [in 1933]." Leftist demagoguery and fear of the kind of "assassinations, atrocities, and attacks against the Catholic religion that had been seen during" 1934 caused the civil war.[26]

Many Spanish historians have dismissed these writings as "nothing less than an up-to-date repetition of what Franco's people have always said." Moa and Vidal "are not historians, but publicists with a police mentality who do nothing but recover the propaganda that the victors have elaborated since the start of the dictatorship." After all, it was the leaders of the Nationalist coup who first "expanded the idea that the law already had been broken in October 1934 and that the July 18, 1936, uprising only sought to restore law and order." Nevertheless, as these historians admit, the works of Moa and Vidal proved much more popular than academic studies of the 1930s.[27] Their combative style and challenge to accepted attitudes attracted notice and was part of their appeal, and they stressed some points that had an undeniably factual basis. Those points caught people's attention against the background of a polemical and once violent debate.[28]

But in addition the sale of their books revealed that older attitudes had not entirely disappeared. Even if they were not applicable to the society of the twenty-first century, the perspectives on what caused the war and who was at fault still had emotional resonance. People like Moa and Vidal and their readers were eager to defend their side of the argument. What was emotionally important was to counter the critics and defend those whose sympathies one had inherited, rather than to take a broader or more detached view. The connections to that era—ties of family loyalty, personal sympathy, or political ideology—still mattered. Such linkages had also proved extremely important in the U.S. South, though far less so in the North.

On the Republican side, the emotional bonds of family launched a major social organization led by *nietos*, the Association for the Recovery of Historical Memory. Late in 2000 Emilio Silva and Santiago Macías began a personal search for the unmarked graves of their Republican ancestors. At first a few sympathetic archaeologists and local officials aided them, and a journalist from *El País*, Spain's largest newspaper, was present at the moving moment when the grave of Silva's grandfather was opened. Word of their efforts spread slowly until 2002, when newspapers began reporting their efforts more widely. Then both men's phones began to ring off the hook. People throughout Spain asked for help in locating their relatives, forensic scientists volunteered their skills, and foreign volunteers arrived from as far away as Japan. Villagers quietly came forward to share information about gravesites known to local residents but never discussed. "In this village," Silva and Macías were told, "there are more dead outside the cemetery than in it." A growing number of common, unmarked graves where summary executions had taken place were found and opened and more relatives finally given a dignified burial.[29]

Initially these efforts were dominated by intense and strictly personal familial emotions. Descendants of executed Republicans told a journalist that "without the body, the pain never ceases." "Never," she reported, "have they spoken of vengeance, of revenge, or of anything that resembles that. In an exhumation, they never raise their eyes from the ground. They are not thinking of reopening wounds, but of closing, for once, their own." This journalist, Natalia Junquera, also quoted a distinguished professor of psychiatry who said, "The hatred dies, it is extinguished, but the necessity of putting a name to the dead, of honoring them, no. There always comes a moment in which one has to put an end to this interminable trauma." Such emotions galvanized individuals across Spain to such an extent that in 2007 the Association for the Recovery of Historical Memory brought to the Audiencia Nacional documentation, collected by family members, of 143,353 people who had disappeared during the civil war, most known to have been executed and thrown into unmarked graves. In April 2010, sixty thousand people demonstrated in Madrid, carrying photographs of the disappeared relatives whom they wanted to find, honor, and inter.

These powerful, personal emotions developed in more public and political directions over time. The two founders of the movement soon declared that giving families the opportunity to bury their loved ones was only one purpose of their organization. Equally important was the desire to allow older Spaniards to transmit to new generations a history that is unknown to them. They saw a need to break the "silence" of the Transition, and they complained that the amnesty laws of the previous generation gave "impunity to the responsible persons of the dictatorship." The association contacted similar groups in nations that have taken action against military regimes and dictatorships, and *El País*' Natalia Junquera writes that "now they ask for three things: truth, justice, and reparation, the three pillars that have supported similar processes in other countries that have applied what is called transitional justice." Emilio Silva and Santiago Macías argue that the "silence" of the Transition meant that "the debate that many people were awaiting" would not be brought to a conclusion in Spanish society and that "the heirs of *Franquismo* would have carte blanche to remain in public life and conserve the privileges that they had obtained through the support of the dictatorship."[30] Questioning whether Spain can have a real democracy without exploring the past, they have raised issues that make their concerns political.

In these changing circumstances, and after the victory of the Socialist Party over the PP in 2004, historical memory became a major controversy in Spanish politics. The new president, José Luis Rodríguez Zapatero, was the grandson of a Republican who had been executed during the civil war. At the beginning of his administration he traveled to León, where he embraced the goals of the Association for the Recovery of Historical Memory and announced that his government would propose a new law to do justice for the conquered.[31] This would become, in fact, one of many laws on the issue that had been enacted over the years, in a piecemeal fashion. But Zapatero's initiative was designed to be more comprehensive. It also would raise the political sparring of previous decades to a new, high level, tie the descendants of Republicans more closely to the PSOE, and reveal the complications involved in using and living with the history of a bloody civil war.

Soon after the Transition's first laws of amnesty, Spain's Congress began a series of small steps either to extend amnesty or to address ill treatment of the conquered. For example, in 1978 officers of Catalonia's wartime (pro-Republican) government were granted amnesty, and Republicans who were professional soldiers before the uprising gained pensions. A 1979 law awarded pensions and medical and social assistance to the survivors of many who had died as a result of battle. In the 1980s one law awarded credit toward the social security system for years spent in Franco's prisons, and another allowed some professional Republican soldiers to recover their active rights or reenter the armed forces. This partial measure of reparation came over the extended opposition of army leaders. By 1990 a law awarded indemnities to those who had spent three or more years in jail under Franco. But critics pointed to shortcomings in all these actions. The laws avoided condemnation of the dictatorship and any language that would praise or legitimize the republic. Citizens who had suffered penalties or damages short of three years of imprisonment received no indemnity. Since the laws arrived years after the conflict, they also failed to help many who had died before approval of the legislation.[32]

The symbolism involved in these actions divided the Congress and posed a particular challenge for the conservative Partido Popular, which had steadily opposed discussing "the good and the bad" of the past. In 1996 there was a commemoration of foreigners who had fought for the republic, and four hundred surviving members of these international brigades traveled to Spain to attend the ceremonies. The Congress of Deputies, with the PP in power, unanimously voted citizenship for these foreigners, but the PP kept a discrete distance, as only officials of the second rank met the honorees in the house's chamber. Three years later exiles were honored, but the PP refused to sign a resolution whose language condemned "the fascist military coup against the legally elected Republican government." After the Partido Popular gained an absolute majority in the elections of 2000, the modest flow of such proposals became an avalanche, and in 2002 the PP decided to change its strategy. Faced with a battery of strong proposals involving aid to exiles and the opening of common graves, the PP announced that it would support a less far-reaching resolution. For the first time and unanimously, the Congress passed a resolution that condemned Franco's uprising, gave "moral recognition" to those who had "suffered the repression of the Franco dictatorship," promised help to exiles and children of the war, urged aid in finding common graves, and declared that the use of violence to impose one's political convictions and establish totalitarian regimes was illegitimate and merited society's condemnation. In parliamentary negotiations and later statements, key members of the PP made it clear that this resolution should smother "the embers of the social conflict" and put an end both to the reopening of old wounds and to the flood of similar proposals. The resolution was to spell *fin* to this legislative concern.[33]

But the issue did not go away. The new initiative of Zapatero's government raised hopes for sweeping measures of aid and recognition, including the legal annulment of most judgments against Republicans and opponents of the Franco regime. When the law finally gained passage in 2007, it was a more modest measure, a law that pleased no one, in the words of many commentators. It was not strong enough for the Left and too far left for the Right. Though popularly known as the Law of Historical Memory, its formal title described it as a law to recognize and aid those who suffered persecution or violence during the civil war or the dictatorship. It required action against symbolic vestiges of Franco's dictatorship and increased aid and recognition for its victims, including support for the reopening of common graves. By May 2011 the national government, aided by the autonomies, had identified 2,232 graves, half of which had never been opened.[34] But the law did not officially annul earlier sentences, merely calling them illegitimate. What it unquestionably accomplished throughout the legislative process was the igniting of a major political controversy as well as the stimulation of many thoughtful arguments over the proper use of the past.

The PP and its supporters denounced the governing PSOE for making political capital out of this measure. *La Razón*, a conservative newspaper, pointed out that in 1999 President Zapatero himself had said that the law passed in that year would be the "last step in this spirit of restitution." This conservative, religiously oriented newspaper also charged that the law catered to the radical Left and harassed Christianity. *ABC*, another right-leaning paper, agreed and charged that the "socialists and communists have raised to the level of law their strategy of division among the citizenry and historical revisionism." The law would "liquidate the constitutional consensus about our immediate past" and "resolve none of the problems that affect the present and future of Spanish society." Moreover, argued the paper, previous governments had already granted 574,000 pensions or indemnities because of the war or the dictatorship. Historian José Varela Ortega claims that the purpose of the law was "the satanization and marginalization of the center-right" or, as *ABC* put it, to paint the Republicans as good and the PP as the incarnation of wrong. Ricardo García-Cárcel agreed, saying that the Socialist government wanted to "reduce the Republic and the Civil War to a simplistic, manichean vision of good and bad." The law, charged critics, broke society's consensus and threatened Spain's greatest success: "the overcoming of the trauma of the Civil War and Dictatorship."[35]

Leaders of the Partido Popular argued that this legislation was unwise and would reopen old wounds. Mariano Rajoy, the party's leader and future president, recalled Max Weber to declare, "It is not the work of the politicians to rewrite history and the past but to construct the future, that is why we are politicians." He also called "the reconciliation among all" one of the great successes of the Transition. Spain's Catholic bishops issued a pastoral letter lamenting that "a society that seemed to have found the road of reconciliation returns to find itself divided and confrontational." The PSOE's law, "guided by a selective mentality, opens anew old wounds." *La Razón* objected that "the memory of a grandfather shot and the pressures of two minority groups were not sufficient motives to revive the old history of the two Spains." Another article charged Zapatero with seeking his political future "in the past," whereas "our democracy is based on . . . the overcoming of the river of blood that divided us." There was a "great difference," argued *ABC*, "between doing justice and imposing a slanted interpretation of history."[36]

Charges of partiality in the law figured prominently in newspapers' attacks and in critical public reaction. Of course, the supporters of the measure believed that the many years of dictatorship and cautious democracy had been overwhelmingly partial, and they argued that it was necessary to focus support on the losing side. Yet it was true that the law restricted much of its aid to organizations that had recently come into being, such as the Association for the Recovery of Historical Memory. A citizen wrote to *El Mundo* saying that his grandfather had been shot by Republicans. He now asked himself "if that recovery of historical memory that is so much talked about will extend to all the Spaniards, and if my grandmother, my mother, my brothers, and I will know someday where rest the remains of my grandfather." The editors labeled his letter, "Historical memory for all or for nobody." In the same vein *ABC* praised a new book that described the suffering of conservatives during the leftist uprising in 1934 and argued that the wrongs committed by Republicans were being ignored. The result was not historical memory but "Historical Dismemory." These articles repeated points made by Ricardo de la Cierva, who once worked in Franco's regime. His book, *113.178 Caídos por Dios y por España* (113,178 Fallen for God and for Spain), presented evidence that 42,617 civilians had been assassinated in Republican-held areas, or what he called the "red zone."[37]

The controversy also stimulated more thoughtful, less immediately political arguments. A sociologist argued that it is pointless to try to place blame on one side or the other, because as Max Weber had said about World War I, "it is the whole structure of a society that is able to explain that catastrophe." Francisco Nieva, a member of the Royal Spanish Academy, refused to blame any side in these disputes, because "the memory of pain is not easily destroyed, it remains as a monumental, subterranean edifice through time immemorial." A winner of the Cervantes Prize, José Jimenez Lozano, publicly shared his opinion that "we all ought to engage in serious mourning for what happened in the Civil War and not take part in valuing those years."[38] Luis María Anson, another member of the Royal Spanish Academy, noted that he had been exiled, censored, or suppressed by Franco, yet he called the law a "blunder" or "stupidity." Both bands had committed atrocities during the war, and in the Transition "victors and defeated ... agreed to turn the page, to look to the future, to establish a pluralist democracy. . . . In that consisted the spirit of the Transition." He urged leaving historical memory to the historians "who are writing about the civil war, about the franquist repression, about the dictator and his regime, with complete liberty." In their work, "in the truth of facts, is found the authentic reparation and the historical justice." However, other scholars argued that "without memory of injustice the past horror is as if it never had existed" and that such deep wounds in society, if submerged and repressed, cannot be healed.[39]

These debates raised important and challenging questions for any society that has experienced a bloody civil war. Was the partial "silence" in Spain a form of social infirmity or sickness inflicted by the dictatorship? Would the passage of generations remove the difficulty of discussing the civil war? When might it become possible for society to confront its past objectively and accept all of its horrors? Who was right, the leaders of the Transition or those in the later generation who demand to reopen old questions? Can a society move beyond or surpass a violent history through amnesty and cooperation, or is some form of justice seeking or settling of accounts necessary?[40]

Clearly the emotional relevance of Spain's civil war was still great. If historians had achieved some objectivity through their research, many ordinary citizens had not. Thus it was not surprising that when the Law of Historical Memory went into effect, there was critical comment on some of the changes as well as some new issues that came to light. The law required the removal of statues of Franco and other Fascist leaders and of street signs that honored Nationalist generals. Such measures had been fought out in various localities before the law took effect. In 2005, for example, the Socialist mayor of Guadalajara, in central Spain, had ordered statues of Franco and José Antonio de Rivera taken down under cover of night, a step that angered the PP and others. Now actions *had* to be taken. In general the removal occurred without resistance amid only quiet protests. *ABC* reported in August 2008 that Santander was removing the last equestrian statue of Franco in all of Spain. The paper's tone was factual, but it evidently was incorrect about remaining statues, because in 2010 it reported that in a town in Galicia an equestrian statue of Franco was being removed. This took place "in compliance with the Law of Historical Memory" but at the insistence of the Ministry of Defense, which would put the covered statue in a military warehouse. In other scattered parts of Spain towns or cities dragged their feet in acting or placed new street names above the older ones of the Franco era.[41]

The opening of *fosas*, the hastily dug common graves of executed Republicans, occasionally sparked social conflict. This symbol-laden act raised political issues, both for relatives of murdered Republicans and for conservatives who might rebel against the implied criticism of Franco and his Nationalists. In Poyales del Hoyo, a town of fewer than one thousand in the province of Ávila, tension mounted as the local government prepared to move, at the request of one family, the remains of three women assassinated by Falangists in 1936. Friends and relations of the other two families objected and planned to read in public a document of protest. Instead, they encountered an angry, jeering crowd, urged on by four recently elected local officials from the PP. Assailed by cries of "Red whores" and accusations that they were not from the town and not even Spaniards, they feared violence, as only three members of the Guardia Civil were available to protect them. There was pushing and shoving, and the anti-Republican crowd destroyed some placards reading "We are the grandchildren of the workers you were not able to shoot." "If Franco could raise his head," shouted one man in the crowd, "he would cut your throat." Both the angry confrontation and the disagreement among the families of the three murdered women testify to the conflicts that burials and reinterments can unleash.[42]

Conservatives have objected strongly to changes in the Valley of the Fallen. The law and the government decreed that this former gathering place for pro-Franco or pro-Falangist ceremonies was to be treated as a place of worship only. The Catholic Church's basilica would take precedence over the memorial to Franco and José Antonio. New rules, reported *ABC*, "do not permit political celebrations or the exaltation of the Civil War and Franco-ism," and in the future the complex must "honor the memory of all" the victims. The changes that soon were implemented were striking even for the casual tourist. A restricted path for entry denied the visitor an opportunity to view the Fascist architecture of the complex in its entirety, and the atmosphere was both more constrained and constraining.[43] By 2010 the government had also eliminated Francisco Franco from the official website that listed heads of the Executive from 1823 forward. *ABC* complained that most of the money appropriated for the Law of Historical Memory had gone into the making of documentaries, the creation of archives, or the gathering of testimony—all activities that would strengthen Republican interests. Only 25 percent of the funds had been spent in exhumation and reinterment of family members.[44]

That same year new issues appeared. One involved the controversial, crusading judge, Baltasar Garzón, and another shed light on a terrible abuse of the Franco regime that rarely had been noted. Garzón was well known in Spain for his high-profile prosecutions of drug lords, ETA terrorists, and politicians, and for his effort to extradite and prosecute Chile's former dictator, Augusto Pinochet, for violations of human rights. In 2007 the Association for the Recovery of Historical Memory sought the legal system's help in investigating the disappearance of tens of thousands of

Republicans in the war years. The Ministerio Fiscal issued an opinion that these complaints should not be processed, citing in part Spain's laws of amnesty, but Garzón launched an investigation anyway. He issued a ruling that the military uprising had "the character of a crime against humanity" and that the state and the judiciary could not ignore international law or such crimes. A few months later, however, Garzón backed away from his initiative, recommending merely that authorities in the various autonomies should proceed with their own investigations. Two ultra-right organizations, Clean Hands and the Spanish Falange, brought complaints against Garzón for *prevaricación*, which means issuing a ruling that he knows is contrary to law. Soon other complaints were added relating to some of his other cases, and the Tribunal Supremo suspended Garzón pending resolution of his case. International organizations, such as Amnesty International, organized protests, but judicial scrutiny of the judge continued. Eventually Garzón was barred from his profession for eleven years, but not supposedly for his rulings on the disappearance of Republicans.[45] Issues raised by his case will receive further discussion in chapter 4.

Although Garzón's attempt to scrutinize Franco's regime was suspended, a very different issue arose to throw light on the dictatorship's crimes. In January 2011 citizens who were seeking their birth parents and mothers who had been separated from their children exposed the thefts of infants, a practice that had taken place under the dictatorship and even into the 1980s. The National Association of those Affected by Irregular Adoption filed evidence with the fiscal general that at least 261 babies had been stolen from their parents. The Congress of Deputies called on the government in February 2011 to investigate, and the government appointed a special prosecutor. Less than a month later the number of suspected cases, dating from 1951, had risen to 750 thefts of infants in at least forty provinces. By June 2011 judicial authorities were investigating 849 cases. Journalists tracked down a ninety-six-year-old nun who had been the sister superior in a Tenerife nursery which various mothers described as part of the infant-stealing network. The nun acknowledged that she had cooperated with a Basque identified as a key figure in the robbery of babies. Her story was somewhat confused, but she acknowledged, "We preferred to give infants recently born" and felt she was doing good. Mothers who were told that their children had died charged, however, that Republicans were the targets of these thefts and childless friends of the dictator's regime were the beneficiaries.[46]

In matters such as these, the past plays a large role in Spain's present, despite the effort of the Transition to leave the past behind. The two institutions most closely connected with Franco's dictatorship—the church and the army—have also been affected by that history, though their situations today are strikingly different. The Catholic Church wholeheartedly embraced the military dictatorship and used its powerful position to try to force Spaniards to conform in religion and politics. That decision has proved disastrous, or at least has cost the church dearly. For when Spaniards regained liberty and democracy, many discarded a church that had discredited itself and was deeply resented. Spaniards rebelled against the church's censorship, repression, and puritanical vigilance over their private lives. Seventy-two percent in a 1975 survey expressed their support for laws allowing divorce. "With the democratic change," a young bishop admitted in 2011, "[the church] is seen as the right hand of the dictator."[47]

Divisions within the church complicated the institution's stance toward the future. Cardinal Tarancón wanted to separate the church from its envenoming embrace with the state, and he courageously aided the Transition in significant ways. But one thousand and sixty-one priests signed a protest in 1976 that communism was trying "once again to subjugate our *Patria*" and urged the church to close ranks in opposition as it had during the "glorious national Crusade" of 1936. Younger priests, by contrast, were far to the Left, with 47 percent of those under thirty favoring a "political system based on socialism," according to a 1970 survey. By the early 1990s "more than one third of the clergy opposed" the Vatican's position on birth control. But the Catholic Church is a hierarchical institution, and beginning with the papacy of John Paul II in 1978, the hierarchy—both in Rome and in Spain—moved once again in a strongly conservative direction. Spain's leading bishops "returned to a modified version of . . . the idea of a defensive bastion surrounded" by hostile "social, political, and cultural forces." In 2007, when the then-head of the Episcopal Conference said that "we should ask for forgiveness" for "concrete acts" during 1936–39, most bishops in the audience "appeared stunned," including Cardinal Antonio María Rouco Varela, a conservative who had headed the conference and soon would do so again. Within a few days the conference insisted that the words that appeared to ask for pardon had been "taken out of context."[48]

The result of past and persistent ultra-conservative attitudes in the church was decline. The number of seminarians plummeted, and more priests left the Catholic Church in Spain than in France. By 2000 the number of priests had fallen from 25,000 in 1970 to 19,000, and a large majority were over sixty years of age. The number of males in religious orders also fell, from almost 28,000 in the 1960s to 18,557 in 1986–87. The number of nuns declined more modestly, but many convents were financially strapped. Polls in the early 1990s indicated that a majority of young adults did not consider themselves "religious persons," and more strikingly, the traditional tendency of Spaniards to identify with the church in rites of passage was waning. In the mid-1980s, 87 percent of Spaniards self-identified as Catholic, 83 percent of newborns were baptized in the church, and 94 percent of all marriages took place in the church.[49] But in 2010 *El País* noted, under the headline "Weddings flee from the altar," that the previous year civil ceremonies had outnumbered church weddings, ninety-five thousand to eighty thousand. Seventeen percent of Spain's couples were not married, and that number was growing. By 2011 one of every three babies was born outside of matrimony. A large-scale survey of public opinion in 2010 found that the social image of the church "is in free fall." One of every two Spaniards "consider that . . . it transmits an image of harshness and condemnation rather than goodness and pardon," and three of every four, including half of those who are practicing Catholics, "think that it has not known how to adapt itself to the current social reality."[50]

In contrast, the armed forces enjoyed an extremely high level of approval, with 84 percent of the population evaluating them positively. This surprising result, only thirty years after the failed coup attempt of 1981, reflects that fact that the public now sees the army as a profoundly and solidly renovated institution that has placed itself "perfectly within the constitutional system." The same percentage, 84 percent, believes that today the army is composed of professionals "very committed to the Constitution and the defense of liberties." Seventy-nine percent regard the army as a source of pride, and 77 percent feel that its missions abroad, often in humanitarian roles, have brought international prestige for Spain.[51]

The army, unlike the church, has changed greatly. Successive governments reduced the bloated ranks of conservative officers, encouraged and inculcated new attitudes, and worked to build a professional force under civilian control. This professional force depends on government support for future funding and modernization. In 2001 Spain ended required military service for young men, as the minister of defense affirmed that at the end of the twentieth century a universal military obligation was not sustainable. By 2002 one-quarter of the aspirants for a professional military career were female, and increasingly Spain's armed forces played a constructive role in humanitarian roles abroad under such international bodies as the United Nations. That same year an opinion piece in *ABC* took delight in the idea that antimilitary leftists no longer could criticize the army, since it had been transformed into "the most efficient humanitarian organization."[52] A surprising statement in 2006 by one general, who seemed to feel that the army's constitutional duties might require intervention in politics, was greeted by shock and opposition among the entire political elite. That general was promptly retired, and the incident seemed to strengthen the national consensus that the army must never again interfere in political life.[53] Its professionalization and integration into the constitutional, democratic system has been rewarded with respect and approval.

In this one area, an important Spanish institution, the military, seems to have escaped the grip and continuing influence of a troubled past. In many other ways, as this chapter has shown, clashing ideologies and verbal battles to justify the past have continued to shape the present. The situation in the United States, which ended its Civil War seventy years earlier and recently commemorated the conflict's 150th anniversary, provides insight into how a longer history might affect such forces and thus what the future might hold for Spain.

Ideology and Memory: The United States after Appomattox

> The black masses of the South ... are as ignorant upon all public questions as the driven cattle. ... To put the ballot in their hands would be not simply a mockery, but a cruelty.
>
> *New York Times*, December 29, 1864

> In fifty years the defense of slavery will be deemed the world over to have been as barbarous as we now deem the slave-trade to have been.... [We must] prevent the impending disaster.
>
> Thomas Nelson Page, *The Negro*, 1904

> I have a dream that one day this nation will rise up and live out the true meaning of its creed: "We hold these truths to be self-evident, that all men are created equal."
>
> Martin Luther King Jr., August 28, 1963

The battle of words in the United States has been at least as intense as that in Spain, and it has extended over a greater period of time. There is ample evidence in the American experience that these old wounds have remarkable power to endure in society and politics. The action or inaction of groups can have a direct effect on their strength, yet clearly the rancor of past conflict does not dissipate rapidly. But the experience of the United States also points to the way that time and social change can alter the verbal battles and gradually allow a society to free itself from a blood-stained heritage.

For almost one hundred years, leaders of the white South managed to freeze race relations and racial ideology in something close to the Confederate pattern, thus demonstrating that the passage of time by itself does not erase a conflicted past. Elite southern men and women created an ideology of the Lost Cause that wrapped antebellum society, the Confederacy, Reconstruction, and postwar racism in the mantle of a protective, laudatory myth. The Lost Cause portrayed the white South as cultured, chivalrous, and superior while making the North into the aggressor—crude, unprincipled, and vindictive. The power of the Lost Cause ideology resulted from determined and energetic efforts by generations of southern leaders.

At the core of this constructed historical memory was a fierce attachment to white racism. Like the religious beliefs that motivated Spanish clergy, southern racism insisted on a certain kind of social order and decreed what the roles of different individuals should be. It was an encompassing formula that laid down rigid rules for personal and social life. Through three postwar decades this myth strengthened until it combined with political interests to place southern thought in a straightjacket and solidify a social system based on racial domination and class privilege. Even after 1900 the Lost Cause ideology continued to gain strength under the leadership of a new generation, until most southern whites came to believe that their history and the myth were identical.

Two rival ideologies—competing interpretations of the meaning of the United States' Civil War—suffered from the absence of dedicated partisans or adequate public support and faded into the background. The ideology of the Union cause could explain the Civil War from the perspective of the victorious North, but few northern leaders advocated its case with zeal. Having won the war, most northerners turned their attention to new and pressing regional issues and showed little interest in imposing the Union's ideology on the defeated South. The emancipation cause related the enormous costs of war to the ideals of human equality, equal rights for African Americans, and the Declaration of Independence. Such ideas collided, however, with pervasive white racism that blunted the persistent efforts of black people to claim their citizenship and advance their interests. Doubly disadvantaged both racially and as a numerical minority, African Americans were unable to make the emancipation cause a dominant historical interpretation.[54]

Thus human efforts proved crucial to the outcome of the postwar battle of words. The Lost Cause ideology gained strength, even influencing parts of northern society, as southern partisans proved every bit as determined to establish their views as Franco was after his victory in 1939. Meanwhile, the Union cause declined from neglect, and racism vitiated the emancipation cause. Eventually the balance between these ideologies would shift as decades and generations advanced. The passage of time played a role in altering people's attitudes. But social change across the spectrum of people's activities has proved more important, especially when it combined with time to distance people from their past in daily reality as well as historical memory. There is evidence in the American case that, after 150 years and great social change, a much smaller, less influential, and diminishing portion of the South's population now pays homage to old Confederate arguments.[55]

As in Spain, the pattern of conflict over memory and meaning highlights generational changes and demonstrates the great adaptability of historical memory to new conditions or new social needs. Both northerners and southerners have changed their arguments over time, modernizing them to better serve the needs of the present. White southerners added to and elaborated the Lost Cause ideology through different eras. Northerners paid more attention to the emancipation cause as the civil rights movement gathered strength. Currently, Lincoln's image is changing, as people use it to ratify and respond to new directions of American society.

The pages below will argue that there have been four periods, generally speaking, in the ideological struggles over historical memory of the Civil War. From 1865 to about 1900, a southern ideological offensive won substantial ground in many areas, and especially on race, from the victorious but passive North. That victory led to an ugly period of consensus on racism and segregation that lasted, despite growing threats, from 1900 to about 1945. The inspiring mass movement that we call the civil rights movement profoundly altered the landscape between 1945 and approximately 1990, with consequent changes in the use of history. The years since that date seem to show that pro-South or pro-Confederate arguments now have a new and different kind of appeal, but a more restricted one, while the Lincoln myth has elaborated its influence in new directions.

* * *

At first glance, the most striking difference between the experience of Spain and the United States is the failure of the victorious American side to impose its ideology. Even in the North that fact is often overlooked or deemphasized in the public's tendency to celebrate the nation's history as an unblemished record of great accomplishments. The North's apparently negligent attitude toward its victory in the postwar period had deleterious consequences, but it actually was not surprising. It was a natural product of the limited war aims of a society still in the grip of racist beliefs, and it reflected assumptions that had remained strong throughout the war.

The North went to war to preserve the Union, not to end slavery. With no societal consensus against racism, Abraham Lincoln had worried greatly that his decision to use emancipation as a tool to win the war would divide the North and palsy its military efforts. Bringing the South's rebels back into the Union was a dominant priority.[56] Lincoln's repeated pledge to Confederates that he would allow apprenticeship of former slaves was intended to reassure slaveholders that "they may be nearly as well off . . . as if the present trouble had not occurred." That attitude also reflected his hopeful but unrealistic assumption that there remained a strong substrate of Unionism in the South, and that he could find a way to appeal to his rebelling countrymen and gain their cooperation once more.[57]

The idea that the rebels were countrymen, a part of the Union that must be restored, was very strong in the wartime North. The Democratic Party defended the South and southern rights with its slogan "The Union as it was, and the Constitution as it is." Instead of advocating ferocity against rebels, Democrats accused Lincoln of oppressing southerners and endangering liberty through tyrannical policies. Even the *New York Times*, whose editor was the chairman of the Republican National Committee, defended states' rights as "the great balance wheel of our government" and predicted that the North would preserve states' rights "to the last iota." The editors of the *Times* also expressed great optimism about "The Future Southern Feeling Toward the Union." Rejecting the idea that defeated southerners would be "exceedingly embittered," the *Times* predicted that "most of the Southern people . . . will welcome the restored Union. . . . Being of the same race . . . with a like past history, [southerners] will undoubtedly settle themselves down quietly and contentedly." After General Sherman captured Savannah, the paper urged aid for that city as "The Way to Restore Fellowship," illustrate "brotherhood," and "welcome back those who have been estranged from us."[58]

Defeating the South and returning its rebellious citizens to the Union was the one aim on which all could agree despite racial, ideological, and partisan division. Southern whites were seen as brothers in the American experiment, part of the American family.[59] In contrast to Spain, several factors protected them from attitudes that they must be exterminated, exiled, or repressed. Among these were their constitutional right to have held slaves, the racism of the North, and a shared pride in America's recent war for independence and democratic system. Once the Union was preserved, northerners had achieved their central goal, whether or not other matters went smoothly. Emancipated slaves with black skins, however, were not part of the white "family." Rights and opportunity for them had never been part of the accepted plan—although fundamentally these were necessary for a true solution to the war's issues.

As in Spain, the victorious North did not forget to honor its dead. Those whose sacrifice had helped to save the Union deserved a respectful, dignified burial. The government had begun establishing cemeteries for Union soldiers during war. Between 1861 and 1870 seventy-three national cemeteries were created. When rumors of desecrations of graves arose, the North reacted quickly. "From 1866 through 1868," writes historian John Neff, "officers and work crews from the Quartermaster Department fanned out across the South" to locate and protect gravesites. "Every avenue was exploited. Circulars were distributed and reprinted in the newspapers asking for any information" about "graves of Union soldiers." Southerners who aided the search often received cash payments for their help. The federal government extended its honors to black soldiers who had died for the Union, since they were part of the army. Confederate soldiers were not interred with the Union dead.[60]

But the North wanted to move away from conflict and the emergency war footing. It quickly demobilized its army of almost two million soldiers, sending the citizen-draftees and volunteers home so rapidly that before the end of 1866 the number of men in the armed forces was only around sixty thousand and falling.[61] As men and women returned to their peacetime pursuits and routines, the public gave its new president, Andrew Johnson, ample room to implement his lenient ideas of putting the Union back together. Even though Johnson was a former Democrat and a southerner, people hoped that he would have success in the place of the martyred Lincoln and that their lives could resume, with the Union restored.

It was not to be that simple. After the fighting stopped, the North encountered hostile and determined southerners instead of family members ready to settle down "quietly and contentedly." The pride of the master class had suffered two heavy blows: defeat with the loss of slaves and the reality that nothing had gone as they had expected, that all their boasts had been mistaken. Even more significant was their fierce determination to control the former slaves in some manner and maintain a rigid system of white supremacy. The "*status* of the negro," in Alexander Stephens's words, was not to change, at least if Southern whites had anything to say about it. If "slavery" was gone, they would enforce "subordination to the superior race." Thus, from the beginning of Reconstruction, their ideology asserted that secession had not been a crime, that the North had violated the Constitution and their rights, that African Americans were inherently inferior, that the former slaves must be compelled to work, and that the subject race—unable to compete and deprived of white care—would die out in freedom. The harsh black codes that they enacted under Johnson's plan of reconstruction documented their hostility toward freedom and ensured "the failure of self-reconstruction in the South."[62]

Such intransigence forced the northern Republicans, who controlled Congress, to take stronger measures. As Senator James G. Blaine admitted, the "Republican party was forced to its Reconstruction policy" by the South, because defeated Confederates rejected lesser steps with "scorn and defiance." Not wanting to "surrender to the rebel Legislatures," Republicans turned to Negro suffrage, which Blaine excused and apologized for as something "the Southern whites knowingly and willfully brought . . . upon themselves." Soon after black suffrage was enacted, the *Atlantic Monthly*, New England's respected journal, declared that "the blacks were, as a general thing, ignorant" and that Republicans had distrusted any suffrage that was not "conferred on the educated alone." But Reconstruction's continued battles "swept forward government and people . . . converting the distrusted abstraction of yesterday in the 'military necessity' of to-day and the constitutional provision of tomorrow."[63]

Southern whites reacted to black suffrage and new governments with outrage that added new items to their list of suffered wrongs and injustices. Vindictive Radicals, they charged, were subjecting the now-loyal South to "black domination," the rule of "ignorant and depraved" Negroes who turned government into a spectacle of "Ethiopean minstrelsy" and "Ham radicalism in its glory." Fighting back with fraud, intimidation, and the rampant violence of the Ku Klux Klan, southern leaders frustrated the timid efforts of the national government to enforce the law. By 1871–72 they had regained control of most southern states, and in 1876 they completed their reconquest of power. Aware of northern racism, they charged that Reconstruction had been "a disgrace and a danger to the country," as unacceptable "as if four million Mexicans or Chinese took over New England, New York, and New Jersey."[64]

The North recoiled from the problems of Reconstruction and the intractable resistance of southern whites. Despite the fact that the Fourteenth

Amendment prohibited states from infringing citizens' rights, the Supreme Court held that "regulation of civil rights" remained a state function.[65] The northern Congress, caught up in issues of industrialization, immigration, and a sharp recession, soon desired "that this Southern question be eliminated as a disturbing element from our national politics."[66] Even before the disputed election of 1876, it was obvious that the effort to change the South would soon be over. Rutherford B. Hayes criticized southern rebels in his campaign as the Republican Party's nominee, but as president he promptly toured the South with a message of unity and accepted a large portion of the South's self-justifying arguments. The Lost Cause was triumphing over the Union cause, and the emancipation cause was being ignored or forgotten.

Thanking southern audiences for their "friendship and welcome," Hayes implicitly suggested that the white South now was loyal. Conflict was now, in 1876, a matter of old history. "We have differed in the past," said Hayes in Tennessee, "but we have fought out that difference." The soldiers of both sides, former enemies, were "ready to clasp hands," because they respected each other's courage and sacrifice. Men who fought for their convictions "can meet and look each other in the face with respect always." This simplistic formula for reunion elided many crucial issues of the war. Hayes expressed an ill-placed confidence that southern whites would respect the rights of African Americans. To blacks in his audience in Atlanta, he declared, "After thinking it over, I believe your rights and interests would be safer if this great mass of intelligent white men [in the South] were left alone by the General Government." He even endorsed what was becoming a new element of ideology among Confederate veterans by saying that initially they were better marksmen and better horsemen, but eventually the North prevailed. "When the issue comes to . . . Greek against Greek, that army will conquer which has the most Greeks."[67]

This argument about the skill of Confederate soldiers was one of three influential movements—one led by men, another by women, and a third by writers of both genders—to reinforce the South's ideology and justifications. Officers in the army of General Robert E. Lee launched the Southern Historical Society in the 1870s to remember and document their military successes. Led primarily by Virginians, these men developed an argument that southern soldiers had actually been the "better men." They did not lose the war but had been "overwhelmed by numbers," and General Lee was both a military genius and moral exemplar. These widely publicized ideas were a salve for wounded egos and damaged pride. They explained why fearless and gallant soldiers—some of whom were compared to chivalrous medieval knights, as in the case of Jeb Stuart—went down to defeat. Military failure was no fault of their own but simply the product of a larger population and immigrant hordes in the North. Robert E. Lee became a military saint in this scenario, and any reverses that he suffered were explained away by the supposed failures of others. After Lee's trusted "old war horse," Lieutenant General James Longstreet, became a Republican, Jubal Early and others attacked him unrelentingly, blaming him for the critical defeat at Gettysburg.[68]

Instead of a crucial, tide-changing loss, Gettysburg became the high-water mark of Confederate glory, a moment in time that would be lauded in countless speeches and celebrated in literature. Even Thomas Wolfe wrote emotionally about Pickett's Charge: "Then morning came and the end of the rebellion, as the ragged men charged straight across the fields against that hill of death and union. They melted, formed again, toiled to the cannon's barrel, and were erased." William Faulkner captured that moment in southern mythology even more romantically: "For every Southern boy fourteen years old . . . there is the instant when it's still not yet two o'clock on that July afternoon in 1863, . . . and . . . it's all in the balance. . . . *Maybe this time.*"[69]

The apotheosis of Lee by the Southern Historical Society resonated with defeated southern whites, and he—rather than Jefferson Davis or Stonewall Jackson or others—became an enduring cultural symbol. The dominance of the Lee legend was due in part to the fact that he fought throughout the war, as compared to Jackson, who died early in 1863. Lee embodied Victorian ideas of rectitude and character, ideally suited to peace, whereas Jackson had been an eccentric, violent warrior-chieftain.[70] In comparison to Jefferson Davis, Lee also was a far more serviceable symbol. Davis's personality was aloof and prickly, whereas Lee was quiet and reserved, a dignified southern gentleman. In the prewar years Davis was known for his aggressive and contentious defense of southern interests. Lee, on the other hand, had been out of political controversies as an army officer and had hesitated before joining the Confederate cause; he thus was a more useful figure to prove that southerners were loyal but had been forced to secede after suffering northern wrongs. In defeat Davis remained combative, writing lengthy, turgid tomes, whereas Lee's profile was lower and his work at Washington College seemed to suggest an intent to rejoin the nation as a constructive citizen. Thus Lee could symbolize the idea that virtuous southerners fought against the Union only because of constitutional principle and loyalty to one's state.

Lee's legend grew swiftly, and within a couple of decades stories such as those of Virginia's John S. Wise were common. Writing in the *Atlantic Monthly*, Wise claimed that he was sent by Jefferson Davis to see Lee near the end of the war. Only when he arrived did he realize that "our army was literally worn out and killed out and starved out." The Confederacy was not going to be defeated but simply worn away. Stoically Lee told him:

> "A few more Sailor's Creeks and it will be over—ended—just as I have expected it would end from the first." [This statement] elevated him in my opinion more than anything else he ever said or did. It revealed him as a man who had sacrificed everything to perform a conscientious duty against his judgment.

Substitute southerners for Lee in these descriptions and the benefit of that image is apparent.[71]

Just as important as the speeches and writings of Lee's former soldiers was the work of southern women, who organized in countless communities to bury and honor the Confederate dead. Numerous chapters of the Ladies Memorial Association, led by elite women, quickly sprouted up in Richmond and other southern cities. One year after the surrender, three hundred elite and middle-class women in Richmond had organized three different memorial associations; by 1868 there were at least twenty-six such societies in the state, with an estimated one thousand three hundred active members. Georgia, South Carolina, North Carolina, Mississippi, and Alabama were not far behind, and one authority estimates that there were "between seventy and one hundred such associations . . . throughout the South."[72]

These women were supporting the South's defeated and emotionally wounded men. In the process they also were modifying prewar gender roles by taking on a public responsibility that had political, civic, and cultural connotations. As women they could provide "domestic legitimization of mourning" in a way that men could not. They worked energetically at this task, raising money, hiring agents to search for Confederate remains, and filling southern cemeteries. In Virginia alone records indicate that five memorial associations were responsible for reinterring 72,520 fallen soldiers. They also erected monuments to the dead and to the Lost Cause, and by the 1880s they contended with men, such as Jubal Early, who tried to take over their efforts. By organizing displays of public support, they eventually succeeded in imposing a "public" interpretation of the war's meaning that echoed their own. Their Lost Cause was a valiant, principled defense of constitutional rights by brave and gallant men who fought against impossible odds. With the passage of time another generation and a successor organization, the United Daughters of the Confederacy (UDC), would take up and expand their task.[73]

The ideology of the Lost Cause emphasized romantic images of courage and gallantry in a principled but doomed military effort. Before long, however, other southerners were creating new arguments to rehabilitate the region's image and strengthen its influence. Much of this work was literary, and it aimed to reverse the North's hostile view of the prewar South as a backward, uncultured, and violently oppressive slave society. Instead, through stories, essays, and memoirs southern writers crafted a romantic picture of the Old South. It was, supposedly, a land of grace, culture, and refinement, an appealing and humane world now lost. In that mythical Old South, time moved slowly and life held more beauty than could be found in the increasingly hectic, polluted, and tension-filled world of industrializing America. Southern planters were principled and honorable, men of strong character combined with generosity and personal warmth. Slavery, rather than an instrument of oppression, was the key to lasting ties between white and black, a personal relation that promoted understanding and familial affection.

Thomas Nelson Page was one of the most effective writers in this romantic genre. An elegiac tone often suffused his stories, which brimmed with warm appreciation for a lost, golden era. One of his best-known tales, "Marse Chan: A Tale of Old Virginia," defended relationships in slavery. In this story a traveler happens upon Sam, an elderly black man who shares the history of his relationship with Master Channing, the planter's son.

Sam grew up with his young master, who always "wuz good to me.... He nuver hit me a lick in his life." Sam's white folks loved the Union and opposed secession. "Dem wuz good ole times ... de bes' Sam ever see." But when the war came, Marse Chan answered the call of duty despite his love for the Union. Sam accompanied his young master to the war, and when Marse Chan died in battle, Sam faithfully brought the body of his young master home. In the years that followed, Sam served the bereaved white family and mourned with the beautiful young woman from a neighboring plantation who had loved Marse Chan. After the grief-stricken parents died, Sam tended the family's graves through his own declining years. In Page's story, the Lost Cause of the South symbolizes much that Sam had lost, as well, and the message to northerners was obvious: they had misunderstood the nature of slavery and the slave regime.[74]

Page added further elements to his message in other stories. In "The Burial of the Guns," for example, he describes a courageous rebel artillery unit that ultimately buried its weapons rather than let them fall into Union hands. This story evokes the themes of "Marse Chan": life on the plantation was quiet and peaceful, with pleasant daily routines interrupted by holiday merry making. Slaves and masters were united in a close relationship. Upon secession, "white and black, all," were eager to defend the South, with "the servants contending for the honor of going with their master." But Page also emphasizes the skill of the soldiers, whose commander "had bitterly opposed secession" but leapt to defend Virginia against federal "coercion." Every morning this colonel "read prayers at the head of his company," and volunteers from a pious, united South "seemed to spring from the ground," until "starvation" brought down the Confederacy. In defeat, the men of the artillery unit went home to be "honest, brave, self-sacrificing, God-fearing citizens" rather than troublemakers.[75]

Others who cultivated the romantic myth of the Old South included John Esten Cooke, who described Civil War soldiers as idealistic medieval knights; Susan Dabney Smedes; and George William Bagby. Bagby was most famous for his essay on "The Old Virginia Gentleman," which closed with these serious words: "In simple truth and beyond question there was in our Virginia country life a beauty, a simplicity, a purity, an uprightness, a cordial and lavish hospitality, warmth and grace which shine in the lens of memory with a charm that passes all language at my command."

Susan Dabney Smedes published *Memorials of a Southern Planter* in 1887 to honor her father and defend southern slaveholding. She emphasized that her father, who had owned a large plantation in Mississippi, was generous, benevolent, and paternalistic and cared for his slaves so faithfully that some refused his offer of freedom in order to remain with their kind master. When the war ended, many of the family's slaves refused to leave their home and their white folks. By the time her book appeared, so many southern writers and politicians had sounded these themes that the *Atlantic Monthly* accepted the portrait without question. Uncritically praising the book's "veracity," the *Atlantic Monthly* described it as "all the more valuable for being artless." Mr. Dabney's treatment of his slaves "was so humane, so liberal, and, as Southerners used to be fond of saying, so patriarchal" that one could almost miss the wrong of slavery. The magazine urged its readers to have "greater charity for the unfortunate men who formed" slave society.[76]

In defending the *nature* of slavery before the war, southerners made one bold change of strategy. They discarded completely their former insistence that slavery was the cause of the war and that the South seceded to protect the institution and white dominance from a hostile Republican Party. The war had *not* been about slavery, they said. Ignoring the historical record, they now insisted that slavery was merely the occasion, rather than the cause of war. Sacred principle was their motive for war. Southerners had gone into battle to protect their constitutional rights; they had fought for liberty in the same spirit as George Washington. This new argument obviously identified a defeated South with foundational American values that the North would respect. It also was likely that it felt more comfortable to the southerners themselves. Although they had not suffered from relentless, debilitating guilt over slavery, they had always known that the "peculiar institution" was inconsistent with the founding values of the United States, as well as the growing convictions of the western world. Even Alexander Stephens admitted, in his "cornerstone" speech, that "as late as twenty years ago" many in the South agreed with Thomas Jefferson that slavery was a "violation of the laws of nature" and "wrong in principle, socially, morally and politically."[77] Defeat in the Civil War destroyed slavery, the North condemned it, and it was easier, in practical and emotional terms, for former Confederates to drop their previous rigid defense.

Thomas Nelson Page was daringly frank and explicit in explaining the reasons for this change in his book *The Negro: The Southerner's Problem*. It was necessary so that "the verdict of posterity" would not be "against us." Writing at the beginning of the twentieth century, he warned, "It is not unlikely that in fifty years the defence of slavery will be deemed the world over to have been as barbarous as we now deem the slave-trade to have been." Therefore it was essential to establish "the real fact" that the South fought for "the principle of self-government and ... her inalienable rights."[78] Page's concern was for "the South's place in history." Southerners must insist that a right of secession had existed: "Without this we were mere insurgents and rebels; with it, we were a great people in revolution for our rights."[79]

This multidimensional southern offensive was not the only reason why the North gave ground before the Lost Cause offensive. A distrust of democracy and a belief in superior and inferior races combined to submerge the emancipation cause still further and to undercut the rights of blacks. There was no shortage of southern voices complaining that the former slave was "yet half a savage" and that Congress had "elevated ignorance into a power" since it could not make blacks "intelligent, responsible, conscientious citizens."[80] But influential northern writers and periodicals began to make that case even more strongly. As early as 1874, Brooks Adams, grandson of one president and great-grandson of another, used a prominent magazine to condemn black suffrage, describing it as the "wholesale creation of the most ignorant mass of voters to be found in the civilized world." Respected academics quickly joined in. Yale's William Graham Sumner declared that it was "a corruption of democracy to set up the dogma that all men are equally competent to give judgment on political questions." Francis Parkman, historian and Harvard professor, warned against the danger of "organized ignorance ... marching ... under the flag of equal rights." Inequalities of "character, ability, and culture" were "real and intrinsic," he argued. "Hordes of native and foreign barbarians" were bewildering democracy. The popular biographer James Parton condemned "the mental inferiority of the black man" whose race "has contributed nothing to the intellectual resources of man." He predicted that in one way or another "gross ignorance shall be put out of politics." With such elite opinions, it was merely repetitious when Senator Henry Cabot Lodge wrote in 1891 that "one of the greatest dangers to our free government is ignorance."[81]

These elite prejudices explicitly equated "intelligence and virtue" or "wealth and intelligence" with being qualified to vote. The "great majority" of African Americans were "unfit for the suffrage" and "manifestly disqualified for political life."[82] Quickly and easily this elitism shaded into harsh theories of permanent racial inferiority. As early as 1878 the *Atlantic Monthly* interpreted the failure of Reconstruction as proof that "the superior race leads and controls the inferior race." "Race distinctions," declared the magazine in 1880, "ought to be maintained for the sake of the best development of the race." Professor Nathan Shaler of Harvard wrote that the freed people were a danger to America's "modern Teutonic society." This peril was "greater and more insuperable than any of those that menace the other great civilized states of the world." Why? Because African Americans' "animal nature" overshadowed their minds, leaving them with little "continuous will" and "very weak" family ties. In an age of social Darwinism and European empires, an article in the *Atlantic Monthly* observed that races were now the dominant actors in international affairs. It predicted "the domination of the world . . . by some one racial type." The United States "may assume . . . that position of leadership . . . and . . . make the world-empire of the Anglo-Saxon a certainty."[83]

The voices raised against this tide of discriminatory attitudes were few, primarily abolitionists or African Americans. Gamely but in vain these individuals defended the emancipation cause. The abolitionist Wendell Phillips blamed the failure of Reconstruction on "white ignorance and hate." Daniel Chamberlain, the white Republican governor of South Carolina from 1874 to 1877, defended the record of black southern voters, saying that "the race exhibited qualities entitling it to all the political privileges conferred by the reconstruction measures." Frederick Douglass never stopped denouncing the injustices suffered by black Americans. Neither did T. Thomas Fortune or Robert Smalls. On an important strategic point, Douglass attacked the idea that political rights meant "social equality." Black people's constitutional rights did not affect decisions by individuals as to whom they would entertain in their homes or choose as friends. Despite the increasingly oppressive climate, Douglass believed that blacks had "a moral and political hold on this country" because they were identified with the theme of "American liberty," a theme that would eventually triumph. The "low and unjust estimate entertained of their abilities," he believed, was the product of slavery, and he urged members of his race to work, study, and elevate themselves so as to change racial stereotypes.[84]

Other black leaders agreed and counseled patience, education, and hard work with no surrender of self-respect. Richard T. Greener, the first black graduate of Harvard and dean of the Howard University Law School, wrote that his race's "drawbacks are the concomitants of slavery" and political controversy, and Bishop W. J. Gaines of the African Methodist Episcopal Church agreed that "prejudice . . . originated in and was perpetuated by slavery." Yet African Americans would "advance," Gaines believed, with "religion and education" and the acquisition of "virtue, intelligence, and wealth."

H. C. Bruce blamed "the unwarranted prejudice against us" less on "color" than on "our condition" and urged self-help and self-reliance. As a hostile white consensus grew, leaders like Reverend J. C. Price and Professor W. S. Scarborough urged "development from within" and counseled "the negro" to "make the most of his opportunities, winning respect and confidence by his moral and intellectual attainments and his financial worth."[85]

But in the 1890s southern whites became more aggressive, saying that "barbarism" was the "natural state" of black Americans, who were "incapable of self-government" and were assaulting white women. At this point northern class and racial prejudices gave added support to the Lost Cause ideology. The North's interest in suffrage restriction grew as old-stock residents reacted against immigrants from southern and eastern Europe, who were arriving in large numbers in their cities. Alexander Kelly McClure, a Pennsylvania journalist, Republican, and biographer of Abraham Lincoln, published a book on the South that called "universal suffrage" a "problem" and declared that "ignorant and thriftless masses" should not be permitted to control "great states." Dismissing some able black leaders in the South as "convicts," he judged Reconstruction "a terrible failure" and declared that "the white man will rule the inferior race."[86]

When Professor James Bryce, the highly respected British historian, political leader, and author of a well-known work on American political institutions, spoke out, his views seemed to many northerners to give objective approval to the assault on black rights. In an 1891 article about the "Negro Problem," Bryce described "the vast majority" of African Americans as "confessedly unfit for the suffrage," something that "was demonstrated on a colossal scale and with ruinous results in the reconstruction period."

The "swarms of ignorant immigrants from the most backward populations of Europe" also contributed to the "mischief" caused by universal suffrage. Bryce endorsed the first southern efforts to disfranchise blacks and wrote that the entire country needed "an educational or a property qualification" or both.[87] After these developments, it was not surprising that in the 1890s the North accepted southern disfranchisement in the 1890s and the Supreme Court's 1896 decision in *Plessy v. Ferguson* that "separate but equal" treatment by a state did not violate the Fourteenth Amendment.

If this first period of ideology and memory in the United States brought the triumph of racism and southern viewpoints by 1900, the next twenty or so years saw a deepening and extension of race prejudice. America's racial attitudes descended to their "nadir." "At no time in American history," observed historian Stanley Elkins, "were Southern race dogmas so widely accepted throughout the entire nation as in the early years of the twentieth century."[88] The triumph of southern ideology seemed complete, as dominant as the ideology of National Catholicism during Franco's early dictatorship.

Foreign affairs added a new dimension to the idea that some races had a right to dominate others. As a result of the Spanish-American War of 1898, the United States became part of the expanding web of Western imperialism. Inevitably this involved further compromise of the nation's democratic ideals, as the United States took control of and denied self-government to the Philippines, Cuba, and Puerto Rico. The justifications for exerting power over those countries and their darker-skinned and ethnically different populations relied upon ideas of Anglo-Saxon racial superiority. President William McKinley grafted onto these a claim that Christianity *required* the United States, as a higher duty, to shoulder its imperial responsibilities.

In a famous interview with a visiting church delegation McKinley stressed that he "didn't want the Philippines" and "did not know what to do with them." "I walked the floor of the White House night after night until midnight" and often "went down on my knees and prayed to Almighty God for light and guidance." Finally he realized that he could not "give them back to Spain" or turn them over to European commercial rivals. Nor was self-government possible because the Philippine people were "unfit for self-government." The only solution, McKinley piously related, was "to take them all, and to educate the Filipinos, and uplift and civilize and Christianize them, ... as our fellow-men for whom Christ also died." These paternalistic ideas, so similar to the claims made by slaveholders and southern apologists for segregation, soon found a stronger echo in the words of William Howard Taft. While serving as governor general of the Philippines before he would himself become president, Taft told McKinley that "our little brown brothers" would need "fifty or one hundred years" of tutelage before they could "develop anything resembling Anglo-Saxon political principles and skills."[89]

This brand of racism—emphasizing imperial Western, Anglo-Saxon superiority—strengthened white racism at home, and the nation's leaders during the Progressive Era gave their endorsement to the racist beliefs so vital to the Lost Cause ideology. Theodore Roosevelt's rhetoric was more egalitarian than that of McKinley or Taft. His stated position was that all should have "equality of opportunity, equality of treatment before the law." But aside from a much criticized meeting in the White House with Booker T. Washington, Roosevelt did little to change race relations, and this during years when lynching was sharply on the rise. Instead, in celebration of the United States' new power in world affairs, he rejoiced that the Civil War had made the North and South "one people." Since America was now the world's "mightiest nation," it was clear that preservation of the Union had been "essential to the welfare of mankind." No longer, he argued, was there any cause to "divide brother from brother," North from South. African Americans were "the backward race," and therefore progress in race relations "must necessarily be slow" for "it is not possible in offhand fashion to obtain or to confer the priceless boons of freedom, industrial efficiency, political capacity, and domestic morality."[90] To Roosevelt, the Union cause guaranteed national unity and power. In social matters it comfortably accommodated the Lost Cause.

Woodrow Wilson, the successor of Roosevelt and Taft in Progressive Era reform, endorsed racism more strongly, in both word and deed. As a leading scholar of American political history, Wilson had written accurately about the dynamics of Reconstruction law making, in which southern intransigence had led to stronger northern policies. But his attitude toward African Americans was approvingly southern. In an essay in the *Atlantic Monthly* in 1901, Wilson had described the freedmen as "unpracticed in liberty, unschooled in self-control, never sobered by the discipline of self-support, never established in any habit of prudence, excited by a freedom they did not understand, exalted by false hopes, bewildered... insolent and aggressive, sick of work, covetous of pleasure—a host of dusky children untimely put out of school." As president, Wilson gave free rein to southern Democrats in his Cabinet, who proposed and achieved segregation of federal employees. He also arranged a screening in the White House of D. W. Griffith's film *Birth of a Nation*, which was based on Thomas Dixon's incendiary, racist novel about the Civil War and Reconstruction. The film depicted black men as lascivious brutes eager to rape virtuous white women. Woodrow Wilson is believed to have said that the film was "like writing history with lightning. And my only regret is that it is all so terribly true."[91] In this environment it was not surprising that bloody race riots in northern cities followed the end of World War I.

As racist ideology consolidated its hold on the nation, social and political elites were at work in the South to make the Lost Cause and its version of history the accepted truth for generations to come. Disfranchisement had put southern Democrats securely in control of their region's politics. In the ensuing decades they used seniority to increase their power in Congress, and they continued to use racism to secure their hold on the small number of southerners who voted. Whenever a challenge arose to the power of the business, industrial, and agricultural interests that dominated the party, Democratic politicians warned of racial dangers. Repeatedly southern demagogues agitated for the repeal of the Fifteenth Amendment—an impractical idea but one that gave them opportunity to slander black people and reinforce segregation.[92]

Closely linked to many members of the economic and political elite were the women of the United Daughters of the Confederacy. The energetic work of this organization, often in association with male groups such as the United Confederate Veterans and the Sons of Confederate Veterans (SCV), had an immense impact on public and university education, on historical organizations, and on social attitudes. The UDC aggressively promoted the Lost Cause not only because its members remembered fallen ancestors but also because the ideology reinforced their privileged and dominant class position.

The UDC saw an opportunity to control what younger generations learned about history. By policing or dictating what was taught in schools and universities, they could implant the ideas of the Lost Cause in the minds of southern children and ensure a continuation of racist, antinorthern thought about the Civil War. The well-to-do, high-status women who led the UDC had direct connections, through marriage and family ties, to the men who legislated and who influenced government. They used those ties not only to shape and monitor existing institutions, such as the schools, but also to establish new ones, such as the first departments of archives and history in southern states. Naturally, these new institutions would have, as part of their purpose, the propagation of "objective" and "unbiased" history, which to the women of the UDC meant the glories of the Lost Cause. The UDC's work has had a long-lasting influence.[93]

Formed in 1894, the United Daughters of the Confederacy expanded the agenda of the many ladies memorial associations and linked an older generation of elite women with their younger successors. Working within "traditional definitions of womanhood," the leaders of the UDC broadened "the scope of women's time-honored responsibilities." While concerned for the Confederate dead and veterans, this organization achieved remarkable results in controlling southern society's understanding of the past and perpetuating Confederate values. Around the turn of the century, leaders gained legislative support for the first state archives and history agencies in the South. Members donated relics or patriotic materials to these new agencies and to the Confederate Museum in Richmond. They organized chapters of Confederate Children and drilled little southerners in correct thought, just as the Catholic Church trained Spanish children. Cornelia Branch Stone's *UDC Catechism for Children* was a document whose forty-eight questions and prescribed answers made the southern view of history crystal clear. Others published books such as Laura Martin Rose's *Ku Klux Klan or Invisible Empire*, which taught that whites had been "trampled underfoot by ignorant and vicious negroes." Essays in journals, especially the *Confederate Veteran*, insisted that slaves "were the happiest set of people on the face of the globe" and that kind masters cared paternalistically for "their people." For the benefit of schoolrooms, UDC chapters donated portraits of Robert E. Lee and Jefferson Davis.[94]

Most important, and highly successful, were the UDC's efforts to control what was taught in educational institutions. Through what one historian aptly calls a "program of indoctrination," the UDC established its values as societal truth, backed and accepted by male elites. Mildred Rutherford, the historian general of the organization, wrote many primers and documents. Hers and other UDC publications found their way into schools, and certain authors received the UDC's imprimatur through a list of approved and unacceptable texts. But even more important was the pressure the organization brought to bear on publishers. Censoring any departures from orthodoxy, the UDC campaigned against "biased" textbooks and "anti-Southern" authors. Publishing companies, which wanted southern sales, had to conform to the organization's rules of content. "Strict censorship," explained Mrs. M. M. Birge of the Texas Division of the UDC, "is the thing that will bring the honest truth." Arguing that Confederates had been "defenders of Constitutional principle," the UDC's approved version of history endorsed the Lost Cause myth as fact and was "at its core, about preserving white supremacy."[95]

It became unsafe, even in the South's better universities, to deviate from the pro-Confederate line. Anything that departed from the Lost Cause narrative caught the attention of vigilant UDC chapters. Women found offending passages deep in textbooks—such as a word problem, on page 251 of a math book, that referred to a victory by General Grant—and waged campaigns to have the offending volumes removed. The Department of History of the University of Texas came under fire for one book on a reading list, even though it was very hostile to Reconstruction. The strategy of UDC campaigns was first to generate unfavorable publicity and then enlist prominent males, who could force action by a university's governing board. In Florida in 1911 the UDC compelled the resignation of Professor Enoch Marvin Banks, who had dared to say that slavery was an "anachronism" and that "a confederacy with the recognized right of secession was not the best form of union." In other southern states professors considered unpatriotic were driven away, while undoubtedly many more silenced themselves to keep their jobs. The UDC, writes historian Fred Bailey, was determined that the South's white children would be "taught to 'think correctly,' to appreciate the virtues of elite rule, to fear the enfranchisement of blacks, and to revere the Confederate cause."[96]

Nationally racism and the Lost Cause gained acceptance among historians at the North's most respected universities. Ulrich B. Phillips, a native of Georgia, was the recognized authority on slavery and held prestigious positions at, successively, the University of Wisconsin, Tulane University, the University of Michigan, and Yale. His writings advanced the South's interests as much as they furthered knowledge. Phillips did pioneering, detailed work in plantation records, and contemporary historians respect some of his observations. But a profound racism was at the core of his interpretation. In his influential work *American Negro Slavery*, Phillips described slavery as a "school" to "civilize" and Christianize the savage African slaves, whom he also referred to as "darkies" and "pickaninnies." "On the whole," Phillips asserted, "the plantations were the best schools yet invented for the mass training of that sort of inert and backward people which the bulk of American negroes represented." African Americans "were more or less contentedly slaves, with grievances from time to time but not ambition. With 'hazy pasts and reckless futures,' they lived each moment as it flew and left 'Old Massa' to take such thought as the morrow might need."[97] About the same time two important works on Reconstruction appeared: Claude Bower's *Tragic Era* (1929) and Howard K. Beale's *Critical Year: A Study of Andrew Johnson and Reconstruction*. Both these books endorsed the southern view of Reconstruction as a great wrong against the South; black suffrage was a key element in the North's vengeful, unjustified, and unwise policy.[98]

With racism dominant in the nation, organizations like the UDC, the United Confederate Veterans, and the Sons of Confederate Veterans had a powerful influence. Working energetically from positions of social power, they shaped a South that was relatively isolated from outside influences. Given segregation, the political dominance of a racist Democratic Party, and a reflexive fear of change, the South became a "closed society" and Lost Cause ideas almost a theology for many. This pro-Confederate myth became a sort of civil religion or societal faith, whose tenets the UDC and political elites defended as aggressively as the Catholic Church enforced its views under Franco. Their efforts strongly shaped the future. "The generation of children raised on the Lost Cause and Confederate culture in the early decades of the twentieth century," points out Karen Cox, "is also the generation that was actively involved in massive resistance to desegregation at mid-century."⁹⁹ The fact that "racism as an ideology reached its highest point in American history in the Nadir, higher even than during slavery" has had long-lingering effects.¹⁰⁰

There were always some dissenting voices raised for the emancipation cause, but until the 1930s or 1940s they seemed to have little effect. Black leaders such as W. E. B. Du Bois, John Hope, William Monroe Trotter, and even Booker T. Washington on occasion,¹⁰¹ protested against discrimination. Du Bois produced some of his most memorable essays during this discouraging period, and he regularly wrote for the NAACP's magazine, the *Crisis*, which he edited. His book *Black Reconstruction* remains an impressive achievement, but at the time it was generally ignored. Instead, it was the Legal Defense Fund of the NAACP that scored some breakthrough victories. The Scottsboro case, in which lawyers hired by the Communist Party displaced the NAACP, began the rejuvenation of the Fourteenth Amendment by successive Supreme Court decisions. The NAACP's lawyers then won important cases in the 1940s and early 1950s that guarded blacks' rights, undermined the legal foundations of "separate but equal," and prepared the way for the landmark decision in *Brown v. Board of Education*.¹⁰² This revitalization of the Fourteenth Amendment was a constitutional prod to action by other branches of government.

Meanwhile, broad social changes were undermining segregation, just as in Spain the rise of a middle-class, urban society undermined Franco's control. These changes had far greater impact than the best writing, the most impressive intellectual arguments, or the finest legal briefs.

Clearly, cogent and compelling arguments had been made before, and the moral principles requiring equal rights had not changed since the Declaration of Independence. But reason and intellect shape people's actions less than the social environment that surrounds them, exerting a silent influence in support of all the conventions to which they conform. Fortunately, practical alterations in the world, both far and near, were beginning to threaten segregation and expose its dangers.

Internal changes will be discussed in more detail in later chapters, but here we can emphasize the advances that African Americans made as they moved to the North and settled in major cities, where they became a factor in politics and produced literature, poetry, and music that attracted attention and respect. Equally significant was World War II, in which the United

States declared that it was fighting for democracy and human rights, with the aid of black soldiers who resisted discrimination after they returned from Europe or the Pacific. Then the Cold War, and the rivalry with the Soviet Union for support among decolonizing nations around the globe, made racial injustice at home a serious disadvantage in foreign affairs. Attitudes began to change. Historians began to revise their interpretations. In 1948 President Truman ordered integration of the armed forces, which the demands of the Korean War accomplished. He also began a push for civil rights, pressured by some progressive northern politicians.

The civil rights movement was an earthquake that redefined the landscape of race relations in the United States. Despite murders, bombings, beatings, and other types of violence, hundreds of thousands of African Americans marched, demonstrated, and stood up for their rights. Their courage pitted ideals of human rights and the emancipation cause against the Lost Cause's racism. Although the ideals of the Declaration of Independence had been ignored for almost two hundred years, society now started paying attention. The moral vision and inspiring oratory of Martin Luther King Jr. grounded the black struggle for freedom in the nation's core values. In his Letter from Birmingham Jail, for example, King affirmed that he had "no fear about the outcome of our struggle in Birmingham, even if our motives are at present misunderstood. We will reach the goal of freedom in Birmingham and all over the nation, because the goal of America is freedom.... We will win our freedom because the sacred heritage of our nation and the eternal will of God are embodied in our echoing demands."[103]

King's philosophy of nonviolent protest, of meeting hate with love, of violating unjust laws and accepting the penalty to throw light on injustice, received enormous validation from the violent resistance of southern whites. Previously apathetic whites in the North, or those who had conformed to popular racist ideas, saw both immorality and inspiring idealism on their television screens. Bull Connor gave a brutal face to white racism with his fire hoses, police dogs, and jack-booted policemen. In contrast, black southerners, young and old, called Americans to idealism by demonstrating peacefully for basic rights. Many consciences awoke and many citizens began to criticize racist customs that before had seemed normal.

President Kennedy reacted to both the violence and the country's awakening and called for landmark legislation. His words echoed and powerfully expressed the ideology of the emancipation cause. After violence at the University of Mississippi in 1962, he called on every American to "examine his conscience" over racial discrimination. Confronting the nation's history, he said,

> We are confronted primarily with a moral issue. It is as old as the Scriptures and is as clear as the American Constitution. The heart of the question is whether all Americans are to be afforded equal rights and equal opportunities, whether we are going to treat our fellow Americans as we want to be treated. . . . One hundred years of delay have passed since President Lincoln freed the slaves, yet their heirs, their grandsons, are not fully free. They are not yet freed from the bonds of injustice. They are not yet freed from social and economic oppression. And this Nation, for all its hopes and all its boasts, will not be fully free until all its citizens are free. . . . Now the time has come for this Nation to fulfill its promise.

He announced that he would send to Congress a bold package of bills to ensure civil rights and equal access to public facilities, to end segregation in public schools, and to secure the right to vote.[104] After his assassination, the legislative wizardry of Lyndon Johnson helped push a balky Congress, impeded by southern objections, to pass the Civil Rights Act and the Voting Rights Act.

The entire civil rights movement, of course, was broader than King, and analysis of its complexities has filled many books. But the key point here is that a new period had begun. The racism of the Lost Cause had become unacceptable in national politics. By 1970 the Supreme Court was insisting that schools be desegregated immediately, and for another decade or so court decisions extended protections for fair treatment in employment, housing, voting, and other areas. The laws had changed, society had changed, and politics had changed. No longer was it possible to be a racist demagogue and enjoy social respectability. Despite problems that remained, it now was unacceptable to oppose fair treatment or equality before the law.

Senator Ernest "Fritz" Hollings of South Carolina confessed that his behavior underwent a transformation after he read King's Letter from Birmingham Jail. "As governor," Hollings admitted, "for four years I enforced those Jim Crow laws. I did not understand, I did not appreciate what King has in mind . . . until he wrote that letter. He opened my eyes and he set me free."[105] Others, such as Jimmy Carter in Georgia, clearly believed in the morality of equal rights, desired a more just society, and were ready to act on those principles in public office. But even those who did not have a changed heart or a willingness to embrace equality faced a different reality. The nation had a new set of laws, society had new standards for what was within the bounds of respectability, black voters had new leverage at the polls. The generations-old rhetoric of segregation and discrimination no longer was viable, and soon a new crop of southern governors joined in declaring that the politics of race was over, "gone with the wind."

Racist views had not, of course, entirely disappeared. Old ways of thinking die hard. Even in the world of science, observed the physicist Max Planck, a new "truth does not triumph by convincing its opponents and making them see the light, but rather because its opponents eventually die, and a new generation grows up that is familiar with it."[106] Before President Jimmy Carter came into office, the state of Georgia incorporated the Confederate battle flag into its state flag. South Carolina raised that Confederate flag over its state capitol, where it flew until the year 2000.[107] Meanwhile, Republican strategists were identifying new ways to win white southern votes.

In 1964 presidential candidate Senator Barry Goldwater decided to go hunting, politically, "where the ducks are." With a more conservative Republican ideology, he carried the states of South Carolina, Georgia, Louisiana, Alabama, and Mississippi. Campaign specialist Lee Atwater explained that "by 1968 you can't say 'nigger'—that hurts you. Backfires. So you say stuff like forced busing, states' rights, and all that stuff." These code words facilitated a shift toward the Republican Party among white citizens who feared they were losing power in the societies they used to dominate. Coded behavior also could be eloquent. Ronald Reagan launched his 1980 presidential election campaign at the Neshoba County Fair in Mississippi. Most Americans remembered that county as the place where local law enforcement in 1964 arranged the murder of three civil rights workers. Republicans also emphasized issues that had always appealed to southern whites, such as limited budgets, fiscal conservatism, evangelical religion, and strong military policies. Richard Nixon continued Goldwater's gains, and in 1980

Ronald Reagan won every former Confederate state except Georgia. In the next two elections Republicans carried every former Confederate state, and in 2008 Barack Obama won only 11 percent of the white vote in Mississippi and 10 percent in Alabama.[108]

Despite this evidence of racially influenced voting, the basic situation of the Lost Cause ideology has, at length, changed greatly. As in Spain, a new generation is speaking in a different way. In the South since 1990 there is much less interest in pro-Confederate patriotism among the ambitious bankers and businessmen of southern cities or among young people in schools and universities. The events of the Civil War seem increasingly irrelevant to the growing cities of the Sunbelt, where conservative southerners give far more attention to securing a prosperous future than to defending a supposedly glorious past. In debates over governmental displays of the Confederate flag, "its defenders could not rely on the gender, religious, and class structures that had sustained earlier Confederate commemoration. To the contrary, those [previous] established patterns ... more often characterized the mobilization *against* the flag."[109] For younger, elite southern women today the Junior League is far more important than the United Daughters of the Confederacy. Most southerners have entered the mainstream of American culture, and pro-Confederate ideology is concentrated mainly in the backwaters.

New ideological groups, aggressive but much more marginal and isolated from the levers of power, have taken the place of the UDC, whose members are elderly and increasingly ineffective. Fascination with the Confederacy survives, but increasingly it expresses either extreme reactions against modernity and big government or a romantic escape from the anonymity of mass society into a simpler era, where individual courage and commitment made a difference. The racial agenda of the Lost Cause has lost its respectability. When the racism of that ideology surfaces, polite society circumscribes its appeal. Chief among the new organizations whose activities now overshadow the UDC are the League of the South, a newly energized Sons of Confederate Veterans, and the legions of Civil War reenactors. The UDC's influence lives on, to the extent that it is noticed, primarily through awards for military graduates that it established years ago.[110]

The League of the South began in 1994, founded by an Alabamian named Michael Hill, and as of 1998 claimed four thousand members. Hill had studied under two well-respected, conservative historians at the University of Alabama, but they dissociated themselves from him as racist comments from his organization began to appear. The "Core Beliefs Statement" of the league reveals traditional pro-Confederate ideology alongside reactions against modern society, big government, and contemporary problems such as the outsourcing of jobs to foreign countries. The statement "advocates the secession and subsequent independence of the Southern States from this forced union" and urges steps toward economic, social, and cultural independence before that political rupture can take place. The South has a "sublime cultural inheritance" involving the "chivalric ideal of manhood," whereas "cultural rot" dominates mainstream culture in the United States, which fails to respect the Christian family or "the Biblical notion of hierarchy." The Core Beliefs Statement goes on to criticize women's rights; abortion; sexual "perversity"; "abstractions" such as "'the nation,' 'the environment,' or the 'global community'"; paper money; the federal reserve system; and the income tax. An independent southern nation would recognize every state's right to "nullification, interposition, and secession," would "strictly limit immigration," and would respect the citizens' right to purchase and own firearms.[111]

After several years of growth, the league's racism and extremism became more visible. In 1998 one of its board members argued that "somebody needs to say a good word for slavery." Two years later Michael Hill declared on the league's website that "a European population" was the "core" of his desired social system. In another essay he defended "a natural affection for one's own kind" and warned of the "disaster" of "being overrun by hordes of non-white immigrants." Slavery, according to Hill, was "God-ordained," and the terrorist attacks of September 11, 2001, were "the natural fruits of a regime committed to multiculturalism and diversity." This rhetoric and revelations of the radical or criminal pasts of some active members caused a decline in membership, and a strategy meeting in 2005 was sparsely attended. Today the Southern Poverty Law Center, which monitors hate groups, judges that the league has been losing ground and that its claims of twenty-five thousand members are "extremely implausible."[112]

The Sons of Confederate Veterans, which succeeded the United Confederate Veterans, has declared on its website that it is a "non-political" organization "dedicated to ensuring that a true history" of the Civil War is preserved. However, the Sons' "true history" is the old idea that "the preservation of liberty and freedom was the motivating factor in the South's decision to fight the *Second American Revolution*."[113] The fact that this hoary justification is the key element in the organization's mission illustrates, as did Pio Moa's book in Spain, the power of original ideological arguments to persist, in spite of contrary evidence. Members of the SCV reflexively defend their ancestors and the ideas that used to make their social position secure. As national support for the Lost Cause ideology has waned in recent years, they have spoken out more aggressively. In North Carolina they ended their support for a statewide book prize after judging that most winning volumes were too liberal. Dissatisfied with treatment of the Civil War at major museums, the SCV is trying to establish a Confederate Museum, seeking donations at the one-thousand-, five-thousand-, and ten-thousand-dollar levels. Their efforts criticize the mainstream, however, rather than constituting it, and on the group's blog are articles that call the NAACP and the American Civil Liberties Union "hate groups."

Far more active are the thousands of Civil War reenactors chronicled in Tony Horwitz's *Confederates in the Attic*. These individuals spend large sums of money to replicate uniforms and equipment from the Civil War period and cheerfully endure bad weather or uncomfortable conditions to relive a bit of history. Horwitz traveled with hard-core reenactors who sought out opportunities to march to historic battlefields and sleep on the cold ground at night, "spooning" their bodies against one another for warmth. The compelling interest in the Civil War for these individuals was not ideological as much as it was personal and romantic. They lived more for their excursions into a vanished past than for the jobs and daily routines that defined their present. That past seemed more vivid, more romantic, and more dependent on individual actions and character than society at the turn of the twenty-first century. Being a Confederate reenactor was a personal experience rather than an attempt to change the beliefs of society.[114]

An unusual and fanciful excursion into an imagined past attracted attention around the year 2000. Suddenly the notion became popular with a noticeable number of black Americans that they had an enslaved ancestor who had marched and fought for the Confederate armies. These new recruits to Confederate history held conventions, created websites, and shared stories or documents in support of their ideas. Their arguments gained the appearance of plausibility from the fact that many slaves had accompanied their owners to the army, where they cooked, cleaned, and on occasion found themselves in the thick of battle. Newspaper reports from the Civil War era occasionally mention black men seen with the Confederate forces in battle. The record is clear, however, that the Confederate government rejected the idea of enlisting black troops until the spring of 1865, when it was too late for any recruits (encouraged by a promise of freedom from their owners) to go into battle. The African Americans who participated in this movement were more interested in honoring their ancestors' history than in supporting the ideology of the Lost Cause or the racism inherent in it.

Die-hard pro-Confederates are very much alive in the contemporary South, but they tend to be older individuals, interested in history and wedded to the myths that they were taught or that their parents and grandparents believed. Among young people in colleges and universities, the sensitivity about secession, the Civil War, and slavery has faded, despite the fact that outdated interpretations continue to be taught in lower grades.[115] Though interesting, those events for most students now are simply history—not *their* history, which requires vindication. In significant ways the South, with the rest of the nation, has moved away from the Lost Cause myth. It is not yet completely repudiated, but it has been left behind.

It is interesting to compare the contemporary state of Franco's ideology and that of the Lost Cause. In Spain the harsh repression of Franco's dictatorship and the church's suffocating moral control produced a remarkable and strong negative reaction. It is probably true that some Spaniards have rejected Franco's ideologies and consciously reconsidered historical memory to a greater extent than is the case in America. The Lost Cause was not so much repudiated in the United States as bypassed. History overtook the Lost Cause; rather than confronting the old ideology, much of society simply moved on to new constructions of historical memory.

This is especially the case with northern understandings of the Civil War. In the last fifteen or twenty years historians, influenced or inspired by the civil rights movement, have begun to follow the general culture in conflating the Union cause with the goal of emancipation and equality. After the civil rights movement triumphed and respectable, "correct" cultural attitudes supported equality rather than segregation, people started to remember the Civil War in a different way. They thought of it as significant less for the preservation of the Union than for the progress that it brought in regard to race. It had contributed—one hundred years before—to the major change that was taking place in national life. Although, in fact, the progress that lasted was limited to the ending of legal slavery, as opposed to voting rights and equality before the law, popular attitudes linked the war to America's movement toward racial equality. These changes in popular thought have appeared most clearly, and have affected most directly, the Lincoln myth.

Abraham Lincoln has become a sacred icon, a kind of symbol for everything that is good—or that Americans want to believe is good—about their nation. Historian James McPherson writes that Lincoln "became the deity of American civil religion," and an essay in the *New Yorker* magazine observed that Lincoln enjoys a "semi-divine status . . . in American history." In earlier decades of the twentieth century, Lincoln's reputation had rested primarily on his central role in saving the Union, for even when racism and segregation were dominant, citizens North and South agreed that the maintenance of the Union had been a great advantage. Scholars such as James G. Randall had pointed out the limited nature of his policies in regard to racial change, and organizations such as the Ku Klux Klan used to publish newspaper advertisements on Lincoln's birthday in which they quoted his statements against equality. In a changed environment, however, the myth of Lincoln transformed to portray him as a great egalitarian and champion of equality—a new emphasis that contributes to general themes of American ideology.

Recent historical works have called Lincoln "a moral visionary," a "fervent idealist," a leader who promoted equality and was "intent on readying the public for black suffrage." In fact, whatever Lincoln's private and personal feelings were on the morality of discrimination, his public acts did little to pave the way for black suffrage. They were limited to a single public statement, just before his death, that his personal preference was that some black men—the very intelligent and those who had served in the U.S. Army—should be allowed to vote.[116] Ignoring such limiting facts, authors have lavished extravagant praise on his smallest actions and explained away shortcomings. If Lincoln opposed or failed to embrace equality, some argue, he was simply shielding his purpose while he secretly pursued egalitarian ends. According to these arguments, Lincoln used "some very crafty methods" in the pursuit of equality, for he was "an artist in the Machiavellian uses of power."

Another device to elevate the image of Lincoln is the recital of a list of facts and efforts on his part. Although all of the items, individually or collectively, clearly stop short of any campaign to establish racial equality or better the social status of African Americans in an immediate, significant way, the repetition in the list tends to create a sense that Lincoln's accomplishments were sweeping or without limit. Although McPherson had acknowledged that "Lincoln did share the racial prejudices of his time and place," he recently has adopted this method of inflation by itemization.[117] Omissions of lesser known facts can also modernize Lincoln's image, as in declarations that after January 1, 1863, Lincoln never again mentioned colonization. Though true in regard to his public statements, this neglects the reality that Lincoln continued to pursue colonization, including an ill-advised experiment on a Haitian island later in 1863 which ended with many fatalities by 1864.[118]

The interest in portraying Lincoln as a champion of racial equality demonstrates once more the fact that historical memory changes at the command of the wider culture. It transforms itself—or more accurately, people transform it—in service to the felt social and political needs of the society. As the life of the nation changes, people seek to use history to validate changes that are occurring or to support changes they believe need to occur. In the case of the United States, the modification of the Lincoln icon is related to more than the civil rights movement and society's rejection of racism. It also draws strength from the pride citizens feel in the fact that their nation is a world power and from the connection its reputation abroad has had with democracy and human rights. The old idea of American exceptionalism, which began with the Puritans' goal of establishing a "city on a hill," reinforces that pride, and the words and actions of politicians constantly encourage patriotic feelings that eclipse unpleasant facts. The erroneous emphasis on Lincoln as a president who fought for racial equality, instead of for the Union and then for emancipation, gives the backing of a great historical figure to an important goal that has been largely, but not completely, realized. The editing and updating of historical memory, whether conscious or unconscious, is always purposeful and is related to present-day agendas.

The relationship between three different interpretations of the significance of the Civil War—the Lost Cause, the Union cause, and the emancipation cause—has changed repeatedly as society has changed. Determined southern whites, aided by northern passivity, first made the Lost Cause triumphant. Then, during the period when racist ideology was most widely accepted in the United States, a socially negotiated truce gave acceptance to both the Lost Cause and the Union cause. Northerners accepted the South's verdict on Reconstruction and race, while southerners acknowledged the importance of the Union. The rights of emancipated slaves were forgotten and ignored. Later, with a multitude of major social changes and the impact of the civil rights movement, the emancipation cause has risen in power while pro-Confederate ideology has become less relevant to most southerners. The old ideology that glorified the Lost Cause, defended slavery, and condemned Reconstruction survives, but principally among an older generation and marginal groups. Each generation experiences a different reality. That fact suggests that however strongly old interpretations of history persist, there is a possibility of escape from their power, as the issues of the present become more distant from the past.

3

The Past and Political Evolution

> To live next to one another is not to live together.
> Aleix Vidal-Quadros, 1997

After their civil wars, both Spain and the United States faced a challenge of political reintegration. War cannot eliminate differing ideas and viewpoints, and partisans of the defeated side do not disappear. Though subjugated, they become a sizable political constituency in the postwar period. A dictator may be able to repress them, and in democracies a numerical majority may outvote them, but neither can change their thoughts. Since civil wars are, by nature, deep and fundamental conflicts, the competition between the views that led to war is likely to resurface. The defeated side may be chastened or subdued, but its values and ways of seeing the world reappear, in some form, in politics.

In a democracy political parties carry the legacy of the victorious or the defeated side into postwar reality. As parties compete for votes, they face a challenge of accommodating the old to the new, of adjusting to the outcome of the war while also nurturing prewar support. On the one hand, political leaders will seek to retain the loyalty of those who formed one side of the civil war. On the other hand they will try to appeal to a broader spectrum of the citizenry in order to build a commanding majority. Often one party enjoys the advantages of victory, or of a marked change like the Transition, for much of a generation, but its rivals will be working to find ways to put together a different majority and come to power.

In both Spain and the United States, legacies from the civil war shaped postwar parties. Both political systems came to be dominated by two parties that echoed wartime divisions. Of course, in Spain Franco's dictatorship allowed no democratic challengers before his death, but with the Transition two processes of political evolution came to the fore. Competition first developed between Adolfo Suárez's newly formed Union of the Democratic Center and PSOE, the Socialist Party. Both sought a majority that would include the political center, composed of citizens hungry for democracy but wary of too rapid a change, which might bring back military repression. Soon the Socialists grasped this high ground, and they held power uninterruptedly for fourteen years. At the same time those from the Right, and those who had held positions within Franco's regime but saw the inevitability of change, worked to adjust right-wing views to the new democratic terrain so that they might become more competitive and build a majority. They formed first the Alianza Popular (AP) and then its more agile successor, the Partido Popular. Thus as the Socialists emerged as a vehicle for democratic aspirations and the inheritor of Republican values, a second major party became the home for Spanish voters sympathetic to Franco's movement, to his legacy, or to conservative religious and social values.

Perhaps such an outcome was not inevitable for Spain, since its parliamentary system permits a variety of parties to seek support. One could imagine a process in which various and distinct issues flowing from the civil war became identified with several smaller parties, instead of with the Partido Popular or with PSOE. But the division between Republicans and Nationalists in the civil war was too deep; it found an echo in the rivalry between these two dominant parties after the Transition. This was the product of wartime emotions, aided by electoral laws that disadvantaged small parties. The Right did not splinter, and most of the more extreme voters on the Left fell in behind the Socialists in order to make the transition to democracy a success.[1]

The United States had well-established Republican and Democratic parties that carried on after Appomattox, and for many years their competition replicated wartime patterns due to political geography. The Republican Party had never enjoyed southern support before the war and afterward had diminishing interest in southern black voters, yet it could continue to win national elections due to its strength in the far more populous North. For southern Democrats the overriding priority was not nationwide strength but racial control in the South. Thus dominant elements of each party had something they dearly wanted without attracting new voters. After an initial period of flux, both parties relied on their base of loyalists for more than two generations.

This pattern perhaps was not predictable from the situation in 1860, when the Democratic Party had, by far, more strength in the different parts of the nation.[2] But the deep divisions of war shaped postwar political identities in a reflection of battle lines. Although Republicans ignored the interests of southern black voters, the arithmetic of the Electoral College, their identification with national prestige and power, and their growing alliance with wealthy industrial interests helped them enjoy a long tenancy in the White House. The Democrats were disadvantaged and outnumbered in the North, where they bore the stigma of having sympathized with "rebellion." They continued to speak for those who feared strong government, and they built some strong urban machines with immigrant support. But catering to the growing population of immigrants did not endear them to old-stock voters or produce quick victories in the North. Meanwhile, in the South, Democrats concentrated on solidifying political and racial control. That goal—the core of the Confederacy's wartime agenda—was far more important to white leaders than presidential elections. The South became Democratic territory, but with cooperative rather than ideologically close connections to the national party. Thus the divisions of war gave shape to postwar political rivalries in both Spain and the United States.

In historical terms Spain is still not that far removed from the years of dictatorship and Transition, and its political life reveals many identifiable, even plainly visible, connections between the issues of the past and those of the present. A visitor to Madrid on July 18, the anniversary of the date in 1936 when Franco joined the uprising by flying from the Canary Islands to Spanish Morocco, can usually see scores of demonstrators giving the Fascist salute. Protestors against budget cuts in 2012 sometimes carried into the streets the flag of the Second Republic. These echoes of the civil war do not foreshadow armed conflict, but some of the old issues are still strong enough to produce predictable division between the PP and PSOE. The United States, like Spain, saw issues from the civil war dominating political rhetoric for a number of decades. Later, in the much longer period since its civil war ended, American developments illustrate two facts. The issues of internecine conflicts can fade or mutate, and political organizations can prove very adaptable, even shedding their ideological skin as society changes, to become quite different parties under the same names.

National identity versus local or regional loyalty remains a controversial issue in both countries. In the United States separate colonies existed before national unity, and then, under the nation, slavery created a different society in the South. Leaders of the region defended their interests before the Civil War through the ideology of states' rights, which one southern newspaper called "the armor that encased" slavery.[3] Through many postwar decades, states' rights remained the white South's tool to protect its system of racial discrimination and subordination. Even today, with a far larger central government and a nationally integrated economy, the idea of states' rights has not lost all its power.[4] Similarly, in Spain regional identities had played a role in the Civil War. These subsequently became more salient as the dictatorship of Franco sought to suppress Catalan, Basque, or other regional aspirations. Insisting on centralization and referring always to one, united Spain, Franco barred the use of languages other than Castilian and hunted down those he suspected of being separatists. As in other areas of life, his repression only deepened the determination of some individuals to resist, and as a result the question of peripheral identities—in Catalonia, the Basque Country, and Navarre, especially—became an important item on the agenda of Spain's post-Franco democracy. The place of the autonomies within the nation is even more controversial today.

For the United States, the connection between states' rights and the larger question of racism was fundamental. Indeed, race played as enduring a role as did religion in Spain. It shaped American politics, just as religion played a prominent role in Spain's civil war and dictatorship and later in the political battles of democracy. In the United States, however, the political parties changed their ideologies, and southern whites changed their party allegiance. Racial equality became a Democratic goal, and Republicans recruited white southerners into a broad social conservatism. In Spain, the inheritance of religiously influenced positions was much more direct and straightforward. There devotees of National Catholicism's fundamentalist beliefs naturally gravitated to the PP rather than the PSOE.

The transformation of parties in the United States took place in two stages over more than one hundred years. At first the Democratic Party became geographically schizophrenic—dominant, racist, and reactionary in the South and weaker but steadily more progressive in the North. These two divergent wings of the party were able to coexist due to the nation's federal structure and northern willingness to accept the South's racial system. Eventually, however, the influence of Franklin Roosevelt's New Deal and the impact of the civil rights movement produced a different, repositioned Democratic Party. Northern Democrats became advocates for racial justice, and President Lyndon Johnson embraced the goals of the civil rights movement. At that point southern whites, led first by Strom Thurmond and his Dixiecrat revolt, began to rebel against the Democratic Party, and leaders of the Republican Party decided to court them. As southern whites moved into the Republican Party they strengthened that organization and contributed to a "southernization" of national politics and rhetoric on a variety of issues.

Although blatant racism became unacceptable after the civil rights movement, the conservative mindset expressed itself in other ways. Republicans opposed welfare, affirmative action, abortion, and social change as they courted fundamentalist evangelicals and trumpeted both patriotism and a pro-business approach to power in society. These issues, infused into national politics from the reactionary South, created some striking similarities between the Republican Party and the Partido Popular of Spain. Like the Republicans, the PP opposes abortion, gay marriage, an expanded welfare state, and greater regulation of business, and it empowers the elite rather than the poor. The issues of race and religion have proven so basic that they can give shape to the political landscape.

Thus in both countries wartime issues proved persistent and important. Time and generational change do not necessarily alter the political agenda. Generational change may do little more than erode the salience of past issues. Only if the structure of society changes enough to resolve fundamental conflicts or replace them with an entirely different social landscape does it become possible for later generations to leave the most divisive matters behind. The exploration of these connections between today's parties and the past will begin with Spain.

Spain's Parties in the Shadow of the Past

The monotheistic and religious fundamentalisms plant barriers between the citizens. Laicism is the space of Integration.

"Constitución, laicidad y educación para la ciudadanía," PSOE position paper, December 1, 2006

In Spain there has been born a laicism, a strong and aggressive secularism, such as we saw in the thirties.... This collision between faith and modernity ... takes place anew today in Spain.

Pope Benedict XVI, October 6, 2010, quoted in *El País*, October 7, 2010

My government, in short, will better the conditions of life for those who possess fewer resources in this society.

José Luis Rodríguez Zapatero, investiture address, April 15, 2004

Government ought to create a framework so that the enterprising may develop it [society]. More society, as our slogan says, means less regulation ... more liberty. There are too many laws, decrees, regulations.

PP leader Mariano Rajoy, quoted in *El País*, March 6, 2011

In Spain the connection between today's parties and the past remains quite direct. The PP is the inheritor of conservative and pro-Franco sentiment. Many "of its leaders are sons, daughters or grandchildren of leading members of the Francoist political elites."[5] There is no ultra-Right party in Spain, and thus the challenge for the PP is to hold onto voters on the Right while capturing support in the center. The capture of the center was achieved first by the PSOE under Felipe González. Adolfo Suárez's newly formed coalition, the UDC, was inexperienced and unstable, whereas the Socialists had a long organizational history and greater party discipline. They adopted a moderate message reassuring to many Spaniards and supported a capitalist, market economy, while voters further to the Left moved from the Communists to the Socialists for fear of the army's reaction. Aided by González's charismatic personality, the Socialists controlled the government from 1982 to 1996. Some had expected Manuel Fraga Iribarne, a minister in Franco's regime but an exponent of *aperture* (change) to head a powerful Right-center coalition. But Fraga decided to contest elections in the Transition in the company of seven reactionary and distrusted Francoists, whom most voters chose to avoid. Fraga later credited his decision with bringing the maximum number of ultra-rightists into a democratic system, but the short-term result was a weak party incapable of winning a majority, the Alianza Popular. After several years Fraga saw the need to restructure conservative forces and refounded the AP as the Partido Popular. With the ascent of José Maria Aznar to leadership, the PP won the presidency in 1996.[6]

Aznar had first gained notice as president of the *autonomia* of Castilla y León. Then in 1989 he headed his party when it failed to defeat González's PSOE but emerged as the principal opposition group. The Socialists' involvement in numerous corruption scandals certainly aided his victory in 1996, but Aznar also reshaped the image of the PP so that it could establish a center-Right identity. He recognized the need to position the party as conservative but not antidemocratic, nationalist but not repressive, traditionalist but also modern. Voters needed to see the party as safe for democrats and backers of Franco.

In speeches and books Aznar argued that the Socialists had come to power only because the center collapsed and that his mission was to recover and rebuild the center in Spanish politics. The program of the PP would be "national, centered, liberal, tolerant, and broad." Distancing himself from Franco's regime, he pledged to govern with "scrupulous respect for institutions, with moderation and tolerance, with austerity, rigor and national spirit" and to show that the Right could govern not only without risk to the nation but with "the guarantee of an impulse of renovation." When Aznar spoke about history, he skipped over the years of dictatorship to align his party with earlier periods of conservative thought, echoing the nineteenth-century leader Cánovas, for example, when he argued that "the alternation [in power] in the democracy is the best method for overcoming" the dangers of "inertia and resignation."[7]

Franco, of course, had exalted Spanish nationalism and, emphasizing centralization, had used violent repression against peripheral nationalisms and languages, such as those in Catalonia or the Basque Country. The Constitution of 1978 had attempted to incorporate these two different viewpoints, declaring on the one hand that it was founded "in the indissoluble unity of the Spanish nation" but on the other that it "recognizes and guarantees the right to the autonomy of the nationalities and regions that form it."[8] Aznar chose his words carefully so as to affirm national unity without being seen as a centralizer in the brutal manner of Franco. Referring to the wars and conflicts caused by national rivalries in modern times, Aznar stated that he believed in "liberty and in reason" and "therefore, I am not a nationalist." But he also said that Spain needed a grand national project to summon its energies and spoke of his emotional feeling for the nation. Calling Spain "a plural nation," he described the nation as a "suit" rather than a "corset." He called for a common patriotism that would respect the identity of peoples within a national community "understood as a collective task to which all the citizens are called." To subordinate Catalan or Basque nationalisms, he rejected the descriptive phrases "a nation of nations" and "a plurinational state." He also rejected federalism, which, he said, refers to efforts to unite the disunited. Spain's common past and shared commitment to the future, he argued, made it a basically homogenous community. Differences would be respected in a plural nation and an autonomous State that offered to all a path for "living together" and making progress. While criticizing the duplication of positions that was occurring in some autonomies, Aznar worked to reassure the Right and disarm fears that he would crush the peripheral nationalisms.[9]

When he became president, Aznar reiterated some other points that were important in defining the PP's ideology. To distance the party from its far Right roots, he declared that "the old quarrels, the old historic disputes, the conceptions based in the division of Spaniards ought not to reappear in our democratic common life, because what interests us all is building the future, undertaking the tasks that society now asks of us." He also praised the "will of reconciliation" and affirmed that Spain's "position in Europe" was a matter of "basic consensus," though in his government Spain would "contribute in a manner more active and decided, and with its own voice, in the project of the construction of Europe." In a more conservative vein, he pledged strong action against the terrorism of ETA, modernization and strengthening of the Spanish economy, expansion of its international economic ties, and development of armed forces that would be smaller but better equipped, more flexible, and more effective.[10]

While Aznar's rhetoric identified major parts of the PP's ideology, the debates over practical issues reveal in greater detail the connections between today's party and past concerns. Among those that distinguish the PP from PSOE or other groups are the Catholic Church and the proper place of religion in public life; issues linked to religion, such as policies on education, abortion, the family, women's status, and symbolic observances; questions of order or freedom in society, which reveal differing conceptions of what liberty means; the government's use of force, both against internal terrorism and in the projection of power abroad; and policies toward the autonomies and the groups that speak of independence. The salience of issues relating to the church shows that religion has played a central role in Spain, analogous to race in the United States.

The church was central to Franco's regime, and despite decline it remains the dominant religion in Spain, with thousands of devoted parishioners. Almost all deeply dedicated Catholics are politically on the Right, following church doctrine. After Pope John XXIII, both the Vatican and the Spanish hierarchy pivoted sharply in a conservative direction, and leaders of the Spanish church have refused to apologize for its passionate embrace of Franco. These facts guarantee continued disputes in Spain. In what some observers judged to be a first, church leaders followed Cardinal Antonio María Rouco into the streets to demonstrate against the legislative program of the Zapatero government. They also denounced the legalization of marriage among homosexuals as "the worst thing that has happened to the Catholic Church in two thousand years." Although the church has continued to enjoy financial support from all Spanish governments, its leaders and the more conservative or religiously oriented newspapers, such as *La Razón, ABC,* or *La Vanguardia,* naturally see the PP as their principal ally.[11]

Politicians clash not only over substantive matters related to religion but also over symbolic issues, such as perceptions of respect or disrespect shown to the church and the pope. When Benedict XVI visited Spain in the fall of 2010, he condemned an "aggressive secularism" in Spain and described it as similar to that which he saw in the history of the 1930s. His evocation of the divisive period immediately before the outbreak of the bloody civil war immediately aroused concern. Vatican spokesmen, aware that such a reference would ignite controversy, quickly tried to diminish the significance of his allusion, claiming that the pope was merely describing a phenomenon common to Europe. But the issue was joined in public debate.

Leaders of PSOE declared that the pope was "gravely mistaken" and that Socialists had treated the church "better" than other governments. The

PP defended the pope and refused to be on the defensive. A spokesperson for the party backed the Vatican's less-alarming interpretation and criticized President Zapatero for not receiving His Eminence. Not only had Zapatero failed to greet the pope, but he even had left the country to visit Afghanistan. This decision, said the PP, showed his alienation from the "sentiment of the Spanish people, since the Pope is the spiritual and emotional leader of the great majority of Spaniards." The PP's spokesperson in the European Parliament, Jaime Mayor Oreja, went further, charging that PSOE was, in fact, carrying out a project of "radical laicism" that "has no comparison in the European Union." In response, other parties further to the Left than PSOE roundly condemned the pope for his "disconcerting" reference to the thirties and his "unacceptable" interference in politics. They also criticized the PSOE government for making concessions to the church. "The Church has not asked pardon for its support of *Franquismo*," said a legislator from United Left, "and therefore" the pope's statement was even "more unjust."[12]

These controversies quickly rose to the surface again in 2011, when the pope came to Madrid for the finale of a worldwide series of church festivals for young Catholics. A government minister stated strongly that the pope should limit his activities to evangelization and avoid politics. But church leaders indicated that the pope would address the problems in Spain that troubled him, especially laicism and the relativism of Spanish society, and give support to his politically outspoken bishops. In reaction, 150 lay or atheistic organizations, plus a few liberal Catholic and Christian groups, protested against the church's role in politics. They decried the use of their tax revenues to facilitate the pope's visit and chanted, "For a laic state." The primate of Toledo retorted that only in Spain was there such a "radical laicism and dangerous secularism." The protesting lay organizations also spoke out in condemnation of the government. Although Zapatero's Socialist government had promised a law on euthanasia, the legislation that it eventually proposed focused on living wills, palliative care, and the right to a dignified death. Other plans to end the church's participation in a variety of official governmental ceremonies came to nothing. Moreover, the lay critics objected that the government had liberalized the funding of the Catholic Church, by raising the percentage of income taxes that citizens could voluntarily assign to its support, from 0.52 to 0.70 percent. With that change the church was reported to have received 250 million euros in 2010.[13]

The church's cardinals and bishops, both singly and through the Episcopal Conference of Spain, continue to condemn abortion and other government policies to which they object. Laws on abortion have steadily become more liberal over the years, and the Tribunal Constitucional ruled in 1999 that the fetus does not have a legal right to life and that embryonic research was legal.[14] Therefore church leaders and conservative newspapers looked to the PP to change the law on abortion, and possibly other measures, when it would again come to power. Politically, the PP needed to support the church but not antagonize majority opinion. These two stances became evident in 2012 under the newly elected government of Mariano Rajoy. The PP's minister of justice, Alberto Ruiz-Gallardón, first unveiled draft legislation that would have restricted abortion severely. Then, in the face of loud protests from a public that has always, in opinion polls, shown strong support for the existing laws, he retreated. The PP's current position, which at this writing it has staunchly reaffirmed, is that the law will be changed and will forbid abortions undertaken due to fetal malformation.[15]

On questions of education the PP gives active and vigorous support to the church. In 2003, when Aznar's government enjoyed an "unassailable majority" in the Congreso, the minister of education introduced a "radical raft of reforms" for schools and universities. These included making religious instruction mandatory in primary and secondary state schools. Although some aspects of the proposed reforms had to be softened due to mass protest, the compulsory courses in religion became law under the PP.[16] Although the subsequent Socialist government made changes, religion continues to have a prominent place in the educational system.

Modern Spain has three types of educational institutions: Catholic institutions, public schools and universities, and instructional "centers" which can be run by various groups but receive state funding. The centers have to offer religious education, although it is voluntary for students, and the church chooses the professors who teach those courses, although they are paid by the state. A very large majority of students take religion courses—99 percent in Catholic schools, 69.6 percent in private, non-Catholic centers, and 62.7 percent in public schools. Overall 71 percent, or slightly more than 3 million of the 4.4 million students in all of Spain and at all levels, are in such religion courses. Nevertheless, the numbers have been dropping and are lowest at the higher levels. This troubles the church and leads to "confrontations with the Government every year," as bishops complain that the government makes it difficult for students to obtain information or encourages the decision to opt out of religious courses. Legislation under PP governments has aimed "to satisfy the demands of the representatives of the concerted centers and the Catholic Church." For the church's part, the cardinal primate of Toledo declared, "we will never resign ourselves to the idea that moral education might be reduced to the sphere of the private, as if it were only something reserved for believers."[17]

Other issues affecting religion's place in education arise frequently. For example, in 2001 the bishop of Almería fired a woman under contract to teach religion in a public center. His reason? She had married a divorced man, and the church does not recognize divorce or sanction remarriage of divorced people. Rather than accept this decision, the teacher, Resurrección Galera Navarro, initiated legal action, and ten years later the Tribunal Constitucional ruled that as a teacher she had a right "to not suffer discrimination by reason of personal circumstances." Her marriage did "not affect her pedagogical aptitude," the court reasoned, and she was constitutionally entitled to enjoy "ideological liberty in connection with the right to marry in a legally established form." In recent years the Tribunal Supremo has also ruled that the church must pay the costs of such cases.[18]

As another illustration of the many areas for conflict over religion, some students at the state-run Complutense University in Madrid recently protested against church policies and against the existence on campus of a chapel where masses were celebrated. Shouting slogans against the church's treatment of women and homosexuals, some students removed their shirts to show messages painted on their bodies. The archbishop of Madrid condemned their act as "profanation," and the right-wing organization Clean Hands demanded prosecution under the penal code for an offense against religious sentiments.[19]

The PSOE government of José Luis Rodríguez Zapatero legalized gay marriage. In response, a number of PP legislators sued to challenge the law. In November 2012 the Tribunal Supremo, by a vote of eight to three, rejected the PP's challenge and affirmed matrimony for gays. The PP thus demonstrated its fidelity to church doctrine and traditional values but failed. Church leaders responded by voicing their concern for "stable" families.[20]

Closely related to these doctrinal controversies is the support of the PP and its allies for an ordered society that respects traditions and institutions such as the church. The PP praises the family as the foundation of a healthy society and sympathizes with commentators who see an emptiness in secular culture. *ABC* has condemned society's emphasis on sex, and *La Razón* has publicized a well-known writer's view that Spain's elites have become happy nihilists while the young lack a classical education. Supporting the church's concerns about education, Mariano Rajoy, leader of the PP, said that no government should tell "a father how to educate his son" or "convert public education into socialist education." On the International Day of the Woman in 2011, Rajoy tried to combine modern attitudes of women's rights with an emotional tribute to the patriarchal values of General Franco. He began by saying that for women today "the challenge is employment, the challenge is to be independent in your life, and the challenge is to be able to choose." But then, recapitulating a viewpoint from Franco's time, Rajoy added, "But if someone wants to dedicate her time, all or in part, . . . to educate your children or to care for your elders, you are doing a very noble work, the most noble work of all."[21]

The PP, like conservative opinion in the United States, sees liberty primarily as freedom from government rather than as a freedom to act that may be aided by government. The party opposed and then legally challenged a 2007 law requiring all parties to give women at least 40 percent of the slots on their electoral lists. The Tribunal Constitucional upheld the law, and the PP had to comply. The party then adopted the tactic of boasting in local elections in 2011 that its female candidates were not imposed by any quota; instead, they had been recognized for their "intelligence and merits" as "the best among the women and the men."[22]

Commentators on the Right have attacked what they view as an intrusive government. They have assailed campaigns to improve diet or curb smoking and have ridiculed political correctness. An article in *El Mundo* compared Spain's then–health minister, the Socialist Elena Salgado, to a puritanical, health-obsessed Mary Baker Eddy (the founder of the Christian Science Church). It charged that Salgado's work against tobacco, hamburgers, and cholesterol was trying to eliminate "all the vices that make life more pleasant." *La Razón* compiled a long list of the Socialist Party's "Dictatorial Prohibitions." The supposedly evil deeds that the Socialists wanted to ban included smoking, being heterosexual, imprisoning murderers, criticizing modern art, condemning ETA terrorists, and treating anyone on the Right as intelligent. *El Mundo* complained that in the female-dominated modern gynecocracy, "Cervantes, Shakespeare, and Fernando de Rojas would be highly politically incorrect." Less sardonically, Mariano Rajoy has endorsed the classically liberal, hands-off approach to economic and social life. Saying that the government should create a framework for enterprising citizens, he called for "less regulation, fewer interventions, fewer prohibitions, less putting government in the lives of the people, and more liberty. There are too many laws, decrees, and regulations." More freedom for society, he insisted, would mean "better government."[23] One practical consequence of this attitude has been more freedom in his administration for employers to fire workers and the scaling back of benefits advocated by unions.

Another characteristic of the PP's approach to governing—and one that highlights the similarities to the Republican Party of the United States—is a stronger emphasis on the use of force as an instrument of policy at home and abroad. Although both PP and PSOE governments have had contacts with ETA in hopes of ending the terrorist group's violence, the PP argues that it has been tougher against ETA and tries to score points by charging that the PSOE negotiates from weakness. When the courts allowed Bildu, a newly formed Basque party that says it has rejected violence but may have ties to ETA, to contest the 2011 elections, Rajoy and the PP attacked the PSOE's government for this development. In response to Bildu's legalization, key members of the party also encouraged and participated in demonstrations honoring the victims of ETA terror. In this way they tried to signal that the PP was ETA's staunchest opponent and would not sit idly by as those who sympathized with terrorists gained influence. Today the PP continues to insist that it will never negotiate with ETA or be soft on Basque terrorists.

The PP also gave strong backing under President Aznar to George Bush's "war on terror" and his war in Iraq. Before the U.S. Congress early in 2004, Aznar declared that "the most important phase" of "the war against terrorism" was unfolding in Afghanistan and Iraq, and he assured

American legislators that "we are going to fulfill our commitments" in that fight. Without consulting the *Congreso*, Aznar went against public opinion and sent troops, arguing that they would assist peace keeping rather than war.[24] The Socialists, on the other hand, had tried to keep some distance from American foreign policy, and after Zapatero defeated Aznar in 2004, he moved to bring Spanish troops home from Iraq in "as short a time as possible."[25]

Franco's obsession with Spain's national greatness survives in the PP's concern for national unity. Under José María Aznar the party appropriated the German concept of constitutional patriotism. But instead of refounding the political community "on the basis of purely civic values," the PP used this concept "as a new cover" for a historically and culturally based nationalism that rejects all separatist tendencies.[26] In 1999 Aznar campaigned in Catalonia, urging citizens to vote for the PP as a "guarantee against other adventures" such as Jordi Pujol's nationalist Convergència i Unió (CiU) alliance. He deplored the National Basque Party's "splashing around in the mud of a very sterile Radicalism" by calling for a vote on self-determination. *El Mundo* agreed that such a step would be "illegal" and "a rupture of the constitutional pact" and called the "atavistic tendencies of the peripheral nationalists every day more pathetic in the reality of globalization." In 2006 Rajoy put forward some proposals to rein in the centrifugal tendencies of the autonomies and accused the peripheral nationalists of "a tendency to exalt prejudices, mythical attributes, artificial identities, and glitzy nationalisms." Spain, he insisted, was "much more than the sum of seventeen communities. It is a will to walk together and share solidarity." The PP fought against a proposal to give Catalonia greater autonomy, and after that law passed in 2007, deputies from the party challenged the law in the courts and won.[27]

Devotion to the nation runs strong within the PP, although for some Spaniards the idea of national pride has been tainted by the dictatorship. The writer Laura Freixas has described how the sinister harangues of Franco or the "ridiculous" view of José Antonio that "to be Spanish is one of the few serious things that one can be in the world" have sown doubts about pro-national emotions. The PP regrets such doubts, and it fears and opposes Catalan and Basque sentiments for independence from Spain.[28] Past surveys and referenda repeatedly showed that large majorities in these autonomies do *not* favor independence,[29] but those who do are a determined minority, and they have been able to exploit political coalitions to advance their aims. Catalan, for example, is now the language of schools and government offices in Catalonia, and politicians constantly pressure the government for more concessions. In 2012 Catalonia's president, Artur Mas, declared that his government would begin a national project, seeking a path to independence. Surveys in the fall of 2012 showed a majority in Catalonia favoring independence. This crisis, which will be discussed in more detail near the end of this chapter, deeply troubles the PP, which stands firmly against any division of the nation.

One thing that initially would surprise American observers is the attitude in Spanish politics toward homosexuality. On this issue there is no difference between the parties. In apparent reaction against the censorship, repression, and oppressive control of the dictatorship and church, Spanish politicians and editors agree that citizens' intimate relations should be outside the reach or interference of government. In 1999 a deputy in Congress announced to voters that he was gay. *La Razón*, though it is a religiously oriented and conservative paper, quickly declared that homosexuality falls within the "sphere of intimate inclinations" and has nothing to do with politics. "Sexual liberty," wrote the paper, "has taken the place of the repression by which *franquismo* tortured lesbians and homosexuals." *El Mundo* agreed that this matter clearly was in the domain of "his intimacy" and that every citizen "has the right to decide what part of his private life goes into or stays out of the public light." In 2002 a member of the Guardia Civil asked that his homosexual partner be allowed to join him in his quarters, and the director general of the Guardia Civil gave his consent within a few hours. Although the request had been granted quickly, it exposed the necessity of changing a regulation, and that fact provoked criticism of the Guardia Civil for not freeing itself completely enough from an ideology anchored in the past. "All the parties applaud this measure," observed *El Mundo*, and an editorial affirmed that "personal sexuality" was "a free and irreproachable choice."[30]

Apart from sexuality, however, the Socialist Party has many ideological differences with the PP, its main rival, differences whose roots often lead back to the civil war era. Modern European socialism has almost completely abandoned ownership of industries or attempts at nonmarket, central control of the economy, and therefore its identity derives largely from social policy, as well as a somewhat distinctive approach to foreign policy. The social policies of today's PSOE have a clear, though general, connection to the desire of the Second Republic to modernize and secularize Spain, to attack inequalities and social injustices, and to better the educational and social opportunities of all. In regard to the church, the echo of that connection is even stronger, though muted in comparison to the violent confrontations of the 1930s. The heritage of Franco's hostility toward the peripheral nationalisms also finds reflection in the PSOE's posture compared to that of the PP.

When Felipe González took office in 1982, he promptly spoke of the Socialists' goal not only to deepen liberties but also to "revitalize human solidarity weakened by individualism" and conflict among groups. Rejecting an "atomized conception of society," he declared that progress was more than economic development. It also meant attention to "the vital necessities of human beings" and to "their profound desire for understanding, dignity, and equality." After pledging to fight against privilege and marginalizing differences, González described the cultural differences between Spain's regions as creative forces that stimulate and foster unity and praised "the diversity of our peoples." Turning to foreign policy, he affirmed "our Europeanist vocation" and his determination to work for "full integration in the European Communities." Spain's relationship with the Cold War United States, however, would require careful examination, and there would be a rigorous restudy of the previous government's decision to join NATO.[31] Eventually González supported that decision and a referendum narrowly confirmed it, but the Socialists remain wary of the imperial United States.

José Luis Rodríguez Zapatero, in his discourse of investiture, tacitly drew a sharp contrast between George Bush's militarism and "the principles of the United Nations Charter opposed to preventive war and unilateralism." He then spoke even more clearly than González had done about his party's social goals. "The socialist project," he said, was defined by policies designed "to promote the conditions of equality in access to goods and public services . . . to guarantee the cohesion of our society and to make it . . . more human." He specified improvements needed in the areas of housing, pensions, those dependent on others, and the handicapped, and he described government-provided social services as "a right of citizenship."

To amplify people's civil and political rights, he promised to facilitate "the right of separation and divorce" and to fight against "discrimination against women" and domestic violence. Homosexuals and transsexuals "deserve the same public consideration as heterosexuals and have the right freely to live the life that they have chosen," and he promised equal laws for them, including the right to marry. More generally, Zapatero advocated integrating the growing number of immigrants to Spain, and he described Spanish society as "tolerant, laic, educated and developed." One statement served as an effective summary: "My government, in short, will better the conditions of life for those who possess fewer resources in this society."[32]

Zapatero's government acted on these plans. Before the worldwide financial crisis forced budgetary cuts in many new programs, the Socialists had added a wide range of innovations, which Zapatero listed before the Congress in February 2011. Excluding unemployment benefits, spending for social programs had increased by 40 percent over levels under the PP. Expenditures for education rose 86 percent between 2004 and 2011, with 30 percent more scholarships. Pensions had risen 51 percent in total, with the greatest improvement coming at the lowest and middle levels of support, while the reserve fund was far stronger. In addition, new Socialist legislation expanded maternal leave, established "rights" to paternal leave, gave immigrants the same rights as Spaniards in health and dependency, extended to nonmarried couples the same rights as married couples in such matters as pensions and provided a rent supplement for young adults. New laws sought to protect women against violence and increase their participation in elective offices, and new measures of support had been enacted for the deaf and the deaf and blind.[33]

Zapatero was very proud of these steps. Even during the 2011 electoral campaign for municipal and local offices, when his popularity was deeply submerged due to the economic crisis and his slow and ineffective response to it, he boasted of progress. He had had to scale back some new programs or "rights," but during his presidency, he insisted, the basic level of social programs had improved. At the beginning of that electoral campaign he spoke to the central committee of his party, and his listeners sensed that he considered these reforms absolutely essential for Spain. The Socialist Party, he argued, "has been and is decisive for the modernization of Spain," and it would be inexcusable to fail in "the changes that Spain needs." He summed up his party's ideology in this manner: "Our identity, the identity of PSOE, is defined and summed up in three words: modernization, solidarity, and rights."[34]

One right the PSOE promotes, with echoes of past conflict, is freedom of religion and freedom from religious dictation. Clashes between the party and the church hierarchy are frequent. Zapatero's vice president at the time, María Teresa Fernández de la Vega, stated the government's conviction that liberty of ideology and belief is integral to democracy. The Socialists published a document titled "The Constitution, Laicism, and Education for Citizenship." After praising the 1931 Constitution along with the 1978 charter, it described laicism—the nonclerical, secular control of political and social institutions—as "a constitutional principle" that "guarantees the positive co-existence of cultures, ideas, and religions" without subordination to any creed or "religious hierarchy." "Laicism is the space of Integration," declared this document. "Without laicism we would not have new rights of citizenship" and such liberties as abortion and same-sex marriage "would be civil crimes." Without laicism, mistreatment of women and discrimination on the basis of gender "would stop being crimes." For these reasons, the PSOE's law on education included a mandate that the curriculum would include instruction about "rights and fundamental liberties and about the effective equality of opportunities between men and women." The goals of education also would include "the recognition of sexual-emotional diversity, as well as the critical evaluation of inequalities, which allows one to overcome sexist behavior."[35]

These ideas provoked sustained criticism from the Catholic Church, the Right, and the PP. Spain's bishops denounced the law on education, and *La Razón* argued that the constitution is "aconfessional [uncommitted to any one religion], not laic, that it entails collaboration with the religious organizations in general and with the Catholic Church in particular." The paper charged that Socialists were trying to purge religion from public life and nullify "its moral principles and its conception of society." A professor who had written about the state and religion also protested against a laicism that would deny religions a place in public debate and make secularism a "new religion." In *El Mundo* he endorsed the laicism that "guarantees to all the space to propose freely their conception of man and of the social life." But if the state tries to impose its own or some group's ideology, "then it stops being laicism: it transforms itself into the propagandistic State." Politicians in the Partido Popular added that education should teach students how to think, not what to think.[36] The battle over education, linked as it is to religion, continues today, just as descendants of the race issue continue to play a role in the United States. Mariano Rajoy's government, working closely and quietly with the church, has revised the education law, eliminating sections promoting gender equality and social, familial, or religious pluralism. But since the autonomies oversee instruction and have partial responsibility for curriculum, PSOE-dominated regions moved to restore these elements.[37]

The challenge of the peripheral nationalisms also touches chords linked to the Spanish Civil War and the dictatorship. Whereas the PP inherited many strong nationalists from Franco's era, many foes of the dictatorship entered the democratic era with sympathy for Basque and Catalan separatists. Even ETA's terrorists received a measure of sympathy for their fight against Franco as long as the bloodstained dictatorship continued its cruel and repressive measures. For these reasons the Left has tended to be more supportive in general of Catalan and other nationalisms. As was the case even with Aznar, the peripheral nationalisms gain power or advantages when one of the main parties needs additional support and has to entertain the idea of forming political coalitions or cooperative arrangements. Leaders of the peripheral nationalisms then demand concessions or advantages as the price of their support. The future of the peripheral nationalisms is a very complicated question, but most of the heated debate breaks down on a Left-versus-Right axis. Similarly, in the United States Democrats resist and Republicans promote states' rights.

In 2003 candidate Zapatero promised to undertake a revision of Catalonia's statute of autonomy, known as the Estatuto.[38] As president, Zapatero let the Catalans have a leading role in the process by initiating proposals and advancing draft legislation. Then the Congress of Deputies would enter the process to polish and validate a new law. Last-minute negotiations proved necessary, but the Congress approved a new Estatuto. There also was a popular referendum on the proposed law in Catalonia, where it received strong support in 2006, although voter participation was only 40 percent.[39] The new Estatuto devolved some additional or greater responsibilities to the Catalan autonomy, in areas such as culture, education, health, environment, and transportation. Other important points were the inclusion for Catalans of the word "nation" in the preamble, a wider role for Catalan courts, representation for the autonomy in the European Parliament, and new rules on finances.

The Partido Popular opposed this revision of the Estatuto at every step, and only nine days after the final vote more than fifty party deputies challenged the law in the Tribunal Constitucional by filing a lengthy document of objections. Their challenge later was joined by five other autonomies and the legal official who holds the post "Defender of the People" and is empowered to bring legal actions. After a delay of four years, the Tribunal Constitucional handed down a verdict in June 2010, declaring null and void the phraseology in more than seventeen parts of the law that seemed to give Catalonia an exclusive or preferential power. Twenty-seven other articles, it stated, would be constitutional only if they were interpreted in accord with a key precedent corresponding to each article. Among these precedents was a ruling that it was not acceptable to require the use of only one of the two official languages, Castilian and Catalan. Nor was it permissible to confuse the encouragement of Catalan with a prohibition of Castilian. The decision also stated that references in the law's preamble to "Catalonia as a nation" and to "the national reality of Catalonia" had no judicial effect. The large majority of the text in this lengthy statute was approved.

Immediately after the court's ruling, there was a storm of reaction from all sides, including a massive public protest in Barcelona. There had always been controversy over appointments to the Tribunal, and many Spaniards viewed the court as politicized. Artur Mas, the president of Catalonia's government, the Generalitat, declared that many Catalans were outraged, especially since they had gone through a lengthy bilateral process to draft the law, and had little faith in the fair-mindedness of the court. Affirming the value of the nation's diversity, he insisted that the problem lay in the attitudes of Spain, not Catalonia, and that for a solution Spain "has to be disposed to change." Some commentators criticized the Court's long delay in reaching a decision and acknowledged that faith in the independence and objectivity of the legal system was far from total. A Catalan writer and historian lambasted the Tribunal as a Madrid-focused institution that was obsessed with fear for "the indissoluble unity of the Spanish nation," a phrase it used eight times. The Defender of the People, on the other hand, soon brought a new legal action, arguing that in accord with the decision on the Estatuto, Catalonia could not be allowed to require that immigrants demonstrate knowledge of Catalan. The PSOE government indicated that it would try to work with Catalonia to identify remedies within the Constitution for many of the problems, although this would take some time.[40]

Carme Chacón, the PSOE's minister of defense and a Catalan, and Felipe González published an analysis of the controversy. Their opinion piece reflected the PSOE's more tolerant and pluralistic attitude. They viewed Catalonia as a nation without a state but an entity enjoying a high level of self-government. This desirable development, they said, had come about despite the anxiety of two groups: centralists, who fear a weakening of the nation and any affront to Castilian, and Catalonia's extreme nationalists, who dismiss any government-supported advance in autonomy as a mere deception and magnify the slightest friction. The court's decision, argued Chacón and González, recognized a high degree of autonomy, even though its language was often offensive and had produced indignation in Catalonia. The problem lay not in the constitution, the text of which recognizes diversity and has permitted a federalizing process with the autonomies, nor in the Estatuto. The problem, they charged, lay with self-interested politicians. They also blamed the passivity of all those who do not work for greater understanding and for a rejection of the twin evils of conformity or separation. The great majority of Catalans and of Spaniards, they asserted, value the diversity of Spain, and the challenge is to resist the confusion caused by the extreme Spanish nationalists and the Catalan minority. The idea that Spain is a "nation of nations," they concluded, strengthens everyone.[41]

Not everyone saw the nationalities issue in the same way, to say the least. Even though PSOE had supported the change in the Estatuto and was far more comfortable with divergent autonomies than the PP, the ideas and wording of Chacón's and González's article brought at least one shocked response from within the PSOE. Juan Carlos Rodríguez Ibarra, who for twenty-four years had been the party's president in the autonomy of Extremadura, declared in *El País* that he was astounded to see Felipe González describe Spain as "a nation of nations." Through many years they had worked together, and he had always admired González as a "revolutionary" who developed "a diverse and decentralized Spain such as no one had ever imagined." But this statement by González shocked him; it was as if the pope had declared that Catholicism was all a lie. "That was not the idea of Spain that I had elaborated from my experience, my reading, and my conversations with others, and fundamentally with Felipe," protested Rodríguez Ibarra. In the years since the adoption of the constitution, he lamented, Spain had developed into something different, something not described in the constitution. He blamed politicians and their maneuverings for advantage, including particularly the Socialists in Catalonia. By moving over to a formerly Catalan nationalist position, they had encouraged the Catalan nationalists to become more extreme and radical. Now those nationalists, after originally accepting the constitutional model of the autonomies, "have broken the pact of the Transition" and are demanding "the capacity of decision and self-determination." This troubled, longtime PSOE leader urged his party to return to the principle of "equality," or "coffee for all," that was the original idea for the autonomies.[42]

If Rodríguez Ibarra was upset, his emotion were mild compared to those of many on the Right. For some years commentators and PP leaders had been warning of disaster due to the peripheral nationalisms. For example, in 1999 *La Razón* promoted the flag, the hymn, and the shield as symbols of Spain and objected that some autonomies were abusing the constitution and forgetting "the pride of belonging to a super-entity like Spain." President Aznar praised these symbols for the strength they gave to an "integrated patriotism." At the same time Aznar was urging Catalan support for the PP in order to restrain the extreme nationalists there. In another example, a few years later *El Mundo* attacked the president of the Basque Country's autonomy for promoting stupidities based on "indigestion from grandfather's tales, macabre ethnicity, fascist populism . . . and smoke from the sacristy's candles." Discrimination against Castilian and "the immense majority" there who spoke only Spanish could only lead to "social fracture and a civic confrontation." Rightists criticized the government of Zapatero for dropping approximately thirty constitutional challenges that Aznar's government had begun against overreaching laws in the autonomies, and Mariano Rajoy put forward a list of proposals to restrain the autonomies and defend the nation. He accused some autonomies of confusing "historic nationality with privileges" and exalting "prejudices" and myths. The PSOE was guilty of trying to dismantle the state and turn it into "something residual."[43]

In 2008 a past president of the Tribunal Constitucional, Manuel Jiménez de Parga, deplored the loss of consensus about the nation and the autonomies that had existed during the Transition. Spaniards then had proudly explained to foreigners that Spain was neither a federation nor a confederation. It was instead "a complex State, in which the common trunk facilitates the cohesion and harmony among the different branches. It is not a juridical-political organization of various parts with their own roots— the Autonomous Communities—but instead those parts have their origin and reason for being in the Constitution." Lamentably, Spain now, he felt, was in the same condition that Ortega y Gasset described in 1932, something that was not a state and not respected as a state by all its citizens. He blamed politicians on the periphery for forgetting the Transition, the rest of Spain for knowing too little about the peripheral autonomies, and all politicians for their shortsighted maneuvering. Two years later the PP, troubled by Catalonia's adoption of Catalan as an official language, developed an educational proposal that would "guarantee" the "teaching of Castilian and in Castilian in all of Spain." In Catalonia the party demanded that at least one-third of instruction take place in Castilian.[44]

Emotions could run high in all parts of Spain. Aleix Vidal-Quadras, a distinguished physicist from the Autonomous University of Barcelona and a high-ranking PP officeholder from that region, published an uncompromising but eloquent protest in the journal *Política Exterior* in 1997. Feeling no sympathy for Catalan nationalism, he dismissed it, saying that "an invented past leads to an empty future." He charged that the peripheral nationalists were carrying out a "perfectly drawn" plan "for the liquidation of Spain as a nation." The second article of the constitution established that Spain is one, and "it is not possible to confederate that which is already united" any more than you could shatter a beautiful vase and expect it to miraculously reconstitute itself. To Vidal-Quadras the constitutional provisions for autonomies had turned out to be a disaster. Spain's history was being exchanged for the old wineskins of small and arbitrary sovereignties seeking meager dividends: "Spain conceived as a plural nation is not compatible with the plurinational Spanish State." Vidal-Quadras warned that "a State cannot survive if its nation breathes its last."[45] Elsewhere he explained that the peripheral nationalisms were dangerous. They constituted a "rational exploitation of the irrational" and the "fierce exacerbation of instincts." A high-ranking professor of administrative law who believed that "we form a single and solid cultural nation" warned that Spain was in "a critical moment of dissolution as a nation-State."[46]

The fact that the ruling of the Tribunal Constitucional was not likely to settle or end these controversies gained confirmation in 2011, after the Partido Popular won sweeping victories in local elections and in many autonomies. In Catalonia the Catalan nationalist party, CiU, needed additional support in Catalonia's legislature, and therefore it agreed to a cooperative alliance with the PP. But issues of nationalism promptly disrupted the parties' honeymoon. Only a few days after the PP helped CiU pass an important budgetary proposal, the regional president of the PP, Alicia Sánchez-Camacho, went to the Generalitat's Department of Instruction and made two formal demands: that her young son receive more hours of instruction in Castilian and that all of Catalonia's schools establish a true system of bilingual education. She joined with a citizens' organization that has demanded an end to Catalan being the primary language of instruction in the schools. Sánchez-Camacho did this, she said, as a politician, but "even more as a mother" who wants to see Castilian used in the schools. She argued that the Catalan government, according to the ruling of the Tribunal Constitucional, was obliged to guarantee a "bilingual" education to the autonomy's students.[47]

In those same local elections Bildu came to power in many parts of the Basque Country. This controversial party had been barred from the electoral process by the Tribunal Supremo on the grounds that it was too closely tied to ETA, but the Tribunal Constitucional reinstated it on appeal. Soon elected leaders of Bildu took symbolic actions to assert their Basque nationalism. One mayor had a portrait of King Juan Carlos removed from the governmental chamber. Others refused to allow bodyguards for officials of other parties to enter government buildings. In two cities, San Sebastian and Andoain, local officials conducted press conferences exclusively in Euskera, the Basque language. These press conferences communicated little; they left in ignorance and incomprehension the journalists as well as many Basques, most of whom do not speak Euskera. But they gave officials in both cities a chance to declare that Euskera was the "primary and only" language, a position that would contradict the constitution.⁴⁸

Beyond the heated rhetoric are complex issues demanding careful discussion and thought. Miguel Herrero de Miñón, one of the seven individuals who drafted the constitution and an important figure in the AP and then the PP, has challenged the fears of the Right. Basque and Catalan nationalisms, he argued, have made great contributions to politics and government in Spain. The error in the policy of "coffee for all" the autonomies was that it failed to recognize the historic rights and particular situation of Catalonia and the Basque Country. "Treating as distinct that which is different," he argues, is part of living together within Spain. "Nationalism, like it or not, is one of the most important political phenomena of our time, and to marginalize it is equivalent to denying reality." He foresaw two possibilities. The best path forward was to recognize the special status of Catalonia and the Basque Country and in one final, summary action transfer to them important competencies in areas such as education, culture, communication, and the organization of public powers. Those nations then would be true fragments of the State, autonomous except for the supreme institutions of Spain, which would be co-governed by its institutions and those of the fragments. Such a step would require consensus of the political parties and a constitutional convention. The other possibility was more likely—a piecemeal series of adjustments, resulting from demands and concessions, and satisfying no one.⁴⁹

Another thought-provoking perspective found voice in Joxe Joan González de Txabarri, a respected deputy in the Congress and a member of the National Basque Party, or Partido Nacionalista Vasco (PNV), Spain's second-oldest party, which governed the Basque Country between 1980 and 2009. González de Txabarri declared that for him and the PNV it is obvious that Spain is plurinational, pluricultural, and plurilinguistic, and the hostility to those facts spurs defensiveness in the peripheral regions: "The historical tendency toward what is called a 'global village' has put on the table the debate over whether the future of societies is going to be 'uniform cosmopolitanism' or 'universalism based in difference.'" His party, he wrote, is nationalist, democratic, and Europeanist, and both the PNV and Catalonia's CiU, he claimed, favor social cohesion through gaining control of local affairs and supporting internationalization of values, customs, and experiences. The traditional nation-state, which was formed through wars, is being superseded by two forces: "the rising importance of the local, as the form for resolution of concrete and daily problems," and "the supranational structures, as a means of being present in contexts every day more globalized." Europe is redefining sovereignty, independence, and statehood in favor of solidarity, interdependence, and participation. His party, he declared, was forward-looking, open, tolerant, democratic, opposed to violence, and not interested in imposing its will on others. "Nationalities without a State," like the Basque Country, "view the European Community from the perspective of reinforcing their own internal cohesion, and even their sovereignty, without the need of being converted into sovereign states in the classical sense."[50]

Debates such as these, whatever their character, have focused attention only on the differences of opinion. In the process they have exaggerated and accentuated those differences, which may make the problem seem insoluble, while the self-serving strategies of politicians often ignore the possibility of common ground. In Catalonia there are many people who use both languages comfortably and without confusion. These individuals do not feel torn between their two affections. Proud of being Catalan, they also enjoy being Spanish. In the words of Catalan writer Laura Freixas, "We can choose to be Spaniards without being less Catalan for that; being Catalan can be the concrete, personal content that we give to our Spanish identity."[51] Their attitudes are misunderstood—or simply not known and comprehended—by many Spaniards outside Catalonia. Regrettably, most citizens are informed only about the extremes of opinion, by attention-getting stories in the media that may promote misunderstanding.

Voting and survey data were consistent before 2012, and they strongly suggested that Catalans who are comfortable with two identities form the majority in the region. In a survey from 2010, 29 percent of Catalans said that they wanted the communities to have more autonomy, but only 23.6 percent supported the idea of allowing communities to become independent, if they so desired. In the Basque Country the respective numbers were 28 percent and 22 percent. In Galicia the numbers were only 13.5 percent and 1.7 percent, with 49.8 percent saying that the communities ought to have *less* autonomy.⁵² Thus separatist desires were clearly the minority viewpoint, even in Catalonia, even though those views received the lion's share of attention.

Politicians benefited from identifying and promoting tension between Spain and the peripheral nationalisms. At times their actions seem inconsistent or self-serving. For example, in the spring of 2011, Catalan nationalist parties, led by CiU, organized a nonbinding referendum on the question of whether the *autonomia* should seek independence. It was understood that the autonomy's legislature then would take action in response to that canvas of the citizenry. Almost nine hundred thousand residents in 550 towns and cities went to the polls in this special referendum, even though it lacked the attractive power of simultaneous contests for elective offices. The nine hundred thousand participants came close to the 40 percent who voted in 2006, when there was a referendum on the revised Estatuto. Ninety percent of those who voted gave their support to independence.

Yet the fact remained that most Catalonians stayed home, despite anger over the Tribunal Constitucional's ruling. In Barcelona only 21 percent voted. A few days later the Catalan parliament debated and took action. The proposition to seek independence failed by a vote of fourteen in favor and forty-nine against, with seventy-two abstentions. Leaders of the largest party, CiU, had voted in the referendum in favor of independence, but as lawmakers they abstained rather than confront Spain's national government. Artur Mas, CiU's leader and president of the autonomy, even absented himself from the parliament's debate, saying that he did not want to pursue independence when it would divide the Catalans. However, no one needed a referendum to predict that support for independence was not unanimous. Through the years it had varied between 20 and 25 percent. What Mas knew and was counting on was two things: first, that agitation of the question undoubtedly strengthened support for his party from those who desire independence, and second, that the referendum could help him put pressure on the national government.⁵³

These events and the current economic crisis have increased Catalan-nationalist sentiments. In 2012 Mas announced that Catalonia would now pursue a path toward independence. His initiative toward a "national project" for Catalonia has produced a major crisis. The PSOE's leader, Alfredo Pérez Rubalcaba, urged constitutional changes to move Spain toward a federal model. Carme Chacón, his chief rival in the last election for party leadership, agreed and criticized plans for Catalonian independence as "absurd" and the building of a "new Berlin Wall." The PP, on the other hand, denounced ideas of independence through a referendum as illegal and totally illegitimate. It dispatched several of its leaders, including Dolores Cospedal, the party's secretary general and president of Castile–La Mancha, to Catalonia to strengthen the fight against Mas's CiU. The elections on November were a setback for Mas and CiU, which lost strength in the autonomy's parliament. However, with conditional support from other groups favoring independence, Mas still aims for a vote on independence in 2014.[54]

The troubled question of the peripheral autonomies has simmered in Spanish politics for more than two decades, and as Herrero de Miñón predicted, there is no sign that political leaders want to attempt to resolve it in a comprehensive way, or will be able to do so. This troubling legacy of the civil war and Franco's repressive centralization has only a weak parallel in the United States. Talk of secession is a way to complain and draw attention, rather than a serious project. But sectional resentment remains. A belligerent pride in being southern sometimes appears in amusing bumper stickers, such as "We don't care how you did it up North" or "Southern by the grace of God." Clearly what energized much of such sentiments was a sense—accurate enough—that Americans in many parts of the North considered themselves superior to southerners and looked down on the South. That kind of cultural condescension always provokes a strong reaction, just as the lack of understanding among all the groups in Spain's plural culture surely contributes to conflict over the peripheral nationalisms. In both nations the legacies of internecine conflict inhibit communication and complicate the challenge of what the Spaniards call *convivencia* (living together).

The United States' Parties amid Change

> Consider what Lee and Jackson would do were they alive.... Remember the men who poured forth their life-blood on Virginia's soil.... Upon your vote depends the success of the Democratic ticket.
>
> Wade Hampton in Virginia, 1876

> Sustained racial passions meant one-party government, one party-government meant upper-class control, and hence antiunion government.... Racial animosity worked to the benefit of the owning classes.
>
> George E. Mowry, *Another Look at the Twentieth-Century South*

> God made "the various races of the world and ... His purpose will best be served in keeping separate what He has separated.... We condemn any teaching, doctrine, or example that is biased toward racial equality."
>
> Mississippi Southern Baptist Convention, 1946

> The politics of race has gone with the wind.
>
> George Busbee, soon-to-be governor of Georgia, 1974

> Why don't you leave the niggers behind and come join us?
>
> A South Carolina Republican businessman to political scientist Earl Black

Secession attempted to create two nations from one Union. Ironically, though secession was defeated, the resulting war solidified two societies. Four years of bloodshed produced new hatreds, and the emotional divisions grew during Reconstruction. This duality long outlived the war, proving to be very persistent in both politics and culture. It was not just that memories and resentments endured for generations. More importantly, politics became the tool for southern elites to guard and preserve vital characteristics of their region. Consolidating power within the South, and then exploiting power within the federal system, southern elites maintained their region as the reactionary and backward-looking part of the "two United States." This duality was real and long lasting, just as Iberian culture recognized "two Spains." Like that other Spain—the non-European, antimodern Spain—the South stood apart from the American model. It was the other society—hierarchical and elite-dominated, backward looking, nondemocratic, repressive, and fundamentalist in its culture and religion. This other United States proved an enduring legacy, rather than a casualty, of the American Civil War.

For three or four decades the war shaped political discourse in North and South. By 1900, however, it was evident that the North was steadily moving away from an absorption in war-related issues. Endorsing racism, the northern public turned its attention to new issues related to industrialization, urbanization, and immigration. The Civil War became less meaningful for the North, which would not revisit that historical wound until the civil rights movement renewed attention. For the South, on the contrary, historical memories continued to dominate politics and culture.

As the Lost Cause became sacred myth in the South, white elites used it to mold southern culture and society into the future. Through exploitation of the race issue and disfranchisement, these elites consolidated their control within the South by 1900. Through the seniority system in Congress and a tacit bargain within the nation's Democratic Party, they obtained power between 1900 and 1960 to block federal legislation that might threaten white supremacy or their economic dominance at home. The North's indifference to racial equality permitted and facilitated this development for many years. Only the civil rights movement—one of the great mass democratic movements in United States history—made it possible for the other United States to begin to change.

The successes of the movement made frank or brutal racism socially and politically unacceptable, and a new era in southern politics began. But southern culture changed more slowly, creating a mixture of change and continuity. The change was substantial. Just as racial change had liberated black southerners in many ways, it liberated the southern economy and began to modernize social patterns. The post–civil rights South moved quickly toward greater prosperity and closer approximation to national norms. But continuity arose from enduring cultural differences, even as they modified themselves and diminished in degree. Racial prejudice declined but did not disappear. The changing South was rejoining the Union but at the same time "southernizing" the nation politically. The South's identity as the other United States emerged in a new form and found significant reflection in politics as the Republican and Democratic parties switched racial identities. The once-racist Democrats advocated equality, and the party of Lincoln and emancipation captured most of the white southern vote and grew more conservative. The formerly Democratic "Solid South" became solid for Republicans in presidential elections, with a concomitant influence on national politics.

Thus the issue that was central to the Civil War—race—affected the structure of national politics long after the war ended. First the South clung to segregation, disfranchisement, and a separate "southern way of life" for generations. Through many decades the North also rejected the ideal of human equality proclaimed in the Declaration of Independence. Then, slowly and reluctantly, the North and the South moved toward their rendezvous with the nation's founding ideals. In politics much has changed, but the cultural transformation is not complete and the past is not yet completely irrelevant. Attitudes toward the Civil War and Reconstruction still affect political and personal attitudes, "how the races perceive each other," how the North perceives the South, and vice versa. Accepting and assimilating a commonly understood history—as opposed to just moving on—remains a challenge for the future. As historian David Goldfield observes, "History is both the problem and the answer."[55]

The incubus of race crippled change in the era of Reconstruction. The victorious North could be aroused to punish southern defiance or suppress continued rebellion, but its lack of commitment to racial justice meant that it had little interest in changing the South. Although responsibility for addressing the legacy of slavery lay with northern Republicans, they viewed the South as an unpromising field for the development of their party or their ideas. Whereas the North had a diversified, industrializing economy fueled by technological change and activist governments, the South was agricultural, inclined to limit government, and unaccustomed to free labor. The logical and natural allies of the Republican Party in the South were the former slaves, but most Republicans regarded them as "at best . . . illiterate, uneducated, and politically inexperienced." Conservatives in the party believed frankly in the racial superiority of whites and had little interest in working with African American southerners. Few had faith that the enfranchisement of former slaves would be a success; they only turned to it as a way to address southern intransigence "without massive federal intervention in the South."[56]

This perspective led to a less than half-hearted approach to reshaping the South and bringing it closer to the national model. Instead of building a party of change in the South, northern Republicans "repeatedly sacrificed Southern interests." They were always "more concerned about maintaining control of the North than about gaining control of the South," and as a result "they consistently and deliberately subordinated the interest of their Southern allies to the demands of their Northern constituency." Those allies received little concern and even less respect from the northern Republicans. Aware that racism remained strong in the North, party leaders frequently worked "at muting or controlling black aims and aspirations." White southern Unionists discovered that they were the objects of suspicion rather than gratitude. When Unionists in the South sought compensation (frequently mentioned by Lincoln) for wartime destruction of their property, Republican leaders feared "a raid on the U.S. Treasury." Not until 1871 did the Congress establish the Southern Claims Commission, and then James G. Blaine, the Republican Speaker of the House of Representatives, commented sarcastically that the number of "suffering patriots from the South who . . . had been true to the Union . . . was so great that the wonder often was where the Richmond government found soldiers enough to fill its armies." Dismissing many claimants as "beggars" and "swindlers," he even criticized them as "scalawags"—an epithet employed by southern white Democrats.[57]

The policies of northern Republicans ignored the needs and wants of their potential southern allies. Banking reforms kept the South from having a reasonable share of national bank currency. Appeals to grant the South "lands for railroad development" usually went unanswered, even though support for railroad building had been generous elsewhere. The 1866 Homestead Act failed to help many poor whites or freed slaves in the South. The northern Congress even taxed cotton during the first, economically difficult years after the Civil War. Republican leaders helped the elite rather than the poor through a national bankruptcy law.[58] They were "particularly eager to get the Southern states back into the Union before the 1868 election, lest their Northern support be weakened by the delay."[59]

By 1872 northern racism was visibly affecting Republican attitudes. A Republican journalist, James Shepherd Pike, published a scathing criticism of Reconstruction in South Carolina, charging that native whites were "under the heel of 400,000 pauper blacks, fresh from a state of slavery and ignorance the most dense." Newspaper editor Horace Greeley denounced black voters as "ignorant and credulous," and Carl Schurz, the leading Republican of German extraction, lamented that they "tend to blindly follow demagogues" and had elected "scandalous" governments. Such sentiments culminated in what was called the Liberal Republican revolt. A number of prominent Republicans deserted their party in the 1872 president election, calling for an end to Reconstruction in the South and reliance on the "best men" of the region—that is, the old elite rather than newly enfranchised

African Americans. The Republican Party prevailed in that election, but its retreat from Reconstruction continued as President Grant refused to counter violence in Mississippi and Speaker Blaine counseled that it was better to "lose the South" than to take strong measures that would "lose both North and South."[60]

In the years that followed, northern Republicans occasionally tried to attract southern support through internal improvements, federal appointments, or tariffs for southern businessmen. But more often they looked to northern support and relied on "waving the bloody shirt." The original bloody shirt was a garment, worn by a northerner whom the Ku Klux Klan had beaten in Mississippi and displayed in the House as evidence of southern outrages. Thereafter "bloody shirt" became a shorthand term for southern violence and rebellion. Although Democrats and white southerners used the phrase mockingly, to many Union veterans and northern voters it could evoke strong memories of the hardships suffered and sacrifices made to suppress the South's rebellion. Consequently, the Republican Party regularly reminded voters during presidential elections of the war years and the dangers posed by unrepentant rebels. "Every man that tried to destroy this nation was a Democrat," declared one Republican speaker. "Soldiers, every scar you have on your heroic bodies was given you by a Democrat."[61]

Throughout the 1880s the popular vote was very close, another reason Republicans waved the bloody shirt. The party's *Campaign Text Book* for 1880 listed many reasons to fear a South-dominated Democratic victory. It warned of an "Impending Crisis," lamented the South's "Hatred of Union Soldiers," and quoted "Confederate brigadiers" and southern leaders who had declared, "The Confederacy still exists." The Democratic Party's "Revolutionary Intentions," Republicans warned, were to steal the election and install a president favored by southern rebels, who were the "Power Behind the Throne." Black Republicans in the South "would be shot down like dogs," and white Republicans "branded as enemies." Southern domination would "bring ruin to Republican institutions" or even precipitate "all the incarnate horrors of a bloody, heart-rending, desolating civil war." Citing a Georgia newspaper, the Republicans charged that the South was demanding $400 million in compensation for its emancipated slave property, and another section of the campaign book recounted "Recent Outrages in the 'Solid South'" against black citizens and Republican supporters.⁶²

Republicans appealed to northern veterans of the Civil War by praising their patriotism and rewarding it financially through pensions, disability payments, and aid to widows and minor children. Republican measures to aid veterans steadily expanded the number of pensioners, and by the 1880s pensions were consuming 20 percent of the federal budget. Under President Benjamin Harrison, the number of pensioners doubled to almost one million. By the end of the century $157 million went annually to soldier's pensions, and by 1911 total spending for Union pensions had exceeded $4 billion.⁶³ Along with appeals to business interests and jabs at the Catholic and immigrant voters, who often voted Democratic, the bloody shirt was fundamental to Republican political appeals throughout the generation following the conflict.

Thereafter, indifference to southern injustices took hold. Increasingly the industrialized, urbanized North looked away from the South and the Civil War. In the "nadir period" of American racism, northerners raised no objection to southern racial policies and focused on their own region's problems, which amid rapid economic change were many. In addition, the population of the North changed with the arrival of millions of additional immigrants for whom the Civil War was not a part of their experience or concern.

Meanwhile, southern politicians who worked to mobilize voters were relying even more heavily on emotions from the war. Performing "mental alchemy" on the war itself, "they spun the straw of defeat into a golden mantle of victory." The Confederacy had been a legitimate and noble enterprise, its leaders and heroes were to be revered, and the principle of white supremacy was to be supported against all northern attacks. The myth of Confederate glories was central to the process by which southern politicians "made a religion" of the region's history."⁶⁴ The Lost Cause embraced both the southern bid for independence and the fierce battle against Reconstruction, and with its elevation into a sacred myth, dissenting views were suppressed, as in Franco's Spain. One South Carolinian who grew up early in the twentieth century "did not learn that the South had lost the war until he was twelve years old. 'It was one of the saddest awakenings I ever had,'" he recalled. Similarly, Margaret Mitchell remembered that she "heard so much about the fighting and hard times after the war that I firmly believed Mother and Father had been through it all instead of being born long afterward."[65]

Southern politicians controlled the region's newspapers and generated voluminous propaganda against Reconstruction and outside interference. Any northern policies that kept whites from having a completely free hand constituted tyranny and oppression. Reconstruction had been "rule by the sword." Greedy "'carpet bag' vultures from the North," politicians declared, had robbed and ruined the South. Black male suffrage subjected virtuous white citizens "to the blighting, brutalizing and unnatural dominion of an alien and inferior race." The violent Ku Klux Klan, on the other hand, arose from "the instinct of self-protection" and acted "purely in self-defense" against dangerous blacks addicted to "crime" and "rape." Hooded Klansmen merged in myth with Confederate military heroes as brave and principled figures who had defended whites, preserved civilization, and saved the South from "blight, crime, ruin and barbarism." According to the approved version of regional ideology, the Democrats had not merely defeated Reconstruction. Instead they had, in a revealing use of religious terminology, *redeemed* the South.[66] Regional racism held the same vital position as National Catholicism.

The first goal of southern white Democrats was to regain control of local and state affairs and to drive African Americans from any positions of political power. Violence, fraud, intimidation, and economic reprisals all contributed to achieve that goal. Then the way was clear to shield white supremacy behind laws as well as customs. When Democrats in North Carolina regained control of state government in 1876, one of their first enactments was to prohibit interracial marriage. South Carolina began restricting black suffrage in the 1880s by means of a cumulative poll tax, which meant that one could not vote if the poll tax for some previous year remained unpaid. Collecting the tax in late summer, before the harvest, also made it more punitive, because poor farmers or laborers had run out of whatever cash they possessed by then.

The constellation of disfranchisement bills and segregation legislation that locked "the other United States" into its backward, elitist pattern came amid crisis in the 1890s. By that time the rising class of southern industrialists—owners and managers of textile mills, railroads, lumber mills, furniture factories, and other enterprises—was gaining influence in the Democratic Party. But the dominance of the party that stressed its Confederate heritage suddenly was threatened by the rise of the Populist Party. Angry farmers, who for years had suffered from falling cotton prices, demanded sweeping changes in the nation's financial and monetary systems. Through the Farmers' Alliance they called on Democratic leaders for help. A few Democrats felt that "the Alliance people . . . are the bone and sinew of the party" and should be heard. But the power of the business and industrial classes was too great, and the Democrats did little to relieve suffering agriculturalists. These southern farmers then made a fateful decision: citing "a nation brought to the verge of moral, political, and material ruin," they formed the Populist Party and challenged the party of white supremacy. Populist leaders such as Tom Watson of Georgia even argued for an alliance of white and black farmers. "You are kept apart that you may be separately fleeced of your earnings," he explained.[67] White Populists sought black votes and, wherever they gained enough power, tried to protect the right of their allies—black southern farmers—to vote. The Democratic Party in the South faced a major crisis.

It fought back with vicious racist rhetoric, white supremacy campaigns, fraud and intimidation at the polls, and violence wherever needed. Democrats declared that the issue was not the impoverishment of once independent farmers or the need for economic reform. Something more important—racial superiority—was at stake. "The Anglo Saxon Must Rule," and whites must unite "against the negroes." "Phalanxes of red-shirted marchers, representing 'the best men,' marched for white supremacy." The political upheaval of the 1890s ended in the victory of the more privileged classes. When they stopped the Populists from winning office, or as soon as they regained control of state governments, Democrats pushed through their program of disfranchisement and segregation. By depriving African Americans of the right to vote, Democrats destroyed the possibility of a successful challenge from some breakaway third party. By stigmatizing black citizens as inferior in every public arena, they deepened the pathological grip of racism on southern culture.[68]

The defeat of Populism ushered in a new era in the South, one that solidified its identity as the very different other United States.[69] Politically the region was completely dominated by one party, the white-supremacist Democrats, just as surely as Franco's Movimiento dominated Spain in the dictatorship. Culturally, the South restricted free thought. One had to conform to the reigning orthodoxies, which were racial and political. Even more than previously, the South now "resembled an authoritarian regime." "There were no jackbooted thugs in the street," writes David Goldfield, "though they did appear from time to time. No; it was more a dictatorship of the mind, a stifling self-censorship.... It took more courage to be a rebel than a Rebel."[70]

W. J. Cash, frustrated and troubled by the region's mental straightjacket, called this situation the "savage ideal." As among savage clans or tribes, he argued, "dissent and variety are completely suppressed and men become, in all their attitudes, professions, and actions, virtual replicas of one another." The typical white was schooled in "violence, intolerance, aversion and suspicion toward new ideas, an incapacity for analysis, [and] an inclination to act from feeling rather than thought."[71] In support of politicians, the United Daughters of the Confederacy and the Sons of Confederate Veterans redoubled their efforts in these years to enforce a single, unitary view of the South's history and social system.

Religion contributed greatly to the closing of the southern mind. As was the case in Franco's Spain, it played a major role in enforcing political conformity. By 1890 one of every two white southerners was a church member, compared to only one in four in 1860. The major Protestant denominations insisted that white supremacy was God's plan; deviations from segregationist norms were not just scandalous but sinful. In the words of a celebrated evangelist, Sam Jones, if God had considered the African American to be equal, "he wouldn't have colored him at the start." "Law and order," Jones declared, "can only be maintained in the South by the supremacy of the white man and domination over the inferior race." Darwin's theory of evolution contradicted the literal words of Genesis, so it too had to be exorcised. Campaigns to ban the teaching of evolution in the schools had their origins in the South during the 1920s, where Reverend Amazi Clarence Dixon tied Darwinism to bolshevism. Evangelical Protestantism also made the prohibition of alcoholic beverages into a religious principle, one that revealed the class bias in southern society. Liquor was widely available for the rich, but local leaders touted prohibition as a way to control poor whites and dangerous black rapists.[72]

Racism and a devotion to segregation were the common denominators for whites of all classes. The rich or well educated might talk of allowing African Americans to progress in some indefinite future time, when they had become more responsible and deserving. But when faced with any specific and immediate change, privileged groups refused to give their support. Black southerners had to live under crushing disadvantages that blasted their hopes for the future. In 1920 only 5 percent of black children were able to attend high school, and "even most cities in the South lacked high schools for blacks into the 1930s." Meanwhile racist rhetoric became, if possible, more hostile. Methodist bishop Atticus G. Haygood parroted the claim that black men were rapists. "Unless assaults by Negroes on white women and little girls come to an end," said Haygood, "there will . . . be . . . vengeance that will shock the world."[73]

Such rhetoric encouraged poorer, working-class southerners to use a more aggressive racism as a means to keep blacks in their place. Lynching increased markedly around the turn of the century, terrorizing blacks and teaching poor whites that they were superior. As Lillian Hellman explained, "To be 'superior' . . . because your sallow skin was white and you were 'Anglo-Saxon,' made you forget that you were eaten up with malaria and hookworm . . . lived in a shanty and . . . worked long hours for nothing." Whiteness gave even the poorest laborer power.[74] Demagogues, of whom the South had many colorful examples, whipped up racial fears or anger for their political benefit, using racism to evade other issues. Pitchfork Ben Tillman, for example, occasionally urged the necessity of repealing the Fifteenth Amendment, even though black men in South Carolina had effectively been disfranchised.[75]

Another crucial aspect of the new order was the dominance of its economic elite. The trappings of this elite varied somewhat from rural, agricultural districts to urban, commercial, or industrial settings, but it was broadly similar everywhere. The antebellum planter gave way to "the county-seat elites" or the "banker-merchant-farmer-lawyer-doctor governing class." Newspaperman Ralph McGill called the South's new social and economic ruler the "village nabob." He owned "the biggest store" or "the gin, the turpentine works, the cotton warehouses, the tobacco warehouses. He was a director of the bank.... He controlled credit" and was "a deacon in his church.... He usually owned and operated a few farms, taken in foreclosures.... He hated all union labor.... He did not want new industries in 'his' town. They competed for 'his' labor."[76] "This village nabob," admits one historian, "may not have been the stuff of which historical romance is made, but his authority in the community at least equaled if it did not exceed that of the storied aristocrat."[77] For the South, these men were the counterparts of Spain's powerful village triumvirate of landowner, priest, and doctor.

Social interchange in rural areas and small towns still had an informal, personal, and face-to-face character that created a certain sense of community. However, that fact did not mitigate a rigid class structure. The South's new, segregated order created, as V. O. Key put it, "a social and economic structure in which the gulf between the rich and the poor has been extraordinarily wide." After disfranchisement, noted George Tindall, "the structure of the southern electorate insured a policy of class distinctions." The elite had the upper hand, and it did not hesitate to maintain and perpetuate its power.

Racism remained a useful tool for solidifying the class structure. As industry grew, manufacturers could tell poorer white workers that they enjoyed a privileged position because of their race. Segregation under Democratic Party dominance was their protection. The *Southern Textile Bulletin*, "by far the most widely read" journal of a major industry that excluded blacks, propagandized relentlessly for white supremacy for more than four decades.[78] A top priority for the southern industrial elite was to resist or crush labor unions. The *Manufacturer's Record* editorialized in 1924 that the "Solid South means security for every manufacturer trembling under the whiplash of the anarchistic labor leaders." Business and political leaders denounced "that unholy, foreign-born, un-American, despotic thing *known* as *labor unionism*."[79]

Their opposition went well beyond words. The South has few unions today, but not because southern workers passively accepted the pittance offered them. Early in the twentieth century hundreds of thousands of southern factory operatives organized, protested, and went on strike to obtain fair treatment and better wages. Repeatedly their efforts failed because the power of government was against them. "The organized power of the southern commonwealths from the governor down to the sheriff and local constabulary broke the strikes and destroyed the unions," even before 1921. Again, "from 1928–29 until World War II the armed forces of the southern states were mobilized to a maximum degree more often against white unionism than against the somnolent blacks."[80] Defeats sapped enthusiasm for unions and made the elite quite secure within a segregated "New South," a South that in its segregation, one-party politics, and anti-union climate was notably unprogressive and backward looking.

Simultaneously southern elites developed ways to protect their "other United States" from interference by the nation. Their methods took shape within the Democratic Party and had their foundation in Congress. At first glance there appears to be a puzzling contradiction between the reactionary policies of the segregated South and its "solid" devotion to a Democratic Party that was becoming more interested, nationally, in reform. But through several decades a silent bargain, or tacit understanding, served the interests of both the national party and the segregated South. Historian George Mowry notes that "until the Truman administration, at least," southern Democrats knew "that their support of the party ... would be repaid by a willingness to permit the South to maintain the existing patterns of racial relations and, to a lesser degree, those characterizing the relations of capital and labor throughout the section."[81]

This understanding derived partly from the racism and indifference to segregation that persisted in the North during the 1930s. Equally important, the bargain worked because the national party and its presidents frequently needed support in Congress, where southerners were serving multiple terms, winning reelection with little or no opposition. The seniority system elevated senators and congressmen from Dixie to heights of power and positions where they could almost guarantee success for a president's program. But chief executives knew that such support came at a price. To attack segregation or the "racial pattern" that was "basic to the mentality of the southern political conservative and his business and professional supporters" would be to forfeit essential support. The compact between southern conservatives and northern reformers was unwritten and probably never formally discussed, yet it was well understood by all.

Democrats from Dixie wielded enormous power in Congress and in Washington. A few statistics from Democratic administrations and

Congresses tell the story. Five members of Woodrow Wilson's Cabinet and two of his important advisers were southern born. In the House of Representatives at that time, the Speaker, the majority floor leader, and thirteen of sixteen important committee chairmen were southerners by birth. At the same time in the Senate, ten out of fourteen major committees had southerners as chairmen. After Wilson left office, southern power in Congress continued year after year. As late as 1969 "twelve of the sixteen standing committees of the Senate were chaired by southerners," and in the House eleven of twenty standing committees were chaired "by southerners with traditional views."[82] Despite those views, southern committee chairmen supported the legislative program of Democratic presidents. Banking reform, antitrust legislation, and other key elements of Wilson's legislative program had depended upon southern support or leadership. Franklin Roosevelt's New Deal would have died aborning but for the prominent role of powerful southerners, who disagreed ideologically with FDR's program.

Southern politicians exploited this inconsistent situation to extract benefits for themselves and their states. Federal pork and federal projects—from roads and river projects to federal offices and post offices—increased many a politician's standing with the voters back home. When Senator Pat Harrison of Mississippi ran for reelection in 1936, he boasted that his state "had received more per capital federal funds than any other state in the Union." The South as a whole received more in New Deal subsidies, compared to taxes, than any other section of the country. The influence of South Carolina's Senator "Cotton Ed" Smith repeatedly saved the Charleston Navy Yard from closure in the 1920s and 1930s, and later, while Congressman L. Mendel Rivers chaired the House Armed Services Committee, the naval yard was a major base and repair center for Polaris nuclear submarines. Examples like these existed in every southern state. Annual figures in the 1960s showed that "returns from federal grants far outweighed the returns from agriculture and were second only to industry in producing income."[83]

For many decades southern congressmen used their power to block or change policies that infringed on "the southern way of life." They were as resolute against change as any member of the "bunker" in the last days of Franco. Their efforts kept regional wage differentials in place in New Deal programs. They tempered labor legislation and made it possible for southern states to pass anti-union "right to work" laws. Even the scandal of lynching could not cause FDR to back the Wagner antilynching bill, and he also allowed southern railroads to escape a Fair Employment Practices Commission order by referring the matter to a mediation committee. Yet in 1938 Senator James Byrnes felt compelled to issue a rare, public warning to the national Democratic Party. Alarmed by growing African American influence in the North, he charged that blacks *controlled* the northern Democrats. What caused Byrnes to speak out? Another antilynching proposal had aroused the white South's obsession with segregation. Whites had believed, said Byrnes, "that when problems affecting the Negro and the very soul of the South arose, they could depend upon the Democrats of the North to rally to their support." Without that support, southerners might have to reassess their loyalty to the party.[84]

Race was more important than any other issue for southern politicians like Jimmy Byrnes. It was "the *sine qua non* of his political demands, the very 'soul' of his particular South." Like National Catholicism in Franco's regime, it bound together a cluster of conservative values. Economic policies that protected the South's agriculture, low-wage industries, and entrenched elites were also very important to the region's leaders, as were restrictive views on religion, social change, and women's rights. But all these things had become wrapped up in the political-social system of segregation and disfranchisement. Unravel one part of the fabric and, the elite feared, all of it might disintegrate. The racial system had to be kept intact, no matter how outrageous discriminatory tactics seemed. Southern leaders were unapologetic and unashamed about their behavior. A journalist once asked an Alabama legislator whether Jesus Christ could pass that state's "understanding" clause, which required a voter to explain some part of the state constitution. "That would depend entirely," the politician brazenly replied, "on which way he was going to vote." In 1936 the national Democratic Party eliminated a two-thirds rule governing nominations at its convention and agreed to seat a few African American delegates. When a black minister offered the invocation, South Carolina's "Cotton Ed" Smith walked out of the convention, denouncing the minister as "a slew-footed, blue-gummed, kinky-headed Senegambian!"[85]

Challenges to the southern political and social system were relatively modest through the 1930s. After 1940, however, change occurred at a quickening pace. Developments at home and abroad began to push the region in new directions that white southerners found both welcome and unwanted. These changes affected the North as well. They slowly forced the nation to confront the race issue and undermined the North-South bargain that had produced a schizophrenic Democratic Party. That undermining led, in turn, to a realignment of parties.

World War II jolted the South's economy and altered its demographics. As the nation geared up to fight a global conflict, the defense department looked to the South, with its warm weather and low wages, as an ideal place to locate training camps. Existing bases expanded, and other defense facilities soon followed. The infusion of federal dollars motivated southern congressmen to defend and continue these benefits, and through their power in Congress, they succeeded.[86] Demographically, the Great Migration of African Americans from the rural South to northern cities took place. As workers became soldiers, northern industry faced a huge need for labor. On a scale far larger than World War I, black southerners moved to northern cities to find jobs in war industries and escape the poverty and discrimination of the rural South. Such migration soon had an important impact on politics in northern cities. In the South it contributed to a rapid reduction in the number of farms and caused a dramatic shrinkage of the South's farm population, which decreased by 83 percent between 1940 and 1979. Although the African American population of the South continued to grow by small amounts, there was a dramatic out-migration of black southerners from 1940 into the 1970s.[87]

Within the South many people were moving to the cities, as places such as Atlanta and Dallas experienced rapid growth. This "great migration from country to city" also supported a marked increase in the level of manufacturing in the South. The demands of World War II had begun this rapid growth, and southern businesses capitalized on it while preserving their "regional hostility to unions." The number of employees in manufacturing soared, with states like North Carolina seeing a substantially higher percentage of their work force in manufacturing than was typical of the rest of the country. At this point, most industrial growth was following traditional southern patterns and was concentrated in low-wage, resource-intensive areas such as textiles or furniture. Few national corporations had done more than locate administrative offices in some of the southern cities, because the "southern way of life" did not appeal to northerners and discouraged relocations. But a shift in the region's economy had begun.

Progress also occurred in public education. At all levels, enrollments increased sharply. In the thirty years after 1940 enrollments in public elementary and secondary schools increased by 67 percent. Colleges and universities saw much more dramatic growth of 542 percent, and a few regional universities aspired to levels of quality that had long prevailed elsewhere. But the South was still spending far less on higher education than the rest of the nation. Alabama, Mississippi, and South Carolina spent less than half the national average per student. Only three southern states—Florida, North Carolina, and Texas—did better than the national average. "Almost sixty-eight percent of the nation's illiterates still were southerners, about equally divided between whites and blacks."[88]

In other ways, too, the South remained behind the curve or had changed little. Per capita income and wealth "were still significantly below" national figures, and a respected historian judges that the South "was still very much a colonial economy." The religious landscape remained familiar, with Protestants overwhelmingly dominant over the few Catholics, Jews, or members of other faiths. Moreover, the influence of Baptists, Methodists, and, to a lesser degree, Presbyterians was so great as to be historically unique. According to Samuel S. Hill Jr., a major scholar of religion, the South's "society was the only one in history dominated by low-church Protestantism." This meant a fundamentalist, anti-intellectual brand of Protestantism typified by the Southern Baptist Church, "a denomination so embracing and influential in the region that it was aptly called 'the folk church of the South.'" In the American South's context, this denomination held power comparable to that of Franco's Catholic Church. Opposed to biblical criticism and modern science, Baptists echoed evangelist Billy Graham, whose hallmark phrase was "The Bible says..." In 1962 the Southern Baptist Convention restated its fundamentalist principles, emphasizing "the unique inspiration, divine authorship, and 'inerrancy' of the Scriptures." The convention directed its seminaries to shun any "doctrines not consistent with this position."[89]

Segregation and this kind of regional culture made political change from inside the South impossible. The few white southern progressives felt vulnerable to racist political charges. Mississippi's Frank Smith, a six-term congressman, described how "the politics of race" served as "the strongest bulwark of economic conservatism" in the Congress. Those who advocated any liberal position usually had made some criticism of segregation, and "in Southern politics it isn't hard to tie the two roles together." That meant that progressive proposals could be attacked and dismissed as integrationist, radical, or "un-American." After leaving Congress, Smith admitted to "the burden of conscience that I carried without public comment during my entire political career." He and a number of other southerners in Congress cringed at racist demagoguery and never doubted "that the South would eventually end segregation." But criticism of the system was impossible. "The paths of communication" were "all closed," and dissent, however mild, would immediately spell electoral defeat. Smith had hoped "that by working for economic progress, without adding my voice to the racial clamor, I could make some genuine contribution to the gradual elimination of discrimination." But he admitted that this strategy "evaded my responsibility" to speak out and tell his constituents that "finding solutions to the racial problems that beset us" was absolutely "urgent."[90]

The impetus for real change would have to come from African Americans and from individuals and institutions outside the South. Like Spain's *nietos*, black people were determined that their story—long suppressed—should be heard. Through the NAACP and political action in northern cities, African Americans were laying the groundwork for an assault on segregation. The NAACP's Legal Defense Fund fought to restore power to the Fourteenth Amendment. In the federal courts it won victories in cases such as *Chambers v. Florida*, *Smith v. Allwright*, *Morgan v. Virginia*, and *Shelley v. Kraemer*.[91] These cases protected citizens' rights by placing limits on police interrogations, outlawing the all-white primary, barring segregation on interstate buses, and declaring that courts could not enforce racially discriminatory covenants on real estate. At the same time the fund prevailed in a series of cases involving higher education and prepared the way for *Brown v. Board of Education*. Meanwhile, the growing black population in industrial cities of the North gave an advantage to liberal northern Democrats. Chicago voters sent Oscar De Priest to Congress in 1929, and black leaders like him began to demand change. The South's discrimination against black citizens seemed especially shameful during World War

II, when the Allies proclaimed that they were fighting for human rights against the Nazis and Axis powers. On many occasions German prisoners of war received better treatment in the South than black GIs—for example, when restaurants served the "Aryan" German prisoners but made black servicemen eat outside.[92]

At this point the national political structure began to shift. Increasingly, northern Democrats seemed dangerously unreliable to their southern allies. Southern congressmen grew livid over President Truman's appointment of the Committee on Civil Rights. In a report issued in 1947, this committee called for an end to poll taxes, action against lynching, a Civil Rights Division in the Department of Justice, and a permanent Commission on Civil Rights. Then, at the party's national convention in 1948, the mayor of Minneapolis, Hubert Humphrey, delivered an impassioned speech calling on delegates to "get out of the shadow of states' rights and walk forthrightly into the bright sunshine of human rights."[93] The convention adopted a strong civil rights plank in its platform. In protest, South Carolina's Strom Thurmond organized a "Dixiecrat" revolt, running as a segregationist candidate on the Democratic Party label in several southern states. Thurmond's move marked the beginning of the movement of southern conservatives away from the Democratic Party.

The integration of the armed forces was slow but a shock to southern leaders. Still, it was nothing compared to the Supreme Court's unanimous decision against segregation in the 1954 *Brown* case. In *Brown* the Court posed the constitutional question squarely: "Does segregation of children in public schools solely on the basis of race, even though the physical facilities and other 'tangible' factors may be equal, deprive the children of the minority group of equal educational opportunities?" Rejecting the 1896 precedent of *Plessy v. Ferguson*, the Court held that in public education "the doctrine of 'separate but equal' has no place." Southern leaders responded with the Southern Manifesto, which pledged to fight the Court's decision by "all lawful means." Signed by almost every southerner in Congress, the manifesto had a certain confidence behind its defiant protest. Southern leaders denounced both the Court and "outside agitators" for interfering with states' rights and long-established racial patterns. Counting on northern racism, they appealed to northerners to respect the "friendship and understanding" that characterized race relations in the South. The manifesto warned northerners that "on issues vital to them" they, too, could become "victims of judicial encroachment."[94]

Like leaders of the army in Spain, the South's political leaders were unwilling to surrender their power. "Massive resistance" was their strategy to maintain segregation. It revealed the formidable ingenuity and imagination of politicians at all levels. Rather than integrate schools, some officials closed and padlocked them. Others designed complicated "freedom of choice" plans that might allow one or two black students to attend a white school somewhere in the school district; meanwhile the vast majority of students would remain in thoroughly segregated and unequal schools. Public facilities, such as parks, golf courses, and swimming pools could be closed to resist integration. Another option was to sell these public facilities to private white clubs at a bargain-basement price. Teams of lawyers went to work identifying ways to stall or evade integration. In the Deep South, especially, Citizens Councils came into being to organize white opposition to every step that would threaten segregation and the racism at the heart of the "southern way of life." Symbols of defiance also were important, as Georgia incorporated the CSA battle flag into its state banner in 1956. South Carolina, similarly, began flying the Confederate battle flag over its state capitol in 1962.[95]

Ironically, in the early days of desegregation and "massive resistance," it was often the southern "moderates" who most effectively stalled civil rights. Governors such as LeRoy Collins of Florida, James P. Coleman of Mississippi, and Luther Hodges of North Carolina received considerable favorable publicity for their refusal to use the language of racial demagoguery. At various times they even spoke of "socially responsible" measures that could help blacks to have "equal opportunities." In Florida, for example, LeRoy Collins said that African Americans needed "improved housing . . . and more opportunities to improve their lives." Such language helped Collins and Hodges respond to *Brown* in a way that was "peaceful, legal, and attuned to northern sensibilities." But as they gave some "moral respectability" to their states' position, they also publicized black illegitimacy rates and "framed the problem of integration as a fundamentally black problem." Integration would come at some point in the future when African Americans made themselves worthy of white respect, and any attempt to "abolish" segregation would cause "many and grave problems." James Coleman, who would soon become an influential federal judge, worked persistently to limit the Supreme Court's decisions by arguing for a color-blind jurisprudence "that did not take historical context into account."[96]

While deploying "elaborate schemes to assign students to schools based on factors other than race," these moderates also changed government to avoid damaging confrontations with the federal government, like the one that had occurred in Little Rock, Arkansas. They "promoted the expansion and centralization of state police, the modernization of state judiciaries, and the reconfiguration of welfare regulations and family law." These steps, plus new laws giving the governor power to declare emergencies and dispatch state troopers to maintain order, were "aimed at preventing violence, preserving as much segregation as possible, and complying, formally, with the Supreme Court." Integration of a few facilities served as "concessions" in a much larger constitutional struggle to delay and debilitate integration. Meanwhile conservative black leaders, often those dependent on some form of state support, were pressured to support these "moderate" measures.[97]

Such tactics achieved a considerable measure of success, but the violent segregationists ultimately seized center stage and provoked federal intervention. In Montgomery, Little Rock, Greensboro, Tuscaloosa, Birmingham, and scores of other towns and cities, black southerners peaceably marched, conducted sit-ins, and protested for basic rights and humane treatment. By contrast, enraged white southerners, their faces contorted with hate, shouted epithets, threw rocks or fists, and descended into violence. Southern police, instead of protecting citizens, often turned on peaceful protestors. These troubling and well-publicized spectacles aroused the North and forced a Democratic president to intervene. The turning point came in 1962 with the court-ordered admission of James Meredith as a student at the University of Mississippi. After Governor Ross Barnett defied the federal courts and the president, a night of violence claimed two lives and injured two hundred. Once again, as in Reconstruction, southern intransigence forced the federal government to confront racism. The "*status* of the negro" was finally and squarely on the national agenda.

In a televised address to an attentive nation, President Kennedy made clear that he had called the Mississippi National Guard into service to impose order and "to carry out the final and unequivocal order" of a U.S.

District Court. His words in the rest of his address were as frank and challenging as they were eloquent. He reminded citizens that the United States was in "a worldwide struggle to promote and protect the rights of all who wish to be free." How could the nation win that struggle when "we say to the world ... that this is the land of the free except for the Negroes ... that we have no class or caste system, no ghettoes, no master race except with respect to Negroes?" It was time for the United States to confront the moral issue and live up to its ideals. A "great change is at hand," he said, and citizens needed "to make that revolution ... peaceful and constructive for all." Kennedy announced that he would send to Congress a bold package of bills to ensure civil rights and equal access to public facilities, to end segregation in public schools, and to secure the right to vote.[98]

With this message, the nonviolent protests led principally by Martin Luther King Jr. and the policies of the national administration came together. The North-South bargain within the Democratic Party was broken. The weight of the federal government began to swing decisively behind African Americans' campaign for justice. The enormous and impressive March on Washington that summer, a peaceful and biracial effort, further mobilized public opinion in favor of reform. Its highlight was King's eloquent "I have a dream" speech, which again called on the nation to realize its ideals and its promise, to "live out the true meaning of its creed" of equality and bring "the sons of former slaves and the sons of former slave owners ... together at the table of brotherhood."

Then the assassination of President Kennedy shocked the nation. Moreover, it brought to the White House an experienced master of the legislative process, Lyndon Johnson. The new president resolved to honor Kennedy's memory by enacting his ambitious package of civil rights bills. Pledging, "We shall overcome," Johnson put the power of the presidency behind equality. Johnson's political skill contributed substantially to the passage, over unbending southern opposition, of the civil rights bill in 1964 and the voting rights bill in 1965. These bills transformed the landscape, not only in social life but also in political affairs. Johnson knew that they would do enormous good; he also expected them to bring political realignment, saying, "We just delivered the South to the Republican Party for a long time to come."[99]

The rights of African Americans to equal treatment in housing, employment, public accommodations, and many other areas now enjoyed the support of law and the federal government. And politicians now faced a new and greatly expanded electorate. In towns and cities throughout the South, federal registrars appeared in courthouses and registered black men and women long disfranchised but eager to vote. Federal law struck down the poll tax, and the Department of Justice gained power to supervise redistricting measures and other laws that might affect the voting rights of African Americans. Newly empowered black voters could not be ignored, even by politicians who had defended segregation at every crossroads. Whether politicians believed in equality or not, they now had to take note of the black electorate.

And take note they did. A new wave of southern governors in the 1970s led the way. In Georgia, Jimmy Carter replaced the outgoing Lester Maddox, who earlier had given axe handles to white customers at his restaurant while he threatened violence to keep black people out. Governor Carter declared in his inaugural address, "I say to you quite frankly that the time for racial discrimination is over. No poor, rural, weak or black person should ever have to bear the additional burden of being deprived of the opportunity of an education, a job or simple justice." In South Carolina, John C. West defeated an opponent who had criticized busing and court orders. In his inaugural West pledged a "colorblind" administration that would focus on housing, education, and hunger, not race. Florida's Reubin Askew promised fair treatment of both races, and Arkansas' Dale Bumpers said, "The future I envision must be shaped and shared by all Arkansans—old and young, black and white, rich and poor." Even Alabama's George Wallace, famous for vowing "segregation now, segregation tomorrow, segregation forever" in 1963, changed his tone and spoke of an Alabama that "belongs to all of us—black and white, young and old, rich and poor alike."[100] The emancipation cause had gained much ground against the pro-Confederate Lost Cause.

Political life changed dramatically. Due to federal intervention, "by 1967 black registration had jumped from nineteen percent to 52 percent in Alabama and from seven to 60 percent in Mississippi." Within a decade black voters made up almost one-quarter of the electorate in the Deep South.

Andrew Young observed that political rhetoric steadily became more polite as more African Americans registered, and once a majority of blacks were voting, all the candidates suddenly were "proud to be associated with their black brothers and sisters." Even once-rabid segregationists such as George Wallace and Strom Thurmond altered their style and their policies in order to appeal to black voters. (Through persistent attention to black concerns, each achieved a considerable measure of success.) Black office holding in the South rapidly outdistanced the rest of the country and proved to be durable. By 1995 African Americans held 16 percent of the seats in southern state legislatures, the same percentage as their numbers in the total population. By contrast, blacks were underrepresented in northern legislatures, where they held only 4.7 percent of the seats. By 2000 there were more than five hundred elected black officials in South Carolina, Georgia, and Louisiana. In addition, "Mississippi and Alabama alone accounted for more blacks in elective office than could be found in the entire country in 1970." Success came more readily for blacks in local and municipal contests than in statewide races, but even so, a mere seven southern states "accounted for forty-two percent of all blacks in statewide office" in the nation in 2007.[101]

School desegregation also occurred rapidly after 1971, when the Supreme Court required that southern school districts take effective steps, immediately, to end segregation. Busing now became the tool used to integrate the schools rather than to keep the races separate. Statistical studies showed that the total number of miles traveled by school children in buses actually decreased in many areas. Although very little integration had taken place before 1971, one year later "thirty-six percent of the region's blacks attended majority-white schools." By 1983 that figure had reached a high of 44 percent, and in 1994 it remained at almost 37 percent.[102] These levels far surpassed the amount of integration in the North.

The new politics also encouraged economic change. Freed of the incubus of Jim Crow and racial conflict, national and international corporations began to invest more heavily in the South. Initially local elites feared and resisted the invasion of companies that would raise wages and compete for established companies' labor. But soon the pent-up desire for greater prosperity carried the day. Industrial recruitment offices opened their doors and welcome signs greeted new investment. The region's economy modernized at an accelerating pace.

Economic progress aided racial and political change, and the traditional personalism of southern culture seemed to make dramatic changes in race relations easier. Observers noted frequent interracial contacts and "a comfortable mixing found less often in the North." Even in traditional bastions of discrimination, examples of relaxed cooperation between community leaders were easy to spot. In South Carolina, for instance, an interracial marriage involving the son of a prominent low country family took place in the Bethel AME Church in Columbia, and the local newspaper covered the wedding with a two-column photograph. South Carolina also witnessed unpleasant racial incidents, such as the refusal of a restaurant to serve black customers or a swimming pool that turned away an interracial group. One country club denied membership to a black executive of IBM, despite business leaders' hopes of landing an important new factory. But, comments historian David Goldfield, "what is particularly noteworthy about these incidents" is "the swiftness with which community institutions and groups came together to denounce the actions." In the examples cited, "the state attorney revoked the restaurant's license" and "the governor of the state invited the youth group over for a pool party." The whites-only country club hastened to change its policy and invited some African Americans to join. Racial etiquette in the South now treats examples of "extreme racism" with "revulsion."[103]

But although some changes could be rapid, social structure and systems of influence altered more slowly. Some racist feelings went underground rather than disappearing. Ingrained patterns of social hierarchy continued to shape society, define attitudes, and influence political allegiances. Rock-ribbed conservatism in the South had customarily served the interests of wealthy elites, and that did not change. In 1967 Senator Ernest Hollings of South Carolina spoke out on behalf of a poverty program targeted to help young children. Large farmers in his state were receiving as much as forty thousand dollars in federal payments not to plant certain crops. But whereas they could take federal money and remain "as red-blooded, capitalistic, free enterprising, and patriotic as ever before," said Hollings, "give the poor little hungry child a 40-cent breakfast . . . and you've destroyed his character . . . ruined his incentive." "Mississippi congressman Jamie Whitten asked whether 'when you start giving people something for nothing . . . you don't destroy character more than you might improve nutrition.'"

He ignored the fact that 350 farmers in his district raked in crop-control checks greater than fifty thousand dollars, including 69 whose payments exceeded one hundred thousand dollars. "Planters in the ten core counties of the Yazoo-Mississippi [Delta]," noted scholar Jim Cobb, "received 22 percent of all federal farm subsidy payments in excess of $50,000 in 1967."[104]

Such large federal payments have continued, as powerful interests oppose federal "giveaways" to the poor and shun any type of progressive taxation. When southern governments have to raise revenue through taxation, they usually look to the sales tax. The sales tax is not only a regressive form of taxation that hits the poor more heavily than the rich, because they have to spend a higher percentage of their income, but also serves as "a buffer against higher property taxes that would affect large individual and corporate landowners." Property taxes in the South tend to be low. In five southern states in 2005, "the per capita property tax burden was less than half the national figure." In recent years already vigorous competition in the recruitment of businesses has increased, with generous incentives and tax breaks luring new factories. State recruiters recite a mantra of "cheap labor, low taxes, and a variety of subsidies," and government officials and business leaders make "no secret of their hostility to organized labor."[105]

Traditional attitudes in areas such as religion and gender restrain political progress as well. Although southern women are moving into the professions and attending college in great numbers, they "lag behind those elsewhere in holding elective office. As of 1997, six of the ten states with the lowest percentages of women in state legislatures were located in the South." The Nineteenth Amendment, which gave women the right to vote, was not ratified by North Carolina until 1971 or by Georgia and Mississippi until the 1980s. Not surprisingly, only two southern states voted to ratify the unsuccessful Equal Rights Amendment. Until the mid-1990s most southern states "did not recognize marital rape as a crime, and of the eight states without laws prohibiting sex discrimination in employment in 1995, all were located in the South." Along with a fondness for beauty pageants, southern culture supports male domination in matters religious. More than 90 percent of southerners are evangelical Protestants, just as the vast majority of Spaniards are Catholic. Most of these evangelical denominations advocate a subordinate role for women. The Southern Baptist

Convention, which long had frowned on women becoming ministers, took a stronger step in 2000. After hearing from a study committee that "Southern Baptists . . . believe leadership is male," it passed a resolution that "the office of pastor is limited to men as qualified by Scripture." Two years earlier the convention had decreed that "a wife is to submit graciously to the servant leadership of her husband."[106]

These conservative cultural attitudes supported the growth of the Republican Party in the South. As southern states started backing Republican presidential candidates, their weight in the Electoral College fed a broader conservative movement in national politics. Lyndon Johnson's fear that civil rights legislation would turn the solid Democratic South over to the Republicans has proved to be insightful, and racism certainly played a part in that startling shift of partisan loyalties. Adept use of racial code words and attacks on affirmative action played an effective role in many state and national campaigns. On occasion the racial motive hidden beneath code words comes out into the open. After political scientist Earl Black gave a talk to a group of South Carolina Republicans, several businessmen from the audience tried to convince him that their conversion to the party had nothing to do with race. As they spoke, another man joined the group, offered a friendly compliment to Black on his remarks, and then said, "Why don't you leave the niggers behind and come join us?"[107]

But race has not been the only factor in the white South's Republicanism. It is true that Ronald Reagan defended states' rights and made other appeals to the racial discontent of southern whites. But he also joined southern conservatism to a growing national mood. He "repackaged" the "old rough-around-the-edges southern strategy" into "a sleeker, more racially modulated 'suburban strategy' that might work equally well in . . . any number of cities elsewhere in the country." With his fervid patriotism, enthusiastic support of the military, hostility toward taxes, and criticism of Washington bureaucrats, he reached a broader electorate. In the 1980s, the "Republicans gained a fifty percent increase in support among southern white conservatives." By 1988, 60 percent of those white conservatives supported the GOP." The South's religious, pro-business, antigovernment conservatism became the conservatism of the nation as a "southernization" of American politics took place. After Reagan's presidency, the nation elected as president three southerners who held office for twenty years. Bill Clinton's ideology could not be described as more than moderate, and the two Republican Bushes took the country in a right-wing direction.[108]

To sum up, change in southern politics has been dramatic for blacks and whites. But although racism has declined, cultural aspects of the "other," hierarchical, conservative South remain. Political scientists Earl and Merle Black conclude, "In terms of real influence and control, the [South's] GOP is preeminently the vehicle of the upper-middle-class, well-educated, conservative whites." It "epitomizes the values and beliefs of the most affluent white southerners"—the same role that the South's Democratic Party played from Reconstruction to the civil rights movement, when it defended the Confederacy and white supremacy.[109] The political system of the Lost Cause and segregation is gone; a conservative social order, buttressed by a fundamentalist religion similar to Spain's, remains.

4

Reconciliation

An End to Civil War?

> Unless justice is done, it's difficult for any person to think about forgiving.
> Churchill Mxenge, brother of a murdered anti-apartheid lawyer

> Personal bitterness is irrelevant. It is a luxury that we, as individuals and as a country, cannot afford.... Instead we must insist with quiet resolve on a firm policy of undoing the continuing effects of the past.
> Nelson Mandela

> Memory is shaped by our changing surroundings and the way we interpret them.
> Michael Richards, "From War Culture to Civil Society," 94.

When emotions have subsided, it is easy to see warfare as a great human and societal failure. This especially is true of internecine conflicts such as those that occurred in Spain and the United States. The destruction in both civil wars was appalling, as hundreds of thousands of the young men and productive male adults lost their lives. Many women and children also died, families were devastated, and farms and factories were destroyed. Both nations squandered immense amounts of their economic resources on killing, an activity that produced only hostility and bitterness. In every war each side demonizes its opponent, but this process is exaggerated in internecine conflicts. "The more the victim resembles the murderer," observes Ian Buruma, "in culture and background, the greater the need for degradation, hence, possibly, the peculiar cruelty of civil wars."[1]

Before such facts, one is driven to ask, What did these wars settle? Did they resolve anything? Or did they merely create more problems? In the case of Spain a related question is, What did the Transition settle or determine for the post-Franco future? Was the Transition flawed? This chapter first will examine the kind of settlement that came out of the civil wars in Spain and the United States, what was sought and understood as reconciliation, and why it was inadequate. Then, in a more abstract or theoretical vein, it will turn to questions such as what reconciliation means, what kind of reconciliation is possible in any large and divided society, and in what way Spain and the United States may hope, eventually, to leave the wounds of history behind.

* * *

For both countries the resolution purchased by violence was limited. In the United States the Civil War made one thing clear: the Union would endure; the United States would be a single country, including both North and South. That, of course, had been the goal for which the states of the North and the government of Abraham Lincoln went to war. The South's goal—to protect slavery and create an independent slaveholding nation— was lost, and the institution of legally established racial bondage perished as a result of the military conflict. There were other important and unplanned effects. The size of the federal government remained permanently larger than ever before, with veterans' benefits and debt service commanding a sizable portion of the budget for decades to come—as much as 20 percent and 40 percent, respectively, in the 1880s. A national banking system and a single federal currency both came out of the war. These monetary changes, along with a series of other measures—higher tariffs, the transcontinental railroad, land grants to states for new colleges and universities—helped to push the North and West toward an industrializing, urbanizing future.

But as we have seen, the question that was at the root of the conflict— what Alexander Stephens called "the proper status of the negro in our form of civilization"—was avoided. The fundamental clash between racism and the founding ideals of the United States received, at best, only a partial answer. Both southerners like Stephens and northern Republicans like Abraham Lincoln knew that the "irrepressible conflict" arose from that issue, which could not be submerged or compromised away. Both the war and Reconstruction failed to create an answer consonant with the ideals of human liberty set forth in the Declaration of Independence. Hostile and embittered white southerners resisted northern legislation and then resorted to terrorism to enforce white supremacy.

After Reconstruction, racial equality under the law existed only on paper. More than two years of southern intransigence had forced the northern Congress to adopt new rules for the South's reunion, including black suffrage. Lawmakers wrote the Fourteenth and Fifteenth Amendments into the Constitution. Along with the Thirteenth Amendment, which abolished slavery, these texts and black male suffrage seemed to confirm a national commitment to the belief that "all men are created equal, that they are endowed by their Creator with certain unalienable Rights, that among these are Life, Liberty, and the pursuit of Happiness." But racial equality had never enjoyed substantial support from a racist white majority, and soon northerners ceded control over the rights of black southerners to their white antagonists. Thus the central issue of the American Civil War remained unsettled, a troubling legacy that future generations would have to address, both North and South.

In addition, reunion was not reconciliation. In psychological and social terms the South refused to become one with the nation. True, in a formal, legal sense, reconstruction occurred, because southern states once again took their place in the national government. But southern whites continued to contest the terms of reunion, insisting on control of their region. Nourishing strong feelings of resentment, white elites elaborated their grievances against the North and charted a separate path for the South's social system. By 1900 the consolidation of a one-party South dominated by white supremacy and devoted to the Lost Cause was complete. In ideological terms any reunion, as a meeting of minds, would have to occur on southern terms. A passive North accepted a limited idea of reconciliation, defined as respect among former soldiers. In social and emotional terms reunion was a fiction. As for true reconciliation, a popular southern answer for more than three generations was "Forget, hell!"

In Spain the results of civil war were at least equally discouraging. War settled the question of who would be in control. The Manichean mentality of Franco's forces and the church guaranteed additional suffering in the immediate postwar period in the form of exile, imprisonment, executions, and economic hardship and hunger through the 1940s. For decades beyond that, the Nationalist victory meant a repressive dictatorship for Spain, the loss of liberty and freedom of expression, and the imposition of an unhealthy public culture. Even conservative newspapers have sometimes seen long-lasting ill effects from the decades of Franco's rule. In an essay in *La Razón*, the award-winning writer Ángel Vallvey declared, "We are heirs of a Franquismo that gangrened the society and promoted mediocrity, social anesthesia, conformism, and a widespread poverty." Others note that the memory of the war and Franco's dictatorship inhibit Spaniards' ability to feel patriotic or to have complete confidence in their own national character.[2]

But Franco's victory, mercilessly enforced, failed in its aims. The crusade did not make Spain a bulwark for the world of reactionary, fundamentalist Catholicism. It did not block secular ideas or aspirations to modernity. Instead, the church's full-throated support for a ruthless dictator discredited and compromised it in the minds of the large majority of Spaniards. Many citizens now are nonreligious, or they are nonpracticing Catholics, or as individuals they form their own religious ideas apart from the conservative doctrines of the church hierarchy. Popular culture is secular, irreverent, and sexually frank. Not only did the crusade fail in its ambitious, reactionary goals, but the church is probably weaker now than it would have been had its leaders not attempted to turn back the clock.

Nor did the militarism and social and political conservatism of Franco survive his regime, for a similar process of popular resentment and rejection led to the Transition. Today Spain is a democratic nation that has been governed through most of the period since 1976 by the Socialist Party. In fact, a profile in *El País* of Mariano Rajoy, leader of the conservative Partido Popular, reported that he and his political strategists view the Spanish electorate as essentially on the Left. They saw their chance to gain power as flowing from disillusion with the management of José Luis Rodríguez Zapatero, and Spain's economic crisis did, in fact, carry them to victory in 2011.[3] By extension we should ask, What was resolved by the Transition? And what remained problematic, after the Transition, as a legacy of the civil war?

Spain came out of a centralized dictatorship amid ETA's escalating violence and opposition from peripheral regions that loathed the dictatorship and its centralization. The Constitution of 1978 attempted to compromise this clash by affirming "the indissoluble unity of the Spanish nation" while recognizing and guaranteeing "the right to autonomy of the nationalities and regions" that make up Spain. Castilian would be "the official Spanish language of the State" and all Spaniards would have "the duty of knowing it and the right of using it." But "the other Spanish languages will also be official in the respective Autonomous Communities in accord with their Statutes." The constitution thus embraced linguistic and cultural diversity, praising Spain's "distinct linguistic modalities" as a "cultural patrimony that will be the object of special respect and protection."[4] However, as noted in earlier chapters, these measures neither diminished ETA's terrorism nor satisfied peripheral minorities who wanted independence. The question of the nationalities and a related matter, the role of the autonomies, remain very troublesome today.[5]

Moreover, what had seemed to be Spain's great modern accomplishment—a peaceful transition to democracy that left the past behind in order to build a democratic future—now has encountered increasing criticism. The "generation of the grandchildren," as observers have dubbed it, often condemned the Transition for an acceptance of *olvido*. Amnesty is not amnesia, many have declared, while demanding that graves be opened, murdered Republican ancestors identified, and an accounting made of the wrongs inflicted by the Nationalist forces. Other critics go further, arguing that there can be no healthy democracy in Spain without an official and legal process that brings justice to the past. The violators of human rights should be punished, or at least condemned if they are now dead, and the unjust sentences against Republicans annulled. This viewpoint passed from questions of personal opinion to matters of law when Judge Baltasar Garzón briefly opened an investigation of human right abuses. Though Garzón soon suspended his efforts, right-wing organizations had an opening to attack him. Charged with "prevarication," or knowingly acting contrary to Spain's laws of amnesty, Garzón faced a judicial process that led to the end his career.[6] Meanwhile the controversy aroused legal scholars around the world who contend that international law prohibits amnesty in the case of violations of human rights.

One also must ask how effectively Spain and the United States reunited their once-warring populations through official ceremonies and commemorations. In the United States there was little unity in grieving for the dead. A pattern of separate commemorations, those for the North and those for the South, developed to honor the soldiers of each region. The federal government created national cemeteries for the Union war dead and worked to locate and give a dignified burial to the remains of northern soldiers who fell in southern states. The various chapters of the Ladies Memorial Association in the South concentrated their similar efforts on finding and interring fallen Confederate soldiers. These separate efforts began while the heated controversies over Reconstruction filled the air with charges and recriminations. President Ulysses S. Grant's first inaugural address, which urged that difficult issues "should be approached calmly, without prejudice, hate, or sectional pride," brought no truce to sectional battles. Four years later, in 1873, he argued that "social equality" was different from "the civil rights which citizenship should carry with it" and called the denial of these rights to African Americans "wrong."[7] Again, his words moved neither the South nor the nation.

The first strong gesture of reconciliation came from President Rutherford B. Hayes. His approach to reuniting the sections amounted to a surrender to white southerners' racism. He journeyed to the South to offer this region his hand in friendship. To African Americans he gave the blatantly questionable advice that they should trust in the fair-mindedness of the South's white leaders. To whites he gave praise for the Confederate soldiers' bravery and defense of their beliefs. Neither offering made much difference—for decades many southern communities refused to celebrate July 4.

The affirmation of the Confederate soldier was key in the next stage of a reconciliation that was very limited, even on southern terms. Editors from the *Century Magazine* solicited wartime recollections from leaders of both armies and began publishing their essays in 1884. After four years these pieces filled four volumes of *Battles and Leaders of the Civil War*. The popular series focused on military campaigns and soldiers' challenges and successes and evaded the conflicts that were at issue. Thus it reinforced the idea of a reconciliation between northern and southern whites that was emptied of troubling content related to race.

By 1900 reconciliation focused principally on veterans' reunions. In the American form of forgetting, the war's causes disappeared from view and the significance of the war was reduced to soldiers' sacrifices. After veterans of the Battle of Gettysburg organized a number of modest-sized reunions, planning began for a large-scale observance on the fiftieth anniversary of that important contest. With support from the state of Pennsylvania, the federal government, and thirty-two other states, a huge encampment of veterans took place. Over fifty thousand elderly former soldiers, most of them from the North, traveled to Gettysburg and lived once more in tents on the battlefield where they had fought. The emotional high point of the commemorative activities occurred on July 3, the anniversary of Pickett's charge, when survivors of two opposing, Union and Confederate, units advanced a short distance toward each other and met at the stone wall where Union forces had stopped the South's attack. There the elderly men clasped hands and embraced each other. President Woodrow Wilson captured the restricted meaning of reconciliation when he declared that northerners and southerners "have found one another again as brothers and comrades in arms." In an unconscious acknowledgment that this veterans' rapprochement had not settled the issues that divided the nation, Wilson went on to say that "our battles" are "long past, the quarrel forgotten—except that we shall not forget the splendid valor."[8]

Forgetting the quarrel was a way to ignore its source. The nation's inability to resolve the conflict between racism and its founding ideals again was evident when the one hundredth anniversary of the Civil War arrived. Southern leaders had just launched their campaign of "massive resistance" to *Brown v. Board of Education* and to any change in segregation. The ideology of the Lost Cause remained strong, and the growing civil rights movement had not yet won its major victories. In addition, the Cold War had shaped Americans' mentalities to automatically embrace national power rather than reflect on national problems. As a result, the national commemoration resembled something that could have happened fifty years earlier. "The official Civil War centennial refused to face the challenge of causes and consequences," writes historian David Blight. "Instead, a reconciliationist, Blue-Gray celebration of soldiers' valor and re-emergent national greatness forged out of conflict dominated the scene." The "master narrative" was still "mutual heroism in a war in which everyone had fought for their sense of the right."[9] One hundred years after the fighting had stopped, official commemorations showed that the United States had neither reconciled nor faced up to the central issue that caused the war.

Public commemorations likewise revealed the difficulty of reconciliation in Spain, where General Franco showed little interest in reuniting his countrymen. There were some calls for reconciliation in the 1940s and

1950s from individuals as diverse as Américo Castro, Indalecio Prieto, Gil Robles, and some of the exiles. In 1956 university students in Madrid called for unity of the conquerors and the conquered against the dictatorship. After the students were jailed, their supporters appealed not only for pardon for the students but also for an amnesty. With the passage of time and modifications in the regime's propaganda, Franco permitted some officials to stop talking about the great Crusade to save Spain and Catholicism. Manuel Fraga Iribarne discussed aperture, or opening, in the 1960s, but the prosecution of dissidents and the execution of opponents, even with the garrote, continued until Franco's death. It is difficult to agree with Salvador de Madariaga's judgment that the civil war ended in 1962, when internal and exiled opponents of the regime met in Munich, Germany, and called for reconciliation among all Spaniards.[10] Reconciliation will necessarily be impossible if one side refuses to cooperate.

Franco had monopolized Spain's national holidays, giving primacy to dates that honored the army's uprising and then its victory and putting his regime's gloss on other holidays, both new and traditional. The date when Franco flew to Spanish Morocco as part of the uprising, July 18, and the day of victory, April 1, were centrally important. Franco designated November 20 as a day to honor the death of José Antonio Primo de Rivera, and he seized the opportunity to identify his regime closely with October 12 (the day of Hispanism) and May 2 (the anniversary of the battle for independence against the French, 1808–14). In the 1960s the regime turned April 1 into Armed Forces Day, with a large military parade. Given the importance of the army and the frequent use of force by Franco's government, the fact that the holiday no longer celebrated "victory" scarcely diminished its connection with the dictatorship.[11]

The Transition to democracy called for a change in these public commemorations. The newly elected governments moved slowly and found that it was difficult to unite the nation enthusiastically behind new and more democratic celebrations. In 1977, July 18 was abolished as a holiday, but what would be done to modify the content of the other holidays? The celebration of Hispanism, which recognized Spain's historical and cultural connection with its former colonies around the world, posed no special problem but did not affirm democracy in any special way. In 1985 the government attempted to modify May 2, when King Juan Carlos added an eternal flame and a short inscription—"Honor to all those who gave their lives for Spain"—to the monument in Madrid that commemorated the 1808 independence movement. Even this modest step aroused opposition. Conservatives and pro-Franco media criticized the change, and the fact that this gesture toward reconciliation avoided mentioning the word testified to its weakness.[12] Even less successful was the effort to create a national holiday in honor of the new constitution. Although December 6 is observed as a national holiday throughout Spain, it has never generated great public enthusiasm or served as a patriotic rallying point.

Thus in both countries change has encountered strong resistance. The victors—whether the passive North in the United States or Franco's Nationalist Crusade in Spain—did not achieve major parts of their goals. White southerners in the United States refused to abandon their "cause," resisted reconciliation, and "won the peace" to a great extent. In Spain Franco succeeded only in repressing his opponents by force. At his death, the Republican vision of a modern, democratic, secular Spain triumphed, though it too faces hostile criticism from parts of the Right that are not fully reconciled. These stubborn facts have stimulated observers to ask, Are there other ways to end bitter civil wars? Can better paths be found to resolve the deep conflicts that led to internal conflict and killing?

"Some societies," observe Luis Roniger and Mario Sznajder, "'move into the future' following a path of progressive and unreflective disengagement from the past, while others ... either cling to the past or consciously attempt to leave the past behind." These different paths create controversy over the demands of justice, the wisdom of amnesty, and the benefits of forgiveness. Those who insist that justice be meted out warn that where "impunity triumphs, state institutions promote collective forgetfulness of violations of human rights.... 'Oblivion must be fought with energy.'" Others place greater emphasis on building a different, healthier future and insist that "reconciliation will have to come through the truth, through memory and through guarantees ... that [wrongs] will not occur anymore."[13] Some democracies in recent decades have chosen to emphasize justice, using the judicial system to identify and punish violations of human rights. Other nations have opted for amnesty, deciding to look to the future and confer legal impunity for the wrongs of the past. A third, new, and much debated path has been the creation of truth and reconciliation commissions.

According to *El País'* Natalia Junquera, more than thirty nations have revisited a bloodstained past and taken steps to compensate victims of wartime crimes or punish the perpetrators. In a number of important cases, these steps occurred early in the process of establishing a new, democratic government, when many of those responsible for killings or crimes against human rights were still alive and active in society. The range of societies that managed to reexamine their troubled past is broad. In Morocco, King Mohamed VI created a commission to investigate "the disappearances, detentions, tortures, rapes, and executions committed between 1956 and 1999." The governments of Guatemala and El Salvador supported an effort to locate secret graves in which victims of state violence had been buried. Even Germany, where the Allied powers had destroyed Nazi symbols following World War II, formally reconsidered its past in 1998, when the Parliament examined the sentences imposed by Hitler's military courts or popular tribunals.

These varied governments took actions to rectify, belatedly, the past. Morocco's Equity and Reconciliation Commission identified and resolved 742 cases of forced disappearances and torture. The government officially asked pardon by letter to the victims, and for several days the television carried live testimony from citizens who described the horrors they had suffered. In Guatemala the government paid the costs of exhumations and indemnified the victims. El Salvador did less, placing most of the burden for initiating exhumations on the families of victims and avoiding prosecutions in the courts. The German Parliament approved a law that annulled those legal or military judgments dictated by the Nazi regime. But perhaps the most important recent examples of government action came from Argentina and Chile, two nations that, like Spain, experienced killings, tortures, and disappearances under military regimes.[14]

In Argentina, the military passed a law, before it yielded power in 1983, to give its members amnesty in cases involving "subversion" as well as "repression." However, the new democratic government that came into existence promptly overturned that amnesty and began some trials. Nine military leaders were prosecuted, and five were convicted of crimes. Angry and nervous military officers then fomented riots, which the government put down before passing laws defining the obedience required of the military. Several years after the transition to democracy occurred, President Carlos Menem issued pardons for most officers, but that did not end the matter. His action had not covered those who had been involved in kidnapping children, and four generals were convicted on that basis in 1998. The courts subsequently opened inquiries, and finally in 2005 the nation's supreme court declared unconstitutional the pardons that Menem had issued. Argentina also has done a notable job of converting a center of military terror into a symbol of democratic values. The Escuela Mecánica de la Armada (Army Mechanical School) was the site where four thousand leftists or suspected leftists were tortured and killed by the military. Now it serves as a Museum of Memory, dedicated to human rights. It documents the wrongs suffered within its walls and displays testimony of the victims.[15]

In Chile the generals of its right-wing regime approved a law of amnesty in 1978, and the new democratic government had to move cautiously as the dictator, General Augusto Pinochet, remained influential for years and headed the executive until 1990. With the leadership of Chile's Catholic Church, some exhumations began while Pinochet was still in power. But not until 1995 (when Pinochet was still commander in chief of the army) did trials for violations of human rights begin. In 2004 the National Commission on Political Imprisonment and Torture released a report which documented the widespread violations of human rights by the military. More than thirty-five thousand individuals declared that they had been tortured, and a large majority of these received monthly reparations payments. Other forms of recognition and reparation, as well as exhumations, have been part of the democratic government's response in Chile.[16]

Recently two other Latin American nations, Brazil and Uruguay, revisited the military repression in their pasts and focused on whether they should cancel or revoke laws of amnesty. These laws shielded individuals who had violated citizens' legal and human rights, but both countries considered steps that would allow the courts to pursue justice and punishment. In Brazil the initiative came from a national organization of attorneys, which petitioned the supreme court to allow revision of that country's amnesty law. The attorneys argued that crimes that were not political, such as torture, disappearances, and the rape of minors, ought to be prosecuted. The government of then-president Luiz Inácio Lula da Silva divided over the question, with the minister of human rights and the former minister of justice in favor of prosecutions and the minister of defense opposed.

By a vote of seven to two, the nation's supreme court rejected the lawyers' petition. In a public session carried by television, members of the court explained their votes. The president of the court expressed the view of the majority in these words: "Brazil made a choice in favor of national concord, and it ought to be respected." Two of his colleagues added, in agreement, that the law had resulted from an ample national debate to make possible the transition to democracy. Defending the importance of the peaceful transition, one jurist said, "The amnesty was an act of love, based in the peaceful coexistence of the citizens." Those who dissented from the court's decision agreed with the association of lawyers that the amnesty law did not include nonpolitical crimes. They also argued that the majority of torturers were not military and that prosecuting those who were would "purify" the armed forces. In any event, had the court decided differently, the Brazilian Congress would have had to revise the law.[17]

Just one year later Uruguay's legislature approached a vote to annul its national law of amnesty. Like the measure in Brazil, this law came at the end of a military dictatorship, which lasted from 1973 to 1985, and it exempted from punishment those in the government who had committed crimes against humanity. By 2011 the nation's president was José Mujica, seventy-five years old, who earlier in his life had been a leader of the Tupamaro guerrillas. The Tupamaros waged a violent campaign against the government in the 1960s, and Mujica had been among those imprisoned and tortured by the dictatorship after it largely suppressed his movement. At least 174 political prisoners were kidnapped and killed during the rule of the military junta, and more than 100 had died behind bars. Mujica's party, the Broad Front, initiated the effort to overturn the amnesty law, while right-wing parties and retired military officials strongly opposed it.

This question generated great debate and individual soul-searching in Uruguay, in part because on two occasions voters in that nation had supported the amnesty law. In 1989 and again in 2009, when Mujica was elected president, the electorate endorsed the law, first by 54 percent and then by 52 percent. A former president of the country, Tabaré Vázquez, who had not criticized the law when in office, now altered his opinion, explaining that "majorities aren't always correct in matters of human rights." In contrast, one member of the Broad Front announced that he would oppose overturning amnesty, saying, "I respect the opinion of the people."

In response, his party expelled him. On the day of the Congress' vote, an intense debate lasted fifteen hours, with the final vote delayed until five-thirty in the morning. A tie, forty-nine to forty-nine votes, produced when one member of Mujica's party absented himself from the legislative chamber, left the amnesty in place. Another member of the Broad Front, a distinguished senator and former Tupamaro, followed party discipline but then announced his resignation, explaining that derogation of the law would have been unconstitutional. Mujica himself had a complex position. He had not backed the proposal, but had pledged to support the measure if it passed and had urged party loyalty. After the legislators' decision, he expressed hope that some way would be found to help families gain information about relatives who were killed or disappeared.[18]

International courts and international law played a role in the Uruguayan dilemma, as they have in other cases. Three months previously the Inter-American Court of Human Rights had issued a judgment against Uruguay for its amnesty, and the possibility remains open that an appeal might be made to that court to modify the law. In a number of ways, international law has been evolving in directions generally opposed to amnesties. The United Nations Human Rights Committee oversees the International Covenant on Civil and Political Rights, which came into effect for its parties in 1976.[19] That covenant recognizes an "inherent right to life," restricts the death penalty to the most serious crimes, and prohibits slavery, forced labor, torture, and cruel, inhuman, or degrading punishments. On those grounds, the Human Rights Committee views amnesties as invalid in cases involving violations of basic human rights. Various regional human rights courts, especially in the Americas, agree and have taken positions against amnesty laws. Three reports from the United Nations criticized Spain in 2009 for allowing its law of amnesty to impede investigation of killings and disappearances. According to one legal scholar, the experience in Latin America, where various nations have refused to honor the amnesty statutes of other countries, suggests that amnesties "have no staying power when considered outside the country where granted."[20]

Spain was prominently involved in developments affecting amnesty and international law between 1998 and 2000. Judge Baltasar Garzón initiated a controversial effort to arrest, extradite, and try the former Chilean dictator, Augusto Pinochet, for crimes against humanity. In 1998, when Garzón learned that Pinochet had secretly traveled to London for surgery on his back, he petitioned British authorities to arrest and extradite Pinochet for crimes of genocide, terrorism, and torture against Chilean citizens and against one named individual. A British judge honored this request, and Pinochet was arrested in his hospital room. A complex and lengthy legal and diplomatic battle ensued. At first Pinochet's counsel won a decision that the former dictator enjoyed immunity as a former head of state. Then Belgium, France, and Switzerland issued orders for Pinochet's detention, the government of Spain endorsed Garzón's petition for extradition, and the Audiencia Nacional ruled that Spain had jurisdiction to try Pinochet for crimes committed in Argentina and Chile. The Audiencia Nacional held that international agreements did not prohibit a trial outside the jurisdiction in which the crimes had occurred, as long as Spanish law, as written, could apply to the facts in Chile. Since the Spanish legal code defined genocide as an effort to destroy, totally or partially, a national, ethnic, racial, or religious group, the Audiencia found the facts in Chile to be applicable. In a series of decisions the British House of Lords considered and supported extradition, and the British legal system ultimately ruled in favor of extradition. However, Chile appealed for Pinochet's release, based on his health, and the British foreign secretary eventually allowed the former dictator to return to his country.[21]

On questions of international law and amnesty, the Pinochet case illustrated both the gains being made against amnesty for those who violate human rights and the inherent weakness of the transnational system. In regard to gains against amnesty, a growing number of countries have entered into international agreements barring crimes such as genocide, terrorism, and torture. In addition, the courts of various nations have recognized their jurisdiction over matters that occurred elsewhere. Mexico's supreme court, for example, ruled that an Argentine naval officer could be extradited to Spain, despite Argentina's law of amnesty, because international treaties "recognized the jurisdiction of any State party to those treaties ... to prosecute ... judge ... and punish." The "principle that domestic amnesties for international crimes have no extraterritorial effect appears clearly to have been strengthened in recent decisions," writes one legal scholar.[22]

In an act that seemed likely to strengthen international law and the prosecution of crimes against humanity, Judge Baltasar Garzón responded to petitions from the Association for the Recovery of Historical Memory and others in 2008. These groups had called on Garzón to investigate the murders and disappearances of Republicans during the Civil War. Their petition pointed out that although Franco's government had tried to identify Nationalists who died or were killed, no one knew where tens or hundreds of thousands of Republicans lay in unmarked graves. Garzón affirmed that the conquered ought to have the same right as the conquerors to efforts by the State to locate and identify the dead. In doing so he went against a report of the Ministerio Fiscal, which argued that the complaints submitted to Garzón should not be examined because "the facts are not constitutive of crimes against human rights or genocide" and "would be affected by the Law of Amnesty of October 15, 1977." In response, Garzón cited various international conventions regarding crimes against humanity, and then focused on the penal code of Spain. That code described crimes against humanity as those committed "for reason of the victim belonging to a group or collectivity persecuted for motives political, racial, national, ethnic, cultural, religious, or of gender and other motives universally recognized as unacceptable with the rule of International Law."[23] Garzón's claim that these could be investigated despite Spain's law of amnesty met continued resistance within the Spanish legal system and from private groups. Their resistance led to the challenges that put his career in peril.

Garzón argued that he was the victim of persecution by segments of the judiciary that were closely aligned with the dictatorship, and some undisputed facts relating to the personnel of Spain's judicial system lend color to his claim. Generalísimo Franco had purged from the courts those with Republican sympathies, but there was no renovation or cleansing of the judicial system when the dictatorship gave way to the Transition. Judges and prosecutors of Franco's regime continued their careers, often with striking success. One individual who had been civil governor of Almería became a member of the Tribunal Constitucional, and one past president of the Tribunal Constitucional is the son of a Falangist who played a role in the murder of Federico García Lorca. A member of the Audiencia Nacional who felt the need to remain anonymous identified four high-ranking judges or prosecutors who are the sons or daughters of prominent Franquistas. He added that the same was true of many currently serving but less prominent figures in the judicial system.[24]

Garzón also has pointed out that Spain is party to various international treaties and functions in a system that includes international laws and tribunals. Citing several recent rulings by the Inter-American Court of Human Rights and the European Tribunal of Human Rights, he argued that his actions in the case brought by the Association for the Recovery of Historical Memory were reasonable. In fact, by some readings of international law they were required. It is "no insignificant thing," stated Garzón, that the Committee on Human Rights and the Committee Against Torture of the United Nations have declared that Spain's law of amnesty ought not to be interpreted in a sense that gives impunity to wrongdoers, or that the Council of Europe called on Spain in 2005 to investigate the disappearance of children under Franco's dictatorship. Judge Garzón acknowledged that his actions can and should "be debated" in judicial circles to clarify whether they are outlandish or "have sense and consistency." But instead, he felt his enemies were trying to impose their more narrow interpretation of a judge's duty "from above, without permitting questioning or liberty of debate." That showed their animus against him and, he warned, threatened democracy, the independence of the judiciary, and the state of law.[25]

The judicial process against Garzón was lengthy. He won some important procedural decisions in his effort to gain a fair hearing. In the end he was not suspended for his short-lived investigation of wartime killings. Rather, he was found guilty of violating the rights of an accused terrorist because he authorized clandestine taping of conversations between the imprisoned man and his attorney. It is widely felt that politics probably played some role in Garzón's condemnation. An additional factor may have been Garzón's unpopularity with other jurists, who through the years had resented his high profile and what many saw as his penchant for seeking publicity.[26]

The case of Judge Garzón illustrates the fact that international law always risks collision with national sovereignties. Its principles and statutes lack force unless they enjoy the acceptance and cooperation of nation states. At one point Belgium seemed ready to apply to war crimes the principle of universal jurisdiction—the concept that under international law Belgian courts could prosecute those crimes wherever they had occurred. Soon there was an avalanche of objections from other nations. That avalanche led Belgium to change and restrict its laws. Despite the warnings to

Spain from the United Nation's Human Rights Committee and its Committee against Torture, it seems clear that internal politics in Spain and elsewhere will often prove far more influential than those international committees.[27] It is easy to cite examples of other nations that have refused to honor international agreements or laws and succeeded in doing so. U.S. congressmen seem particularly hostile to any limitation on their country's sovereign independence. Without a supreme international authority, nation states that are powerful, influential enough, or stubborn enough may defy an international agreement or principle and do so with impunity. The belief that justice must be obtained, for a true resolution of past conflicts, sometimes finds support under the existing system of international law, but that system is no guarantee.

Rather than judicial proceedings, truth and reconciliation commissions have gained popularity and attention as a way to resolve civil wars or bloody internal conflicts. South Africa, as it moved from apartheid to democracy, furnished the most intriguing example of what such a commission might accomplish, and the idea has spread. In Brazil one branch of the legislature recently voted to create such a body, in order to "examine and clarify" abuses during a forty-two-year period that has been veiled in silence.[28] Some observers believe a truth and reconciliation commission is the surest path to social peace and progress.

In South Africa, the African National Congress, before it came to power, had already investigated abuses and violations of human rights committed by its members. It then proposed a more extensive investigation focused on the repressions of apartheid. By contrast, the formerly dominant, white National Party wanted a reconciliation commission that would confer amnesty on past crimes. The resulting compromise, the Truth and Reconciliation Commission (TRC), was authorized by the Parliament and recognized by the constitution. As established in 1995, the TRC consisted of three committees—those focusing on, respectively, Human Rights Violations, Amnesty, and Reparations and Rehabilitation. A key provision was the fact that those who came before the Human Rights Violations Committee and testified to their acts could gain amnesty. The TRC did not have to accept all applications for amnesty, however, and it could use the subpoena power to further its search for truth. In addition, prosecutions and civil suits could still take place against people who did not apply for amnesty or whose application was denied. The Human Rights Violations Committee began its work first, whereas the Reparations and Rehabilitation Committee later had to make applications for aid and legislative support for its recommendations. The hearings of the Human Rights Violations Committee were televised and included many dramatic moments.[29]

Bishop Desmond Tutu, who led the committee, believed that the "past, far from disappearing or lying down and being quiet, has an embarrassing and persistent way of returning and haunting us unless it has been dealt with adequately." Under his leadership, the Human Rights Violations Committee conducted frequent public hearings and in addition received twenty thousand statements by February of 1998. Emotions ran high in some of the public sessions. Confronted with narratives or confessions of heinous and cruel acts, committee members were sometimes shocked, stunned, or moved to tears. In one session Bishop Tutu, overwhelmed by a horrifying story, buried his face in his hands and then bowed down, prone, before the table in front of him. Witnesses often cried or struggled with powerful emotions. The committee consciously tried to be supportive and empathetic toward those who had suffered and needed to tell their stories. Often such witnesses declared that the act of publicly revealing their painful experience was mentally and emotionally liberating. In one hearing, Cynthia Ngewu, the mother of a young man who was killed by apartheid security forces, struggled with her feelings and then declared, "This thing called reconciliation . . . if it means . . . this man who has killed . . . becomes human again, this man, so that I, so that all of us, get our humanity back . . . then I agree, then I support it all."[30]

Psychologists and psychiatrists who consulted with the TRC advised that the act of testifying was vital to the mental health of victims. The effect of the process, as one psychologist put it, was to affirm to those who had suffered, "You are right, you were damaged, and it was wrong." A man who was blinded by a notoriously ruthless police officer testified, "I feel what has been making me sick all the time is the fact that I couldn't tell my story. But now I—it feels like I got my sight back by coming here and telling you the story." A woman who was tortured at age sixteen said that testifying "has taken it off my heart." Bishop Tutu and others saw the healing potential of the TRC in a religious context, that of forgiveness. "There is no future without forgiveness," declared Tutu, who subsequently published a book by the same title. Certainly some victims, some perpetrators who confessed, and even some ordinary white citizens who recognized their silent culpability in the evils of apartheid would agree.[31]

But academics have pointed out that the body of objective evidence for such therapeutic effects is slim, and longitudinal studies have not been done to demonstrate long-lasting benefits. Other problems with the TRC hearings included the opposition of certain key figures. Former president Frederick De Klerk turned against the process and threatened a lawsuit, declaring that the truth commission was biased. Winnie Mandela also refused to be cooperative, denying her own participation in human rights violations and demanding a public hearing, which she then tried to turn into a popularity contest. Moreover, some participants in the truth commission hearings could not share Tutu's positive feelings. Churchill Mxenge spoke for many of those individuals when he said that Tutu "believes in miracles" and that it was difficult for "people who are hurt and bleeding simply to forget about their wounds and forget about justice. . . . Unless justice is done, it's difficult for any person to think about forgiving." When he and others confronted Bishop Tutu on television, the latter cited political necessity—he argued that amnesty was necessary to avoid military conflict. But Tutu has also commended the African concept of forgiveness incorporated in *ubuntu*. "Retributive justice," he explained, "is largely Western. The African understanding is far more restorative. . . . The justice we hope for is restorative of the dignity of the people."[32]

American law professor Martha Minow argues that the TRC, although it sacrifices some aspects of justice, simultaneously serves important purposes of justice. "Litigation," she writes, "is not an ideal form of social action." In an adversarial system legal trials narrow and foreclose some avenues of investigation. The TRC hearings, on the other hand, sometimes opened up new areas of inquiry. When certain individuals testified to their activities, they implicated others, some of whom then came forward. Others who were implicated but did not testify could still be investigated and prosecuted. The goal of a truth commission was also, in some sense, superior to that of a trial. The central task of the TRC was "to write the history of what happened," whereas "for judges at trials, such histories are [merely] the byproduct" of the battle between prosecution and defense. A truth commission can "cut through myths, rumors, and false pictures about the past," whereas trials of individuals may obscure the larger picture. To the extent that the TRC ensured some accountability, identified perpetrators, discouraged violence, strengthened institutions, and encouraged respect for human rights, it also was supporting some of goals of a criminal justice system. If it also restored dignity, aided emotional or psychological healing, and promoted reconciliation in society, the tradeoff with absolute justice was probably well worth the sacrifice.[33]

Jonathan Allen, a political scientist and also a South African, agreed, advancing arguments that concepts such as justice, reconciliation, peace, and unity are not mutually exclusive or at war with each other. To Allen it was not clear that truth and reconciliation commissions always benefited the victims or promoted healing. Nor did he agree that truth is essential for healing, because some truths might be so incendiary that the only viable option for a society is "amnesty and amnesia." But Allen also rejected the unqualified claim that one must do justice "though the heavens fall." Sometimes doing justice without regard to the social consequences "is bound to wreak havoc in politics." South Africa's TRC was never likely to bring about "communal intimacy" in the society, but it furthered some of the goals of punitive justice while educating people's sense of injustice. Allen defended a "principled compromise" between justice and unity, which could retain the central elements of both. He also believed that the TRC could counter a history of "disrespect for justice and individual rights" and help to overcome the tendency toward authoritarianism in South African political culture.[34]

A number of leaders in South Africa used socially oriented arguments to defend the TRC as superior to a purely judicial process. After observing a TRC hearing, Antjie Krog, a South African poet and journalist, wrote that it had "little to do with the past. It has everything to do with the future." "Forgiveness is a personal matter," stated the South African justice minister, Dullah Omar. "However, bitterness can only exacerbate tensions in society," whereas the TRC "can help to achieve a nation reconciled with its past and at peace with itself." Scholars have noted that these comments illuminate the difference between the value of forgiveness for a person and reconciliation for a society. Whereas a person forgives to free himself from the corrosive effects of hating, reconciliation for a society does not depend on the emotional states of individuals. Forgiveness by an individual may involve forgetting, but reconciliation is a social process that requires "the rehabilitation of relationships rather than the refusal to relate." Something shattered in society has to be repaired; relationships of civic and moral equality have to be established or reinstated. That is what Nelson Mandela meant when he spoke of "undoing the continuing effects of the past." In the words of Professor June O'Connor, "Joint action and cooperation" become the path "for constructing something greater than we now have." Grasping the essence of that idea, Kader Asmal, another government minister, said, "We must deliberately sacrifice the formal trappings of justice, the courts and the trials for an even higher good: Truth. . . . We sacrifice justice for truth so as to consolidate democracy, to close the chapter of the past and to avoid confrontation."[35]

This pragmatic but challenging perspective brings us closer to the realities of power that shaped the process of reconciliation in Spain and the United States. Reconciliation—even in the South African experience—is largely a negotiation between the opposing sides. In fact, it is not an open discussion in which both sides consider new directions and new ideas. Rather, it is a negotiation powerfully shaped by past circumstances, one in which each side is likely to insist on certain minimal conditions and stubbornly hold to its beliefs. However valuable truth telling, confessions, pardons, and forgiveness may be, both for individuals and for the society as a whole, these will never involve all the citizens. Many individuals on both of the opposing sides will remain essentially unreconciled, accepting as a necessity some measures of coexistence but refusing to meet their opponents on new mental ground. For a society, reconciliation will have a limited meaning without measures to change the structure of future social relations.

These facts were very evident in the post–Civil War United States, where the war did not remove the cancer of racial inequality. For the victorious North, the preservation of the Union was non-negotiable, but establishing and maintaining equal rights for African Americans never was a priority. Economically, northern textile factories wanted to buy southern cotton once again, but the North's path to rapid industrialization did not depend on southern cooperation. Defeated white Confederates were willing to accept the reality of reunion, but on matters of race they were determined and insistent. Ironically, their intransigence made Reconstruction more demanding and thorough, for a few years, than northerners would otherwise have required. But by 1872 in most states and 1877 everywhere, southern whites had reestablished racist control of their communities. Racism and white domination of black southerners became the currency of postwar reconciliation.

What southern whites further sought, and in a sense demanded, was respect. This the North provided after 1876 in paeans to the courage and dedication of soldiers on both sides. Resentment of northern power, the war's destruction, and Reconstruction continued to be strong in the South, and the work of white-supremacist politicians, army veterans, and southern women turned that resentment into a long-lasting ideology of the Lost Cause. Northerners, for their part, congratulated themselves on winning the war and freeing the slaves; they also took pleasure in feeling superior to the South for many generations, while industrialization, urbanization, immigration, and other social changes diverted much of their attention from wartime issues.

For Spain the concept of reconciliation—limited or more extensive—had little relevance in 1939, because Franco was determined to impose a society shaped only by his wishes. But the nature of reconciliation as a negotiation between powerful interests was clearly evident in the early years of the Transition. The strength of democratic forces derived from the crisis of the dictatorial regime, the continuously increasing resistance to it, and the widespread desire of the populace for change. But conservative forces remained numerous and powerful. Both the army and the inflexible Franquista politicians known as the Bunker presented a real danger to democratic government, and groups that had prospered economically under Franco's system were ready to defend their interests. What emerged from the confrontation of these opposing forces was a two-pronged settlement: democracy was allowed to proceed as long as it was not too influenced by the Left and amnesty became the currency of democratic progress. Spain could move in the direction of a modern, democratic, European society as long as it ignored the past and did not embrace the future too precipitously.

A key fact—and important similarity—in both societies was that there was no wholesale replacement of personnel from the old regime, no purging of those who had been powerful from the political and cultural life of the future. This fact undoubtedly retarded change. The adoption of amnesty in Spain's Transition meant that in all parts of society individuals who had been deeply involved in the system created by the dictatorship continued to hold positions of power and influence. Politically the king avoided reliance on any of Franco's former ministers, and the electorate supported candidates from the center or center-Left rather than those too closely linked to the old regime. But in vital sectors of society—the judiciary, the army, major companies, the universities, even honorary societies such as the royal academies—the men of Franco's era continued to have weight. Their influence would be felt in decisions they reached, opinions they disseminated, and rising leaders they blocked or promoted.

Likewise, in the United States the political elite of the Old South—that other United States that had been dedicated to inequality, aristocracy, and a system of slavery that could not be questioned—continued to run affairs. True, early in Reconstruction white southern voters tended to choose members of the old elite who had been reluctant to secede rather than the fire-eaters who led the region into disaster. The Fourteenth Amendment then barred leaders of the Confederacy from holding public office unless Congress decided by a two-thirds vote of each house to remove the disability. Congress quickly did so at the beginning of the 1870s, and the old leaders returned to power. Before 1876, when white racism had reestablished control of governments, the political elite again was largely that of prewar days. These men continued to defend entrenched economic interests, feed a sense of regional resentment, and praise the Lost Cause. As the South's agriculture went into economic decline, they allied with newer economic interests, continued to promote white supremacy, and set the tone of society around racism and the Lost Cause.

The impact of the continued influence of these old elites was great. In Spain the church, as a privately governed institution answering ultimately to the pope, was able to make its own decisions about change. With the Vatican's movement away from liberal doctrines, the church hierarchy in Spain has remained very conservative. In the army, the police forces, and the judiciary the continuity of personnel was "overwhelming" writes Paloma Aguilar Fernández. In the 1980s and even into the 1990s, when young school children who had been born after 1975 visited the Military Historical Service, they learned essentially the same things children had been taught in 1945. The room where children viewed documents from the civil war was called "The War of Liberation," and a friendly staff screened for them a partisan, pro-Franco video. Fifty-four years after the end of the civil war, the Museum of the Army still described the war as a "Crusade of Liberation" in which the "glorious National army" triumphed over "red hordes." A major newspaper continued to use such terminology in its press archive as late as 1994.[36]

The influence of old leadership in many levels of society could be both obvious and subtle. An illustration of the many ways this influence was felt surfaced in 2011, when the Royal Academy of History published a long-awaited, fifty-volume Spanish Biographical Dictionary. The academy, which was authorized by King Felipe V in 1738 and receives financial support from the Ministry of Education and the Ministry of Culture, had been the subject of criticism from time to time in the past. Some had noted that the academy inducted very few female honorees as members and tended to publish history in the old style, with emphasis on kings and queens or battles of the Reconquest. The historians who enjoyed membership generally were not among those most current with recent trends in professional scholarship, such as emphasis on social or cultural history. Nevertheless, there was surprise and shock in many parts of Spain when people read the biographical essay on Franco and found that it avoided calling him a dictator. That entry had been written by a politically conservative medieval historian, the biographical entry for Valencia's mayor had been written by one of her advisors, and the biography of General Alfonso Armada, who played an important role in the attempted military coup of 1981, was written by his son-in-law. By contrast, many of the most respected historians of the twentieth century in Spain or other countries had not been asked to participate. A number of important entries had a pro-Franco or anti-Republican cast.[37]

After controversy erupted, Spain's largest newspaper, *El País*, interviewed Gonzalo Anes, the director of the Real Academia de la Historia. His answers to the periodical's questions revealed the detached, insulated mentality that had been preserved in and propagated by that prestigious organization. Pressed to explain his view of Franco's biography, Anes stressed his respect for the author of that entry. When asked if that entry was "rigorous and objective," he replied, "I don't want to be a judge." Later he acknowledged that since he had lived in the era of Franco, he "did not feel any curiosity" about what had been written about the *caudillo*. When asked for his personal opinion on whether Franco was a dictator, Anes said, "Look, I am tired and I have to go." With irritation he claimed that in no other European country would there be this kind of criticism. On the issue of editorial policy he said that it would be difficult to make corrections even when a lack of objectivity is clear "because to do that it would be necessary to read all the texts." Moreover, if the academics who commissioned the volumes had taken upon themselves to revise the texts, "it never would have been published." Repeatedly trying to put an end to questions, Anes declared that the authors were responsible for their entries and that the academy trusted in their abilities. To a final question about any deficiencies in the academy, he admitted that it needed "more women." But he explained away this fact by saying that a historian needs to spend many hours in the archives, and "unfortunately, for the women those thousands of hours are dedicated to raising their children and being housewives."[38]

In the United States the continued influence of the old elite meant that southern politics fell under the domination of a Democratic Party that glorified the Confederacy, the Lost Cause, the Ku Klux Klan, and resistance to Reconstruction. White supremacy was made into the fundamental cause of the South, and racism became the tool to enforce white unity behind the Democratic Party whenever a political challenge arose. Another tactic used over and over again to maintain the Solid South was to warn against outside threats and outside agitators. The mentality of a defensive, isolated, but gallant South helped Democratic leaders to deflect attention from the problems of their society and the effects of their rule. These powerful social currents, aided by women's groups such as the United Daughters of the Confederacy, shaped and inhibited the region's culture. Conformity to white supremacy, segregation, and Democratic Party rule was a social imperative for generations of southerners who were indoctrinated in the belief that they had suffered grave injustice with the defeat of their glorious Lost Cause. Had the diverse political leaders of so-called Radical Reconstruction continued to exercise some power or influence, the South would have been a very different society.

Both Spain and the United States have been slow to confront their troubled pasts. Successful avoidance was greater in the United States and lasted for a longer period than in Spain, where debates over amnesty have been frequent since the Transition. In Spain a series of laws, though often partial in nature, have been enacted through the post-Transition decades to give dignity and benefits to those who suffered from Franco's repression. In the United States one hundred years elapsed before the success of the civil rights movement changed both discriminatory laws and the parameters of discussion in respectable society. But social redemption or "communal intimacy" are impossible to achieve in any large society. Attempts to create the religiously inspired "beloved community" of which Martin Luther King Jr. spoke soon lost traction, and more radical ideas have been ignored. Books and conferences have raised the concept of reparations for past wrongs of slavery, but relatively few beyond its advocates see value in the idea. On the other hand, symbolic action by various legislatures and organizations has been forthcoming, in the form of official apologies for slavery or for slaveholding. It is easy (and probably justified), however, to be cynical about such pronouncements. They change little, while they allow politicians to congratulate themselves and then quickly move on to other concerns.

But demands for justice will continue to appear, especially since they now can arise from distant parts of the world. In 2010 Darío Rivas, a ninety-year-old Gallego who has lived in Argentina from age nine, appeared in an Argentine court to demand that it act against the crimes of the Franco era, just as Judge Baltasar Garzón from Madrid had initiated the arrest of Chile's Pinochet. Over the years Rivas had visited Spain and sought information about members of his family who were executed during the civil war, and in 2005 he gave the bones of his father a dignified burial. In 2011 Rivas carried his crusade to Spain and asked, "Why have [the Spaniards] delayed so long? . . . What can one expect of a country that doesn't dare to say that Franco was a dictator? Franquismo isn't finished, and the best proof is the maneuvering against Garzón." Rivas explained his perspective on justice long delayed:

> The most important thing is not to seek punishment of the guilty. I have no intention of putting [Manuel] Fraga on trial at his age, but I want the guilty to be painted as guilty and those [who were] shot [acknowledged] as heroes. Because they were heroes: good men and women who did not deserve to die shot in the back.[39]

Similarly, Argentina's example of turning the Army Mechanical School into a museum to document the wrongs committed there has inspired citizens in Spain. In Navarre a coalition of at least seven civic organizations has launched a campaign to preserve a prison used in the days of the war and dictatorship. They desire to restore it both to recognize the suffering of its inmates and "to strengthen a culture of respect for human rights." Having obtained a royal decree that the site possesses cultural interest, these groups are working to document the structure of the prison and its history as they draw up plans for its transformation. Their effort gains inspiration from, and their reports explicitly cite, projects that have been realized in Germany, Argentina, and the Republic of South Africa. What has been accomplished in those nations illustrates the key role of civil society and citizens' organizations "in the battle for the memory and recognition of human rights, as much during the dictatorship as afterwards."[40]

A sensitive, balanced, and fair-minded perspective on moving beyond the wrongs of the past is difficult. In spite of strong and persistent collective emotions, it sometimes finds a voice in individuals, despite the fact that Spain and the United States have not fully disentangled their present from their violent histories. For example, an opinion piece by Antonio Burgos in the generally conservative newspaper *El Mundo* echoed the words of the Second Republic's Manuel Azaña. Burgos urged "honor to the defeated. To all the defeated." He then explained that "we were all defeated in the civil war, even those born afterwards, and we waited many years to begin enjoying our liberties." In another conservative newspaper, a member of the Spanish Royal Academy, Francisco Nieva, counseled patience and tolerance as emotions welled up over past conflict, because "the memory of pain is not destroyed easily." It endures as a "monumental and subterranean structure." In the midst of the controversy over the Law of Historical Memory, César Hornero Méndez, a professor of civil law, noted but put aside the fact that this issue had triggered considerable political opportunism. Rising above partisanship, he insisted in *ABC* that the law gave Spain an important opportunity—an opportunity "to do justice" to victims of the war and dictatorship, "to repair definitively and in a collective form, the injustice suffered." Hornero Méndez warns that the passage of time often does more to deepen wrongs than to right them. More important than sentimentalism and desires for vengeance or victory, fairness, he insisted, "is something that we owe to our democracy, if we don't want to be weighed down by ghosts. . . . Such phantoms should only inhabit our disgraced past."[41]

Americans are much given to celebrating their history—recounting and praising each of its triumphs—but in public discourse they rarely admit or analyze past problems and failures. Yet a balanced and insightful consideration of the central problem of race is possible, as Barack Obama demonstrated during his 2008 campaign. Under criticism because the pastor of his church had harshly criticized the United States, Obama took on the divisive issue of racism and racial justice and demonstrated fairness to whites and blacks. After noting that the nation's founders wrote a Constitution "unfinished" and "stained" by the existence of slavery, Obama explained his affection for and disagreements with his former pastor. Then he turned to citizens' feelings about race, past and present. Discrimination and inequalities handicapped African Americans and their families in manifold ways. Remarkably, "many men and women overcame the odds," but "there were many who didn't make it," and their frustrations sometimes found expression as anger. "Similar anger exists," Obama then pointed out, among whites who have never felt "particularly privileged by their race," who have "worked hard all their lives," and who fear that "an African American is getting an advantage in landing a good job or a spot in a good college because of an injustice that they themselves never committed." Such legitimate emotions often go unexpressed in "polite company," but they are part of "the complexities of race . . . that we've never really worked through." Recognizing each other's "legitimate concerns" is required to overcome the "racial stalemate." Challenging his listeners, Obama then affirmed that "working together we can move beyond some of our old racial wounds, and that in fact we have no choice if we are to continue on the path of a more perfect union." Effort will be required from all groups to open "the path to understanding" and "insist on a full measure of justice in every aspect of American life." But by "binding our particular grievances . . . to the larger aspirations of all Americans," Obama said, it would be possible to escape the grip of a past that "isn't dead and buried."[42]

The past is the occupational realm of historians—their daily work—and scholars have debated what their stance toward these social issues should be. As citizens and professionals, historians may naturally form a desire, as Carl Becker puts it, "to do work in the world." That is, they might aspire to write history that is not only of scholarly value but also has a salutary impact in society. Becker defines the appropriate impact and the historian's proper role as "correcting and rationalizing for common use Mr. Everyman's mythological adaption of what actually happened." That process is never simple, however, when the subject involves divisions so deep that they led to civil wars. One issue that inevitably leads to controversy is the extent to which history involves moral judgment. Another is the power of myths, exerting their influence on society and acting in opposition to the findings of historical research.

Wars in which thousands or hundreds of thousands of people were killed present unavoidable questions of morality. Bitter debate over the moral positions of the opposing sides can persist long afterward. Some would argue that, in the face of such questions, judgment cannot be suspended and a society cannot heal until it has addressed the wrongs of the past. Without "resolving the problem of justice," citizens cannot reach a "shared vision" that allows them to embrace the future. "A theory of justice that does not bring up the memory of injustice is unthinkable," argues Professor Reyes Mate from a philosophical perspective. "Without memory of injustice the past horror is as if it never had existed." Morality, as one of his colleagues notes, demands a suspension of time and lacks an expiration date, since moral issues claim eternal relevance. But for contemporary social relations, when does it make sense to stop making judgments? Do historians and citizens today need to judge people's actions thirty years in the past? Seventy-five years in the past? One hundred fifty years in the past? Are moral judgments required over events of long-ago centuries? History, argues Eduardo Manzano, can recognize cruelty, extermination, or horror in past events, but "there is no judgment" involved, for making judgments "is not an essential element of our historical approach. We can feel empathy for distant suffering, but . . . we don't judge Roman slavery" since that "is not the mission of our historical knowledge."[43] Absent the need to judge, people become free to leave old battles behind, but such consensus is difficult to achieve; perhaps it never comes merely through persuasion.

Even more problematic for the historian is the difficulty of being heard on deeply emotional conflicts. Scholars in Spain have been investigating all aspects of the civil war, energetically and with complete freedom since the Transition, yet it is the simplistic books that recycled old propaganda and hoary arguments that have become best sellers. Similarly, historians in the United States have dismantled the distortions and inventions of the Lost Cause, yet James Loewen finds that many ordinary citizens, and even the large majority of secondary-school teachers, subscribed to the myths rather than the documented history. Before such facts professional historians can only admit their weakness. The more historians address the live historical issues in contemporary society, observes Eduardo Manzano ruefully, "the more the social debates surpass us." As for those who defend myths, "We are not going to convince them." Nevertheless, insists Ramón López Facal, historians have to counter a mythical history, even if the history in books takes a long time to reach public awareness. Historians have to combat erroneous and biased memories "to avoid that a false knowledge of the past is constructed." Sociologist Julio Carabaña affirms that scholars are needed to supply a brake on historical memories that are biased and partial.[44]

For any once divided society, the achievement of a shared and accurate understanding of its history is healthy but difficult. In the long run, excellent scholarship will be heard, but it is frequently ignored in the short run. Scholars cannot change human nature, and human beings often give their allegiance to fiery emotions rather than cold rationality. Especially is this true when the divisive conflicts of the past still resonate with contemporary problems and issues. Distance from the troubled past is the product of economic and social change more than reflection or the mere passage of time, which may have little effect. To the extent that the basic circumstances of life remain unchanged, time becomes irrelevant; in fact, it may even deepen the hold of former attitudes, turning them into ancient truths. But as the foundations of social reality alter and the circumstances of daily life take on a new character, society can more easily accept hard truths and discard old controversies. It gains an ability to leave its past in the past and move into a different future.

That is happening in both Spain and the United States, as broad-scale economic change in both countries has altered the social landscape. The decades since 1865 and 1939 provide abundant evidence that conflicts from the civil wars have a long life and are prolonged by interested parties, but they also show the way in which change erodes continuity. The desire of a few individuals to "overcome the past,"⁴⁵ to rise above enmity and engage a different future after a destructive war, is laudable but rarely is achievable for an entire society. Substantial numbers of people will defend old positions or insist on the validity of their grievances, and the next generation may revive propaganda or condemn efforts to "forget." Eventually, however, the world moves on, and changed realities allow acceptance of bitter truths about a troubled past. As progressively greater numbers acknowledge the past, historical wounds close, even those of bloody civil war.

5

Economic Change and the Transformation of Cultural Landscapes

> We regard economic conditions as that which ultimately conditions historical development.... Political, juridical, philosophical, religious, literary, artistic, etc., development is based on economic development. But all these react upon one another and also upon the economic basis.
>
> Friedrich Engels to Heinz Starkenburg, January 25, 1894

> The ultimately determining element in history is the production and reproduction of real life.
>
> Friedrich Engels to Joseph Bloch, September 21–22, 1890

On December 22, 2010, members of the social elite in Charleston, South Carolina, gathered for a festive party and dance. This was Charleston's commemorative secession ball, marking the 150th anniversary of the day that South Carolina left the Union. Affluent men and women dressed up in period costume, wearing long-tailed coats or elaborate hoop skirts. The state's history and its devotion to the principle of states' rights were honored by everyone—or almost everyone. One important attendee was David J. Rutledge, the great-great-great-grandson of the man who had been president of South Carolina's secession convention. David Rutledge took part in the festivities, but despite his family's history, he candidly announced to his friends, "You're going to be mad at me.... I believe it was about slavery."[1]

Unquestionably, these words from David Rutledge marked a sea change taking place in the state where secession began. What explains such evolution? How do the scars from deep historical wounds eventually disappear?

In both Spain and the United States the influence of civil war has been strong and persistent. Long after the fighting ended, memories and ideologies, political loyalties and priorities, continued to reflect the divisions of wartime. But history is a constantly evolving mixture of continuity and change, and in both nations economic developments have been dramatic. For the United States economic change came slowly to the South, and that region's economic stasis long reinforced its social and cultural immersion in the values of the Lost Cause. Seventy years elapsed before the currents leading to a new economy gathered force. But then they launched what soon became a transformation affecting many aspects of life. In Spain the pace of change has been more rapid. Only a generation after the Spanish Civil War significant developments in the economy began to alter long-established patterns, and new directions continued to make a strong impact after the end of Franco's dictatorship.

The significance of these changes extended far beyond the economic realm. Citizens in both countries gained new jobs and better incomes, which were welcome improvements, to be sure. But a large proportion of citizens also found that they were living dramatically different lives, for economic change brought social and cultural transformations in its wake. People moved to new locations, took up new lifestyles, and felt the influence of unfamiliar cultural currents. The substance and pattern of daily life changed for millions of southerners in the United States, and for millions of Spaniards, as a changed economy introduced people to a different social reality.

The forces that stimulated these transformations were different in the two nations, but for both the primary impetus came from outside. International politics, tourism, and the policies and opportunities of the European Community played a major role in Spain. In the U.S. South, federal laws combined with migration flows and technological developments to change the labor market and create both an altered incentive structure and more welcoming social climate. These developments broke down the cultural and economic isolation of a South known for segregation and Lost Cause memories; they spurred its integration into the national economy. For both nations different types of changes became mutually reinforcing as they gathered momentum.

With changes in people's daily lives came changes in their thinking. The key elements of daily reality—where one lived, how one worked, who were one's neighbors, and what were one's surroundings—altered, shifting personal experience in new directions. Culture is persistent, of course, and established beliefs and ways of thinking are not taken off and thrown aside like a piece of clothing. But the extent of change in one's day-to-day world—stemming ultimately from economic transformation—enables greater or lesser change in beliefs, ideologies, and values. It is changes of this type that finally can permit the "great historical wounds" to heal or—to put it more accurately—give people reason to feel that their present and future no longer are governed by the divisions of the past. The kind of economic and social transformations that have taken place in Spain and the U.S. South offer hope for reconciliation among the once warring sides and values. For when the memories, myths, and hatreds of the past lose their relevance for the present, other concerns can finally take their place and allow past events to become . . . merely history. Though history, in this sense, remains important, it no longer is controlling but can be understood as someone else's experience in another time.

* * *

Prior to the twentieth century, Spain's hierarchical and rural society was dominated by an agricultural sector that was inefficient and exploitative toward the laborers. Less than a quarter of the population was urban in 1857, even by a standard that defined as urban any town with as few as five thousand residents. Landholdings of medium size were scarce. The north had many small farms, and in Galicia traditional patterns of ownership divided the land into a crazy quilt of many small, noncontiguous parcels. In the south, on the other hand, landholdings were large but generally less efficient. The major political events of the nineteenth century had benefited wealthy landowners at the expense of the poor families that did the work of cultivating the land. When church lands were disentailed in 1836–37, nobles bought up properties and increased the extent of latifundism, or excessively large holdings. In the 1850s, when more Catholic Church lands were sold, the rich again were the major beneficiaries. But these land barons were neither progressive nor productive. They formed a "narrow-minded class of absentee landowners" who dominated politics, enjoyed life in resorts, and "rarely visited their estates except for such pastimes as hunting, shooting and the rigging of elections." Modernization of agriculture took a back seat to pleasure, while tariffs protected their incomes. Meanwhile the farm workers and their families suffered, as did the industrial workers where factories had begun to emerge in Catalonia and the Basque Country.²

The early signs of a more modern economy began to develop after 1875, and by 1900 the percentage of the population that lived in towns larger than five thousand had doubled. Settlement was most dense on the periphery of the nation, which included the developing industrial areas, some of whose products were cushioned in a number of ways from the effects of the loss of Spain's colonies. But conditions in agriculture remained difficult without reform. In 1914 Spain's per capita income was only one-third that of Britain and the nation "could accurately be described as an underdeveloped country, with closer affinity to the backward countries of Eastern and southern Europe than to the advanced nations of the north-west." Spain benefited as a nonparticipant from World War I, and there were some years of prosperity and economic progress during the dictatorship of Primo de Rivera, who encouraged irrigation and improvements in infrastructure. By the eve of the Second Republic, in 1930, industrial workers had grown to become 26.5 percent of the work force and agriculturalists had fallen from 66 percent in 1910 to 45.5 percent. Electrical output and the production of iron ore were rising, but Primo de Rivera could not challenge the large landholders, so little or no agricultural reform took place. The land reforms of the Second Republic were blocked, and with the Great Depression most of the unemployed were agricultural workers, who lacked work much of the year even when they had employment.³

With Spain's descent into civil war, human and material destruction led to suffering that continued through the decade of the 1940s. Counting wartime deaths and exiles from the Republican side, Spain lost as many as a million people in the 1930s, among them many skilled workers, technicians, and scientists. Although a boom in the postwar birthrate would replenish population numbers, regaining economic ground was difficult. Franco initially pursued a policy of autarky, desiring self-sufficiency, and after the Allied victory in World War II most of the developed world shunned commerce with Spain. "Output plunged sharply" after the civil war, "and during the decade of the 1940s gross domestic output was on average little more than 10 per cent above the level of 1931" while the population became one-third greater. Franco banned rural labor organizations and forced wages in the countryside down "to 1936 levels." While rural farm laborers suffered, the regime's supporters enjoyed "a period of remarkable prosperity," especially those large landowners who channeled much of their crop to the lucrative black market. These conservative favorites of the regime purchased luxuries or more land rather than investing in and modernizing their operations.[4]

Although the repression of Franco's dictatorship continued, positive economic changes began to occur in the 1950s. The first strong impetus for progress came, ironically, from the United States' desire to create military bastions against its rival in the Cold War, the Soviet Union. In 1953 the leading democracy of the "Free World" entered into an alliance with Spain's formerly pro-Fascist dictator in order to establish military bases on the Iberian Peninsula. And the United States had a great deal of money to spend. In the first seven years of the agreement, Spain received almost 1.5 billion dollars—$618.2 million in grants, $404 million in loans, and $436.8 million in military aid. Over the next seven years the total amount of money injected into the Spanish economy fell but still amounted to nearly half a billion dollars. Under the terms of the alliance Spain had to spend part of the money it received on purchases of U.S military equipment. Nevertheless, the influx of these sums sent ripples of spending and investment through a formerly enfeebled economy. Moreover, it set off a period of economic success that "was due less to policy action than to [this and other] external influences."[5]

Among the most important of these additional factors was "a boom in tourist earnings." Spain's warm climate and sunny beaches had always had the potential to attract Northern Europeans weary of cold weather and gray skies. Yet only 4.2 million tourists visited Spain in 1959. With increasing postwar prosperity in Europe and a new willingness of the Madrid government to accede to the pleas of local mayors—even if that meant foreigners in skimpy bathing suits—tourism increased. Areas such as Benidorm began to invest heavily in facilities to attract visitors, the British and Germans especially, and hotels and restaurants sprang up along the coast. Spain was on its way to becoming one of the major tourist destinations in the Western world. In the early 1960s tourism became "the principal engine of growth in the services sector." The expansion of tourism helped lift the services sector to the status of Spain's leading industry. "Growing at double the rate of increase of GDP," services "played a key role both as an income generator and as a source of employment." From providing 31 percent of employment in 1960, the services sector expanded to 66 percent of employment by 1999. Tourism directly employed 10 percent of the work force, and by 2001 Spain ranked second only to France in foreign visitors and behind only the United States in terms of tourism earnings. In that year forty-nine million people stayed one night or more, and the total with day visitors exceeded seventy-four million people.[6]

Not everyone in the growing Spanish population could find work in tourism, however, and the birthrate had soared after a bloody civil war. Thus the economic expansion of the 1950s and 1960s also benefited substantially from emigration. With too few jobs in a national economy just beginning to emerge from a stunted condition, many Spaniards looked to other countries in Northern and Western Europe—such as Germany and Switzerland—as places to find steady and better-paid work. Between 1959 and 1973 almost two million citizens left Spain to work abroad, and roughly seven hundred thousand of these individuals never returned. The departure of these people tended not only to alleviate suffering and unemployment at home, but it also provided another source of external stimulus. Spain's emigrants sent large amounts of money back home, and their remittances aided relatives, whose spending then boosted the domestic economy.[7]

Foreign investment by this point began to add its weight to the growth of Spain's economy. As government policy makers paid attention to the benefits that could come from international sources, they began to lay the groundwork for greater involvement by foreign businesses. After joining the Organization for European Economic Cooperation (OEEC) and the International Monetary Fund (IMF) and the World Bank, Spain gained $420 million from the OEEC, $75 million in IMF drawing rights, $70 million in commercial credits from big U.S. banks, and $30 million in loans to foreign companies from the U.S. Import-Export Bank. Between 1959 and 1973, "direct foreign investment . . . increased twenty-sevenfold." In the decade of the 1960s taken as a whole, "foreign investment accounted for about 10 per cent of gross capital formation and 20 percent of gross industrial investment." Money from abroad was continuing to boost the Spanish economy and fuel its growth. It proved especially valuable for the auto industry and for chemicals during the 1960s.[8]

Economic policies adopted by the Franco regime after 1959 deserve some credit for these changes, but not the primary credit. A group of economic technocrats connected with Opus Dei came into office at the end of the 1950s, and they modeled their policies on French development strategies. The regime favored irrigation and participated directly in various industries, such as shipbuilding, steel, aluminum, oil refining, and auto manufacturing. Under the First Development Plan the number of tractors "rose from 53,000 in 1960 to 130,000 in 1964 and 295,000 in 1972." Large landholders benefited most from these changes, as latifundia in the South remained. In fact, as of 1979, "large estates which comprise one per cent of all holdings still occupy 49 per cent of the cultivated land surface in Spain." Moreover, "the Spanish authorities continued to squander vast amounts of funds on the protection of staple crops," especially grains, while consumer demand was shifting toward dairy products and meats. Most economists agree that tourism and external investment did more than government policies to account for a high growth rate of 7.9 percent per year between 1959 and 1972. Cheap imports of petroleum before the oil shock of the 1970s also were beneficial.[9]

The cumulative effect of these changes was to upend the lives of millions of Spaniards and shatter rigid social patterns that had endured for centuries. Between 1960 and 1975 "almost 5 million Spaniards (15 per cent of the entire population) abandoned the countryside." This exodus constituted "the largest movement of people in Spain's demographic history." One part of this movement, the emigration to foreign countries, alone "accounted for 20 per cent of Spain's agricultural labour force and 12.5 per cent of the non-agricultural working class." Those who left the countryside were overwhelmingly the struggling farm laborers who had been locked into an exploitative social system; they or their parents had fought for the Republicans or tried to seize lands during the civil war. Now, however, they moved to large and growing cities and found higher-paying jobs in Spain or abroad. By 1970 cities whose population exceeded one hundred thousand people were home to 38 percent of the nation's population. This figure represented an increase of 60 percent in only twenty years, and the process of urbanization continued. What was once a rural nation now has four-fifths of its population living in cities, with several million people residing in centers such as Madrid, Barcelona, and Sevilla.[10]

After Franco's death, the decision by Spain's democratic governments to enter the European Union strengthened and extended the changes that were modernizing and transforming the economy and society. After a period of stagnation following the Transition, rapid growth resumed in the late 1980s. Both domestic demand and foreign direct investment increased. The growth of foreign direct investment was "massive" and aided much needed industrial restructuring and technological modernization. Foreign capital's control of Spanish industry rose from 11 per cent in 1981 to 36.5 percent in 1990, with the United States now playing a lesser role behind the nations of the European Union (EU). After Spain became a member of the EU, most foreign investment went into high-tech sectors such as "electronics, aerospace equipment, computers and office automation, and chemicals." This fact enabled Spain to move from a position of advantage in unskilled labor, when it joined the EU, to having an advantage in technology-intensive sectors by 2000.[11]

After 1986, when customs barriers were removed, Spain began to run trade deficits with the EU, but it also was the largest beneficiary of funds from the union. These came in the form of agricultural subsidies and regional, social, and cohesion funds. Foreign trade rose from 18 percent of GDP in 1970–79 to 43 percent in 1997, and only a decade after entry in the EU foreign trade amounted to 65 percent of GDP. Agricultural exports shrank comparatively until they made up only 10 percent of this foreign commerce. The leading areas of export goods were chemicals, metallurgical goods, machinery, transport materials, motor vehicles, and horticultural produce. Some of the nation's modernized industries—such as footwear, textiles, clothing, ceramics, glassware, and drinks—have performed well in world markets. Meanwhile, Spanish companies increased their foreign investment markedly during the 1980s, and "in recent years, Spain has become one of the leading international investors." Some Spanish banks and communications companies have developed large operations in Latin America.[12]

All is not healthy in the Spanish economy, especially during the current crisis that Americans have called "the great recession." In Europe this crisis has ravaged countries such as Ireland, Portugal, and Greece and had a severe impact on Spain. The Spanish economy had become overly dependent in recent decades on construction and tourism. Even though the government of the PSOE's José Luis Rodríguez Zapatero was fiscally responsible in balancing the budget, it took no action to burst the economic bubble. The subsequent recession in the West's economies hit tourism and construction hard, revealing overextension in banking. A longstanding problem of persistently high unemployment compared to other European nations became far worse.[13] At this writing the Spanish economy is suffering from a long recession and unemployment of 25 percent. Nevertheless, in broad historical perspective, there has been a transformation of the economy in the past half century.

Such a broad and dramatic transformation has profound implications for social life and social consciousness. As Marx and Engels argued, economic realities condition or influence all the other areas of thought and experience; for the individual living in society, they shape the nature of "real life." Since the most dramatic of the changes in the Spanish economy have taken place since the civil war, they have tended to remove people from the realities and associations of that war and that era. Landless and exploited day laborers in southern agriculture, who were desperate and unemployed most of the year, moved to urban areas and became city dwellers. Their urbanized children have never known the harsh and rigidly stratified rural life—dominated by the local landlord, the priest, and the doctor—endured by their parents. Defeated Republicans lived to see a democratic, Europe-oriented, secular Spain led by Socialist governments and free from the church's domination, a Spain such as the leaders of the Second Republic had desired. Old elites that had ruled the countryside or monopolized privilege under Franco have lost rank and been pushed aside by new leaders in business, banking, and industry. In short, the Spanish economy is not at all what it was at the time of the civil war, and thus the realities of daily life are very different in the modern nation.

As all the other chapters of this book attest, culture changes more slowly than modern economies, and the legacies of the civil war live on in Spanish society in many ways. But just as social connections—through families, organizations, and culture—keep memories and myths of the civil war alive, economic change reshapes the foundations of society and makes a new and different consciousness possible. Many *nietos* have wanted to reexamine issues that war placed out of bounds for their grandparents and that the Transition to democracy made unattractive for their parents. Their demands that graves be identified and notice taken of injustices suffered by the losing side served to revive old issues and arguments. But at the same time there was evidence that this generation was moving on. Opinion surveys repeatedly showed that it had less tolerance than other Spaniards for Franco's dictatorship and a greater identification with democracy and Europe.

The frank discussion of the past has caused discomfort and controversy. It also has provoked cries of "foul" from those who may have been linked, through family or political connections, to long-ago killings or repressions they did not commit. But the recrudescence of debate about the civil war has spawned few new myths or dangerous excuses, and it is likely that succeeding generations will be less burdened by its legacy. As the contemporary world brings new and pressing problems to the table, these can push past divisions further into the background. In this connection, it is worth noting that debates about the civil war held a prominent place in Spanish politics from consideration of the Law of Historical Memory through 2010. But around that point the pressing concerns over recession, unemployment, weakened banks, and sovereign debt crises moved to center stage as economic dangers and distress became acute. Spain's political parties spar over these economic issues now, for they are far more meaningful and immediate than arguments about the past. Although at this moment economic problems seem likely to darken the horizon for a number of years, in the future other issues are sure to become dominant and require attention. Thus a changed Spain will continue to remember its civil war, but there is reason to believe that it will be better able to view it objectively, as the past plays a diminished role in citizens' present.

In a similar fashion, change remade the U.S. South. On the western side of the Atlantic, change came more slowly, even tardily. For eighty or ninety years little that was transformative seemed to occur in southern society. The South's social system was resistant, backward looking, dominated by the elites, and dedicated to maintaining racism and segregation at all costs. Socially and psychologically the South seemed isolated and separated from the rest of the United States. That separation was economic as well, for southern life was marked by rurality, struggling agriculture, low-tech or extractive industry, and a low-wage labor market. The dean of historians of the South labeled this pattern a colonial economy. Until the 1930s most economic developments tended to reinforce the inward-looking, self-isolated, and racist "southern way of life."

After the American Civil War, southerners had poured much energy into regaining their supremacy in the world's production of cotton. Competitors from Egypt and elsewhere had seized their opportunity when the war greatly reduced shipments of cotton from the South. At war's end, since cotton had always been the road to wealth, southerners concentrated on becoming once more the dominant supplier of that staple. Many small, formerly self-sufficient farmers, encouraged by the expansion of railroads, joined planters in focusing their cultivation on cotton. By the late 1870s southerners had achieved their goal, only to find that theirs was a pyrrhic victory.

The structure of demand for cotton had changed. In the decades before the Civil War, the British textile industry had expanded rapidly, selling its products to a succession of new and expanding markets. As a consequence the demand for cotton grew steadily and strongly through those decades, averaging 5 percent increase per year. By 1860, however, the British had established their dominance in all the major markets for textiles, and thereafter the demand for raw cotton to be manufactured into cloth grew much more slowly—barely 1 percent per year. As southern farms produced more cotton, the demand for their crop was slowing. The result was predictable: prices began to fall. When individual farmers or planters earned a disappointing income from the sale of their crop, they did what was logical for them as individuals—they grew more the next year. Thus cotton production continued to expand, outstripping the rate of increase of demand. Prices for cotton, therefore, fell steadily from the 1870s through the 1890s, impoverishing farmers, sharecroppers, and the region. From being the richest region of the United States early in its history, the South rapidly became the poorest region of the country.[14]

Postwar southern agriculture and the regional economy were handicapped in other ways as well. Banking reforms that had been passed by a northern Congress during war were tailored to meet the needs of urbanized, industrializing areas of the North, not a rural, undercapitalized South where defeat had spelled a great loss of wealth and the failure of every bank. As a result, the postwar southern economy suffered from a dearth of banking resources and credit. Many farmers or sharecroppers lived most of the year with little or no money in their pockets. They bought fertilizer, tools, or necessary household goods on credit from a local merchant, who charged them interest on the funds he advanced. When the harvest came in and farmers sold their cotton in a market where prices were falling, more and more ordinary southerners found that they could not "pay out," or settle their debts with profit to spare. Farm wages fell "and carried wages in many other southern labor markets with it." Small farmers lost their land. By 1900 "nearly half of the white farm operators were tenants" and the situation for former slaves was substantially worse.[15]

The high birth rate in the postwar South also tended to depress wages. Whatever the gains in productivity of the regional economy, the rapidly expanding population held down average gains in per capita income. The prevalent low wages also meant that other sectors of the economy were not able to compete for immigrants. Those who came "would not stay long in the low-wage South once they arrived.... By 1910 no more than 2 percent of the southern population was foreign-born," in marked contrast to the North, where heavy immigration was a vital support for industrialization.[16]

Advocates of the New South, of course, were intent on industrialization, and they promoted it as a way to lift the South out of poverty into prosperity. The low wage scales in the region would seem to have given their businesses an advantage, and, in fact, textile manufacturing began to expand "after 1875, when the Southeast emerged as the lower-wage region in a national context." Numerous studies have confirmed that cheap labor was the key element in this development. But it was not a guarantee of regional progress. For many years southern textile mills were known for relatively coarse fabrics, rather than the more valuable and expensive types of cloth that could boost income and lift wages. On the one hand, there was an abundant supply of laborers hoping to flee from failing farms. But on the other hand, these "hands" had no experience and had to learn what was involved in industrial labor, just as their managers were learning how to advance the industry. "The process of industrial development involved an extended period of adaptation ... not just to the factory and the tasks, but to the entire social setting" of a mill village and work in a factory. For fifty years "the industry did not provide the revolutionary regional dynamism of its New England predecessor, because the center of machinery production and associated technological development was still in the North."[17]

Other southern industries before 1930 did little to transform the character of the region. For decades the largest southern industry classified as "manufacturing" was not textiles but lumber and timber products. Some workers felled trees, but most in this sector worked in sawmills or in some aspect of processing lumber. They labored in an extractive industry that could flourish, temporarily, because the postwar South had far more unharvested timber than other parts of the nation. But logging camps were often isolated and dependent on "single, homeless" workers, and even the saw mills were "temporary establishments" that operated for "only a limited number of years" until the nearby supply of timber was used up. Using cheap labor, the lumber and timber products industry "made no lasting contribution to local development."[18]

An offshoot of lumbering was the furniture industry, which developed great strength around the town of High Point in the North Carolina Piedmont. After beginning with the simplest, cheapest grade of products, furniture manufacturers raised the quality of their goods and began to compete nationally by 1920. But furniture making, in the region as a whole, was a small industry. It "accounted for only one-tenth the employment and one-ninth the value-added of cotton textiles and related industries." The same was true of the scale of all other industries in the New South, even iron and steel. Iron making got an early start in Chattanooga, Tennessee. Soon thereafter impressive-looking mills grew up around Birmingham, Alabama, which was close to both iron and coal deposits. But inexperienced labor, a weak regional market, the problematic content of Alabama ore, and other problems caused the iron and steel industry to be "the biggest disappointment of the New South." The cigarette industry, concentrated in North Carolina, was more profitable and technologically advanced, but it too did not pay high wages.[19]

The limited impact of New South industry, joined to the social and political influence of the Lost Cause, disfranchisement, and Jim Crow racism, meant that the southern region seemed frozen in time. Although some things changed, the South remained so far behind the rest of the nation that it seemed not to have moved in relative terms. Ubiquitous, often violent discrimination against African Americans trapped them in low-paying agricultural labor, and although whites might earn more, the modal or typical wage for white workers was not substantially higher than the modal black wage. The pay scales of textile workers remained "closely linked to farm labor," and "the southern labor force remained overwhelmingly agricultural" in 1930. That fact held down wages, but it had social implications as well. Mechanisms of social control function more stringently in rural and small town settings than in bustling cities, and southern industrial development did little to change that pattern. The most important industry—textiles—generally preserved low population density and a dispersed population, as mill builders avoided cities and their lawyers. Small mill towns dotted the countryside throughout the Carolinas rather than creating metropolises.[20] An entrenched political and economic elite seemed determined to preserve a "southern way of life" that was rural, impoverished, poorly educated, and suffused with the racism of segregation and white supremacy.

The mentality associated with this society had not only racial consequences but economic and political ones as well. The fact that the South was a low-wage region in a high-wage nation created a set of perverse incentives. Employers ignored human capital because cheap labor was readily at hand. In fact, "The region was reluctant to invest heavily in schooling and higher education." A common saying was that education ruined a good field hand. Landowners feared that education for laborers "only had the effect of 'making them discontented with farm work and not improving their morals.'" Similarly, "a high school diploma was as good as a ticket to leave the mill village." For this reason, wealthy southerners and business leaders were "concerned with preserving the isolation of their regional labor supply" and were "suspicious rather than welcoming to outsiders and outside ideas." In most states political power was "firmly lodged in the white minority of the plantation districts, which is to say, in the group with the least interest in promoting integration of national capital and labor markets." Industrialists in the Carolina Piedmont similarly depended on cheap labor and were wary of outside investment that might raise wages and steal their workers.[21] This situation was an effective formula for stagnation and social stasis.

The key to progress, argues economic historian Gavin Wright, was the breaking down of the isolation of the South's labor market. The separate labor market was also the basis "for the isolation of the capital market" and a key to southern backwardness."[22] Forces outside the South were responsible for eroding the South's isolation and setting in motion a series of positive changes. As the South's separation declined, perverse incentives that worked against education, investment, and progress crumbled. When the South's labor market and economy became integrated with the national economy, a new set of incentives came into play and new attitudes took hold. Investment from outside became more attractive and popular as the "other United States" moved toward national customs and norms, and after 1950 transformation was rapid.

World War I began the dismantling of the South's economic separation. More than anything else, the South's vast pool of low-skilled, poorly educated black agricultural workers, held down by discrimination, created its separate labor market. When World War I halted European immigration, northern businessmen energetically recruited for laborers from the South: "Perhaps as many as a half-million southern blacks went North between 1915 and 1920." White workers also left the South for northern jobs—in fact, they left in greater numbers. More than a million southerners left the region between 1910 and 1920, and more than 1.6 million left between 1920 and 1930. This northward movement often involved southerners who had previously left the farm and were living in cities, so its effect on agricultural wages was slight. But it established social pathways that future emigrants from the South could use to find housing and jobs in the North. World War II turned the migration into a flood, as almost two and a half million southerners, roughly two-thirds of them black, moved to the North.[23]

Even more important was the New Deal, the reforms of which affected the southern labor market more directly. A variety of New Deal measures affected wages. The National Industrial Recovery Act (NIRA) reduced the workweek in southern textiles and "nearly doubled the hourly wage" before it was declared unconstitutional in 1935. The Fair Labor Standards Act in 1938 then "reestablished the minimum" wage level, bringing "national wage standards" to this southern industry.[24] The NIRA had a similar effect on other industries, from furniture to iron and steel, paints and varnishes, lumber, and tobacco. Increases in hourly wages "ranged from 21.5 percent ... to more than 70 percent." Although the Roosevelt administration permitted wage differentials, North to South, in its relief programs such as the Works Progress Administration, it raised southern rates of pay between 1935 and 1939 and reduced the existing regional difference. The majority of workers whose pay was affected by the Fair Labor Standards Act's minimum wage were southerners, and the reaction of the old, established elite was predictably negative. South Carolina's Senator Cotton Ed Smith denounced the minimum wage as a nefarious effort "by human legislation, to overcome the splendid gifts of God to the South."[25] The New Deal also encouraged unions and political mobilization among southern workers.

Agricultural programs of the New Deal reduced sharecropping in favor of wage labor and produced modest incentives for landowners to move toward mechanization. Plantation areas began to purchase tractors "much faster than the rest of the South." Then World War II brought a "massive out-migration of unskilled labor" which "focused technological energies" on mechanizing the cotton harvest. With more and more planters interested in machines to pick cotton, manufacturers saw more reason to build and perfect them, and by the end of the 1940s International Harvester, John Deere, and Allis Chalmers were all selling mechanical harvesters. Machines harvested only 5 percent of the cotton crop in 1950. By 1960, however, that was true for half the crop, and ten years later almost all cotton was harvested by machine. In the 1970s the same thing happened for tobacco. The number of farm operators plummeted as southern agriculture mechanized. Between 1950 and 1970 the number of southern farms declined by 58 percent, and the number of people employed in agriculture dropped by 69.5 percent. Large, modern operations replaced the old pattern of low-wage, small-scale sharecropping.[26]

The effect on incentives and patterns of thought was dramatic. Initially, as black southerners moved to the North, southern landowners worried about holding on to their labor force, and "concern for the loss of labor led Southerners to upgrade the level of spending on black schools." Despite the maintenance of segregation, the extent of "racial inequality in education," as measured by expenditures, declined between 1945 and 1950.[27] Soon, however, as out-migration continued and landowners began to consider mechanization, landowners saw the advantages of dispensing with low-skill labor. "At first the farmers wanted to keep industry away from their labor," observed one Mississippian, but "then they wanted to see them gone. They were careful not to do anything that might keep blacks here." Between 1940 and 1970 more than four and a half million blacks left the South and three million whites moved in. The foundation for the traditional, rural South of agriculture and sharecropping was disappearing. As

Gavin Wright concludes, "With the decline of the tenant plantation and the effective abolition of the low-wage industrial labor market, southern political and economic leadership no longer had strong interests in regional isolation from outside labor and capital markets."[28]

At this point the federal government proved helpful. Significant investment came from federal defense spending in the South, which had begun to soar during World War II. "The South led the nation in defense salary expenditures by the mid-1950s," notes historian James Cobb, "primarily because of the sheer number of military bases it boasted." Nowhere else did military spending do so much to aid personal income: by 1955 one out of every ten dollars of southerners' personal income came from military expenditures. In the poorest states of the region, such as Mississippi, as much as 20 percent of the increase in income was due to the federal government. Between 1952 and 1962 even more prosperous southern states such as Texas, Florida, and Virginia derived at least 10 percent of their increased income from federal spending.[29] It would be a mistake to ignore the complementary impact of the civil rights movement. At the same time that economic forces were ending the South's isolation and moving it into the nation's economic mainstream, the movement was weakening the perception of the South as another and inferior America, a backward and socially undesirable region. Northerners had done their part to make racism and discrimination a national pattern and national failing. But they also had assured themselves that they were not like their southern counterparts, not as prejudiced or culpable. Moreover, lynching and Jim Crow segregation convinced them that the South was a violent, uneducated, and unpleasant place. In the days before air conditioning, it was also a physically uncomfortable place for northerners accustomed to cold weather. For all these reasons national businesses had little interest in opening offices or building factories in the South. Their employees would not want to go there.

At first the civil rights movement deepened these negative impressions, as news coverage filled television screens and front pages with images of violence and hatred directed at peaceful demonstrators. But the victories of the movement, nationally and in the South, brought a new day and created changed images of a more open, progressive South. A new generation of governors publicly affirmed that the era of harsh racial injustice was over. Evidence of equal access to public accommodations and public transportation showed that daily life was now similar to other parts of the country. Integration in southern schools actually ran far ahead of northern schools, where there was much-publicized resistance in Boston and elsewhere. The personalism that had long been a feature of southern culture also seemed to suggest that many southerners were adjusting to racial change in ways that could become a model to the nation.

Consequently, it now became feasible, even appealing, for national businesses to consider new ventures in the South, where local governments hastened to inform them that they were welcome. After 1950 southern leaders began to act in accord with the changed conditions and new incentives that were surrounding them. State, county, and municipal governments began a determined campaign to sell the South to business—first to northern business and later to international firms. This new mentality, eager for growth and accepting of change, was plainly visible in the ambitious and growing cities of what soon would be called the Sunbelt. There business leaders understood that "civic renaissance and future economic growth ultimately will depend on the ability of many interest groups to work together." Charlotte, North Carolina, for example, was a community eager to emulate Atlanta, the booming city "too busy to hate." The Charlotte Chamber of Commerce, which had been working to attract new businesses from outside the region, led the decision to integrate restaurants and stores early in the 1960s. Leaders of the chamber appointed a special committee to investigate the business climate in Little Rock, Arkansas. It found that not a single new business had come to Little Rock in the years immediately after its bitter confrontations over school integration. Resolved that racial strife would not stop Charlotte's growth, Chamber members made contact with black leaders in their city. On the following day they went together to restaurants, shops, and stores, and integrated public facilities throughout the downtown.[30]

Changed attitudes like these facilitated economic progress. "In 1940," notes historian Numan Bartley, "the raison d'être of southern state governments was the protection of white supremacy and social stability; thirty years later their central purpose was the promotion of business and industrial development."[31] By 1972 the value of southern manufactures was forty-five times greater than it had been in 1939. Southern governments issued bonds to create industrial parks and build factories, which they then leased to businesses. They dangled tax breaks stretching far into the future to make the decision to locate in the South much more attractive. They moved corporate tax rates lower than the national average, stepped up their efforts to obtain federal grants and facilities, and developed state offices to contact and recruit potential enterprises. Some notable and well-publicized successes—such as the Research Triangle Park in North Carolina or General Motor's decision to build a huge Saturn plant in Spring Hill, Tennessee—encouraged other states to do more and catch up.[32]

In the thirty years after the Montgomery bus boycott, the structure of the southern economy underwent a transformation. According to census figures, the number of agricultural workers in the Southeast shrank from almost 4 million to fewer than 1 million, while the number in manufacturing almost doubled to 6 million. Government employees rose from about 2 million to 6 million, while those in trade more than doubled to more than 8 million and the number of service workers soared from 1.5 million to more than 7 million. In Texas and Louisiana, petrochemical expansion helped to fuel the growing economy, and income levels at long last began to approach national norms. White families enjoyed their new prosperity and suburbs boomed. But the black middle-class population also benefited. In South Carolina, for example, the black middle class grew from 17 percent in 1969 to 38 percent in 1989, and in North Carolina it expanded from 21 percent to 44 percent. In the 1970s the tide of black migration out of the South reversed, and more African Americans began coming home to the South than those who left for the North.[33]

In recent decades southern governments have pursued outside investment more aggressively than ever, raising the bidding for international firms to surprising, almost astronomical levels. South Carolina offered a massive package of incentives to BMW, which built a large plant near Greenville. Before 1975 South Carolina had been luring European textile companies to the corridor around I-85, but in that year it landed a large Michelin plant and expanded the scope of foreign investments. At the end of the 1970s "only West Germany could claim more West German industrial capital than South Carolina." In Alabama the "total estimated subsidy contributions to foreign automakers alone stood at $874 million" by 2002. To keep these companies happy, the southern states have relied heavily upon sales taxes to raise revenue rather than property taxes, which could hit both corporate and large individual landowners hard. The anti-union attitudes of southerners, the historical product of previous failures of unions suppressed by government power, also have appealed to business investors.[34]

Federal defense spending has continued to buoy the South, as appropriations for the military in recent decades have tracked the political importance of southern voting power. "By 2000, 47 percent of all military personnel on active duty were serving in the region," and five southern cities "enjoyed military investments of over $2.25 billion." In 1994 "the eleven states of the former Confederacy received 32.3 percent of federal expenditures on military contracts," but by 2000 that figure had grown to "51.8 percent." The fortunate economies of Texas and Virginia enjoyed increases of almost 50 percent. "Of the top ten destinations for military investment, the South has five of them, and Washington, D.C.," adjacent to Virginia, "is the sixth."[35] Federal military spending strengthened the South's economy while changing its society.

Other factors have contributed to the rapid transformation of the South's economy after World War II. Some have argued for the importance of the Sunbelt phenomenon—the idea that in contemporary society a warm climate and various natural amenities that support leisure are increasingly important to citizens in general, and to professionals and managers in particular. Other economists have pointed to higher year-round energy costs and other problems in the North and have argued that capital was simply flowing to an area where it could offer a higher return. Still others maintain that growth in the South has benefited from the fact that the region had a "clean slate," meaning "the relative absence of labor unions, entrenched bureaucracies, restrictive legislation, and the overall hardening-of-the-arteries that inevitably comes with economic maturity." Gavin Wright acknowledges that all these have contributed, but he emphasizes the end of southern separateness. "When southern property owners no longer had an economic stake in maintaining the separateness of the southern labor market, they opened the regional doors to much larger flows of outside labor and capital, with the result that the South as a distinct economic entity has all but disappeared."[36]

This different, socially reshaped South has left most visible signs of its past behind to resemble the social environment of most parts of the United States. After 1940 "regional trends of standardized occupational wages have been clearly ahead of the national average" and per capita income "has persistently grown at rates well above the national average." In 1950, for example, per capita income in the South was only 72.9 percent of the U.S. figure, but by 1974 it has risen to 87.7 percent of the national average. In 2010 one southern state, Virginia, ranked seventh in per capita income, well above the national average. Three others were located between twenty-fourth and twenty-eighth place among the fifty states, and only Alabama, in the forty-second position, and Mississippi, in fiftieth, stood out as markedly different and disadvantaged.[37] The formerly rural South also has become urbanized. The number of people living in metropolitan areas increased by 60 percent between 1950 and 1970 and reached a total of 55.2 percent. That rate of growth was twice the national rate, and urbanization has continued. Southern population growth now relies significantly on the arrival of nonsoutherners. Three million moved into the region between 1940 and 1970, to raise the figure of non-natives to 18.7 percent. By 1980 nonsouthern whites made up 20 percent of the region's white population overall and 25 percent outside the five Deep South states stretching from Louisiana to South Carolina.[38] Black migration to the south was producing net losses for every other region of the United States by the late 1990s. The scale of net black migration into the South in 1995–2000 (346,546 person) was three times as great as it had been in 1975–80.[39]

Thus economic and demographic changes have combined with the political consequences of the civil rights movement to erode the longstanding southern distinctiveness that was rooted in poverty, racism, and segregation. By an abundance of measures the South and the rest of the nation are far more similar today than ever before. Religion has become the leading aspect of regional difference today, as a national poll in 2011 found that southerners were not only more Christian but also more likely to believe that the Bible is the literal word of God. That difference affected attitudes on a variety of other issues as well. Given the marked difference between the United States and other Western nations in the intensity of religious belief, this may be evidence as much for the southernizing of America as for southern distinctiveness.[40]

Culture has a persistent influence on individuals and society, and historic attitudes about the Civil War and Reconstruction have not disappeared in the South, or in the North, for that matter. But it also is undeniable that the powerful forces of change that have swept over the South have made the Lost Cause less relevant to daily life or to relations between the South and the North. A strong sense of southern identity survives, nourished by such things as local pride, sports rivalries, and the long history of a visible assumption of superiority on the part of the North. But for the vast majority it more often takes the form of a desire to "show" the North than to fight the old ideological battles over the Civil War. As a proud NationsBank executive in Charlotte, North Carolina, explained, after his company had taken over Bank of America, "we didn't need to tolerate their looking down their noses at Southerners."[41] Young people in the South today are far more likely to admire and identify with modern business leaders or leaders in sports or entertainment than with military heroes of the Confederacy or defiant politicians from Reconstruction. They do so because these figures have a stronger relevance to their present-day lives and future aspirations. Because the South as a region is no longer mired in its Civil War history, southern thought can enjoy more freedom from the weight of the past.

Gaining distance from the controversies and enmities of the Civil War has taken longer in the United States than in Spain, but the reason that is so seems clear. Society in the southern United States changed very slowly for three or four generations, roughly a hundred years. The dramatically faster pace since then has had a correspondingly dramatic impact on attitudes. The rapid pace and broad scope of change offers more than the strong promise that the South will leave its Civil War battles behind. It also suggests that Spain can recover from its historical wounds in fewer generations than those that marked the United States' slow progress. An altered social landscape creates new realities and brings new attitudes.

Notes

Introduction

1. Aguilar Fernández, *Políticas de la memoria*, 414. The number of postwar executions, like many other issues concerning the civil war itself, are contested by defenders of the regime and by some historians. Stanley G. Payne puts the figure at thirty thousand in his review of Paul Preston's book, *The Spanish Holocaust*, which appeared in the *Wall Street Journal*, April 14–15, 2012.

2. Aguilar Fernández, *Políticas de la memoria*, 414. Cuesta Bustillo, *Odisea de la memoria*, 384; Carme Molinero, "¿Memoria de la represión o Memoria del franquismo?" in Juliá, *Memoria de la guerra*, 221. Josep Sánchez Cervelló notes that 450,000 people crossed the border into France in the first two months of 1939 alone. These would be in addition to exiles who fled earlier or went to North Africa, Mexico, and South America, or other destinations. See his essay in Viñas, *En el combate*, 501.

3. Professor Harry Stout, Yale University, in Beecher Lectures, 2005, lecture 1, p. 3, http://www.yale.edu/divinity/convocation/lectures.htm/.

4. Molinero, "Memoria de la represión," in Juliá, *Memoria de la guerra*, 221.

5. Friedrich Nietzsche, "History in the Service and Disservice of Life," in Nietzsche, *Unmodern Observations*, 89; Aguilar Fernández, *Políticas de la memoria*, 43–60, especially 59–60.

Chapter 1. Background

1. Don Doyle points out that in the modern era the United States was not exceptional but was "a scarred and grizzled veteran of nationalism and its discontents." See Doyle, *Nations Divided*, 10 and chap. 2.

2. References to the "two Spains" may be found in the distant past, but one of the most famous uses of this phrase was by the poet Antonio Machado, who in the twentieth century wrote, "Españolito que vienes al mundo te guarde Dios / Una de las dos Españas ha de helarte el corazón" or "Little Spaniard who comes into the world may God watch over you / One of the two Spains is going to freeze your

heart." These lines come from poem LIII of Machado's *Proverbios y cantares*. Here and elsewhere in this book the translations are my own.

3. Carr, *Modern Spain*, 1, 4, 13, 5, 12; Merry y Colón and Merry y Villalba, *Compendio de historia*, 160.

4. Carr, *Spain*, chap. 8, p. 207; Carr, *Modern Spain*, 209, 215–16, 236–37, 206–7, 231.

5. Syllabus of Errors Condemned by Pope Pius IX.

6. Ibid.

7. Carr, *Spain*, 235–43.

8. Callahan, *Catholic Church in Spain*, 286–91; Carr, *Spain*, 246–47, 249.

9. Carr, *Spain*, 247–50.

10. Sebastian Balfour, "Spain from 1931 to the Present," in Carr, *Spain*, chap. 9.

11. "Exposición de agravios hechos a la Iglesia," June 3, 1931, and "Sobre el Proyecto de Constitución y deberes de los Católicos," July 25, 1931, in Iribarren, *Documentos colectivos del episcopado Español*, 133–35, 137–38, 146, 141; Lazo, *Familia mal avenida*, 11; Rodríguez, *Problema social*, 127; *Dilectissima Nobis*, title and points 6, 18, 5, 17.

12. Father Hilario Yaben in 1931, quoted in Callahan, *Catholic Church in Spain*, 276, 146, 251.

13. Volunteers, perhaps as many as thirty thousand in all, formed the International Brigades. Those from the United States were called the Lincoln Brigade.

14. The measure of General Franco's determination and hostility toward his opponents is suggested by an interview that he gave to a journalist on July 28, 1936. In this interview he said, in relation to his enemies, "We fight for Spain. They fight against Spain. We are resolved to go forward at whatever price." When his interviewer replied, in apparent surprise, "You will have to kill half of Spain," Franco smiled and with a firm look answered, "I have said at whatever price." Quoted in the auto of Spanish jurist Baltasar Garzón, October 16, 2008, which is reprinted in Cierva, *113.178 Caídos*, 33, and is available at http://www.meneame.net/story/28-julio-1936-entrevista-franco-jay-allen/.

15. Stanley Payne, article in the *Wall Street Journal*, April 14–15, 2012 (for the estimate of 325,000); Callahan, *Catholic Church in Spain*, 358 and (last figure of paragraph) 370; Molinero, "Memoria de la represión," 221; Aguilar Fernández, *Políticas de la memoria*, 414.

Incomplete records, the destruction of records, and political controversies have created varying estimates of the death toll in Spain. (Similar problems make figures for the United States' Civil War inexact as well.) Hugh Thomas, *The Spanish Civil War* (London: Eyre & Spottiswoode, 1961), 632, wrote that in the war and immediate postwar years up to 600,000 people perished. Of these, he calculated that 410,000 died violently as a result of battles or executions. In 2008 a citizens' organization, the Association for the Recovery of Historical Memory, appeared before the Audiencia Nacional (on September 22, 2008) and presented 143,353 names of Republicans who disappeared during the Civil War. In many cases family members knew that their relative had been executed and often knew the approximate location of a common grave. Thus the figure of 150,000 executions surely is credible. See Pérez Garzón and Manzano Moreno, *Memoria histórica*, 18–19. The Association for the Recovery of Historical Memory, or ARMH in Spanish, will be discussed in later chapters.

A study of records by José Antonio Argos concluded that 113,178 supporters of Franco's uprising died "for God and for Spain" during the Civil War. Of this number, Argos concluded that 42,617 civilians were assassinated in what he called the "red zone," that 13,940 military men were executed or assassinated, and that the remainder were nationalist soldiers killed in action. See Cierva, *113.178 caídos*, 322–23. Francisco Espinosa and José Luis Ledesma give the following "approximate" but admittedly incomplete number for the wartime victims of *franquista* repression and executions: 130,199. See Viñas, *En el combate*, 493–95.

16. Molinero, "Memoria de la represión," 225–26, 228; Callahan, *Catholic Church in Spain*, 370, 467–68, 486–87.

17. Opus Dei, founded in Spain in 1928, is composed of priests and many more lay Catholics who believe in the church's teaching that all are called to be saints and that daily occupations can be a road to sainthood. The organization's influence was strong in Spain among many talented members of the professional and business elite.

18. Balfour's chapter in Carr, *Spain*, 268–71.

19. Quoted in Marañón, *Conversaciones*, 95, 100, 89, 275, 182. On the idea that the Right gave democracy to Spain, see 245. Fraga had responsibility for interior affairs in 1976, and he opposed street demonstrations with tough shows of force, saying, "The street is mine." A little later, when democratic elections were taking place, he allied himself with several rigid conservatives instead of forming a centrist organization.

20. Cercas, *Anatomía*, 347.

21. *Cortes* is a traditional Spanish name for a legislative body. In the dictatorship the Cortes that Franco created was a rubber-stamp body subject to his control.

22. Cercas, *Anatomía*, 112, 243; Linz and Stepan, *Problems of Democratic Transition*, 94–95. Adolfo Suárez was King Juan Carlos's second president of the government, after Arias Navarro.

23. In Spain's long history, certain regions—Catalonia, the Basque Country, Galicia, and Navarre—had at earlier times enjoyed special rights or greater independence than other areas. Cultural and language differences, as well as protonational aspirations, also had tended to be most pronounced in those areas. When

the Spanish constitution was written, many politicians hoped that the system of autonomies, involving a substantial measure of self-government, would help to bring peace to the Basque Country and might appease ETA. But provision also was made for the organization of autonomies throughout Spain, in a spirit of equal treatment or *café para todos*, "coffee for everyone."

24. Fernández, *Políticas de la memoria*, chap. 4; Santos Juliá, "Memoria, historia y política de un pasado de guerra y dictadura," in Juliá, *Memoria de la guerra*, 52–55; Ley 46/1977, de 15 de octubre, de Amnistia. The Communist Party thus gained the right to compete in the elections, but only a few months before citizens went to the polls. Santiago Carrillo, the longtime head of the Communist Party, notes this disadvantage in his book, *La difícil reconciliación*, 24. The vote in favor of the constitution was 88 percent.

25. Marcelino Oreja quoted in Marañón, *Conversaciones*, 272; "Discurso de dimisión," January 29, 1981, http://www.retoricas.com/.

26. The Guardia Civil had been created in 1844 as a governmental security force, employed especially in the early days to suppress banditry or lawlessness in the rural countryside. It had earned a reputation under Franco as a harsh and feared instrument of his repression.

27. "¿Qué fue de los golpistas del 23-F?" *El Mundo*, February 23, 2011, 10–11. For additional newspaper coverage, see 1, 3, and 13–15 of the same issue of *El Mundo*; *El País*, February 23, 2011, 14–16, and February 20, 2011, 1, 16–17, and section Domingo, 1–18. Book-length accounts include Blanco, *23-F*; Merino, *Tejero*; Perote, *23-F*; Rubio, *23-F*; Segura and Merion, *Jaque al Rey*; and Javier Cerca's fascinating book, *Anatomía de un instante*. In the end, none of the convicted *golpistas* served a terribly long sentence.

28. Interview with Felipe González by Juan José Millás, *El País*, November 7, 2010; Juan José Millás, "Vidas al límite," *El País Semanal*, June 27, 2010, 58.

29. Interview by Millás in *El País*, November 7, 2010. It should be recognized, as well, that the government of Calvo Sotelo, after the attempted coup of February 23, 1981, had taken strong measures to purge and control the army, including a total replacement of the council of chiefs of staff, many retirements, shifts in command responsibilities, and close control of promotions. González's measures came after those of Calvo Sotelo and added to them. See Cercas, *Anatomía*, 424–25.

30. Santos Juliá, "History, Politics, and Culture, 1975–1996," in Gies, *Cambridge Companion to Modern Spanish Culture*, 116; Balfour's chapter 9 in Carr, *Spain*, 278–79.

31. For an insightful assessment of Aznar's years in power through 1993, see Tusell, *Aznarato*.

32. For example, see "Los españoles dicen no al Gobierno y a la oposición," *El País*, March 27, 2011.

33. Zilversmit, *First Emancipation*. See also Litwack, *North of Slavery*. Although controversies over slavery before the 1820s and 1830s were not as intense as they would become thereafter, the issue was present in the early Republic. See Hammond and Mason, *Contesting Slavery*.

34. For valuable information and analysis on the economy of the slave South, see Wright, *Political Economy of the Cotton South*.

35. The classic text on transportation and changes in the North's economy is Taylor, *Transportation Revolution*. For more recent and broad coverage, see Howe, *What Hath God Wrought*; and Griffin, *Ferment of Reform*. See also Foner, *Free Soil*.

36. There are many works on proslavery thought, but extremely useful as a starting point are Jenkins, *Pro-slavery Thought*; and Tise, *Proslavery*. For background on the seceding South, see also Freehling, *Road to Disunion*, particularly volume 2, and Escott, *Confederacy*.

37. South Carolina Resolutions on Abolitionist Propaganda, December 16, 1835.

38. One of the best treatments of the sectional conflict, in addition to Freehling's *Road to Disunion*, is Potter, *Impending Crisis*.

39. In addition to the works cited above, see Fehrenbacher, *Slavery, Law, and Politics*; and Davis, *Slave Power Conspiracy*.

40. Lincoln's words are from his Peoria speech of 1854. For the southern states' declarations, see Escott, *"What Shall We Do with the Negro?"* especially 10–15.

41. Freehling, *South vs. the South*, 19, 61.

42. Many of these issues are treated in greater detail in Escott, *"What Shall We Do with the Negro?"*

43. McDonald and McWhiney, "Antebellum Southern Herdsman," 147–66. See also Escott, *Confederacy*, 137.

44. Escott, *Confederacy*, 115; McPherson, *Ordeal by Fire*, 380, 459–60.

45. Escott, *Confederacy*, 134; McPherson, *Ordeal by Fire*, 450, 353.

46. For a cogent and concise narrative of these events, with documents, see Benedict, *Fruits of Victory*. Elections for the new southern governments, with participation by black male voters, took place the following year, in 1868.

47. Emphasis added. Those three words were important qualifiers, because they allowed other types of restrictions that need not be phrased in terms of race, color, or previous condition of servitude yet would affect African Americans disproportionately

48. For articles reflective of these attitudes, see the *New York Times*, December 1, 1864, 4; January 15, 1865, 4; July 14, 1863, 4; October 18, 1863, 4; December 25, 1864, 4; December 27, 1864, 4; December 19, 1864, 4; January 6, 1865, 4; January 16, 1865, 4; and February 9, 1865, 4. The editor of the *Times*, Henry Raymond, was a founder of the Republican Party and chairman of its national committee in 1864 and 1865.

49. Foner, *Reconstruction*; and Gillette, *Retreat from Reconstruction*.
50. Wright, *Political Economy of the Cotton South*.
51. Harris, *Life of Henry W. Grady*, 83, 86, 88.
52. Goodwyn, *Democratic Promise*; and Kousser, *Shaping of Southern Politics*.
53. See Key, *Southern Politics*.
54. Mowry, *Theodore Roosevelt and the Progressive Movement*; Mowry, *Era of Theodore Roosevelt*; Mowry, *Progressive Era*; Link, *Woodrow Wilson and the Progressive Era*; Link, *Progressivism*; Wiebe, *Search for Order*; Hayes, *Response to Industrialism*; Watts, *Rough Rider in the White House*.
55. Logan, *Negro*. Note also the statement of Stanley Elkins: "At no time in American history were Southern race dogmas so widely accepted throughout the entire nation as in the early years of the twentieth century." Elkins, *Slavery*, 13.
56. There is a vast and growing literature on the civil rights movement. See Jacquelyn Hall's online project on "The Long Civil Rights Movement," http://www.torightthesewrongs.com/long-civil-rights-movement/, and such standard texts as Branch's, *Parting the Waters*, *Pillar of Fire*, and *At Canaan's Edge*. Still useful is Lewis, *King*.
57. The Atlantic Charter, http://usinfo.org/docs/democracy/53htm/.
58. Kluger, *Simple Justice*, 688–91.
59. Dallek, *Flawed Giant*, 116–21, 211–21.
60. Ibid., 120.
61. Black and Black, *Politics and Society in the South*, especially pts. 3 and 4.
62. Dennis Rash, quoted in Goldfield, *Still Fighting the Civil War*, 8.

Chapter 2. Ideology and Memory

1. Goldfield, *America Aflame*; Blum, *Reforging the White Republic*, 11–16 and chaps. 3–6.
2. *Dilectissima Nobis*, quotation from point 6; Rodríguez, *Problema social*, unpaginated introduction, 13, 28, 31–32, 43, 63; Villada, *Destino de España*, which is quoted rather extensively in Morodo, *Orígenes ideológicos de franquismo*, 144, 147.
3. Juliá, *Memoria de la guerra*, 27–30; Cuenca Toribio, *Relaciones Iglesia-Estado*, 72; Callahan, *Catholic Church in Spain*, 349; Plá y Deniel, *Dos ciudades*, 29–31; Moradiellos, *1936*, 21–22. For centuries the archbishop of Toledo was the primate, the head of the Catholic Church in Spain. In 1979, however, the Spanish Episcopal Conference, rather than the archbishop of Toledo, was recognized as the official representative of the Catholic hierarchy before the government. See Callahan, *Catholic Church in Spain*, 556–57.
4. *Episcopado Español a los obispos de todo el mundo*, July 1, 1937, in Iribarren, *Documentos Colectivos del Episcopado Español*, 222, 229, 224, 227, 230–32, 225, 238–42.

5. Paul Preston's important book, *El Holocausto español*, documents in chilling detail the beliefs and attitudes that served as justification for exterminating one's enemies. On pages 22–24, Preston estimates that away from the front lines and the fighting there, 200,000 Spaniards were murdered. The Republican forces killed 50,000, which Preston judges to be a firm figure, whereas the Nationalists killed 150,000 or possibly more. These deaths were in addition to the many killed in battle.

6. The languages suppressed were principally Catalan and the Basque language, Euskera, but Franco's government also opposed the use of Galician and a number of other languages or dialects spoken by smaller numbers of people in the Iberian peninsula.

7. Juliá, *Memoria de la guerra*, 32–37; Molinero, "Memoria de la represión," 221–28, 233–37.

8. Carolyn P. Boyd, "De la Memoria Oficial a la Memoria Histórica: La Guerra Civil y la dictadura en los textos escolares de 1939 al presente," in Juliá, *Memoria de la guerra*, 83–87; Callahan, *Catholic Church in Spain*, 455.

9. Callahan, *Catholic Church in Spain*, 462–88, especially 467–68, 462, 478, 486–88; Shubert, *Social History of Modern Spain*, 214–16.

10. Callahan, *Catholic Church in Spain*, 462–88, 462, 478; Shubert, *Social History of Modern Spain*, 214–16; Molinero, "Memoria de la represión," 231–37.

11. Juliá, *Memoria de la guerra*, 39, 88–89; Moradiellos, *1936*, 26–27; Carsten Humlebaek, "The 'Pacto de Olvido,'" in Alonso and Muro, *Politics and Memory of Democratic Transition*, 185. It is worth noting that Ricardo de la Cierva's term "War of Spain" avoided the term "civil war," which would have given too much legitimacy to the losing side.

12. Aguilar and Humlebaek, "Collective Memory and National Identity," 121–64, especially 124–46.

13. Moradiellos, *1936*, 22, 28.

14. Among the best and fullest discussions of these matters are Cuesta Bustillo, *Odisea de la memoria*, and Aguilar Fernández, *Políticas de la memoria*. For a recent perspective on *olvido*, see Humlebaek's essay in Alonso and Muro, *Politics and Memory of Democratic Transition*, 183–98. Humlebaek analyzes the political balance between avoiding or addressing conflicts arising from the past and how and why that balance changed (sometimes subtly) over time.

15. Carrillo, *Difícil reconciliación*, 15–16, 28.

16. Aguilar Fernández, *Políticas de la memoria*, chap. 4; Juliá, *Memoria de la guerra*, 52–55. The Law of Amnesty of October 15, 1977, amnestied "all acts of a political intention, whatever may have been their result . . . prior to 15 December 1976." Actions of the same nature that took place between December 15, 1976, and June 15, 1977, were amnestied if they involved a motive to "reestablish the public

liberties or reclaim the autonomies of the people of Spain." Ley 46/1977, de 15 de octubre, de Amnistia.

17. Carrillo, 17; emphasis added.

18. Juliá, *Memoria de la guerra*, 57–67; also essays in that volume by Roman Gubern, "La Guerra Civil Vista por el Cine del Franquismo," and by Paloma Aguilar Fernández, especially, 290–95; Moradiellos, *1936*, 27–30. The interest in the civil war continues to be strong. "The War Is a 'Best Seller,' generating tons of paper and polemics," *El País*, May 21, 2011, in the section *Babelia*, p. 4.

19. Aguilar and Humlebaek, "Collective Memory and National Identity," especially 130–31, 140–41, 145, 149–50; Paloma Aguilar Fernández, "La evocacion de la guerra y del franquismo en la política, la cultura y la sociedad españolas," in Juliá, *Memoria de la guerra*, 295–315.

20. Debates over Franco's dictatorship and the legacy of the civil war naturally affect Spanish politics, as today's parties are descended from supporters of one side or the other. The relationship between the ideological battles of the civil war and the modern political system will be treated in much more detail in chapter 3.

21. Cuesta Bustillo, *Odisea de la memoria*, chaps. 10 and 11; *El Mundo*, November 2, 1992, 8, and November 23, 1992, 5.

22. Juliá, "Memoria, historia y política." Santos Juliá, "Echar al olvido: memoria y amnistía en la Transición a la democracia," in Juliá, *Hoy no es ayer*, especially 324–30; Cuesta Bustillo, *Odisea de la memoria*, Epílogo Inacabado.

23. Juliá, *Memoria de la guerra*, 20–25; Richards, "From War Culture to Civil Society," 94.

24. Paloma Aguilar Fernández, "La evocacion de la guerra y del franquismo en la política, la cultura y la sociedad españolas," in Juliá, *Memoria de la guerra*, 304–15, which shows that in public opinion surveys the grandchildren of the wartime generation are most likely to see the dictatorship as a negative period and most interested in revisiting the war and identifying its victims. In this book see chapter 3 for a more complete analysis of the legacy of the Spanish Civil War on contemporary politics and political parties.

25. Juliá, *Hoy no es ayer*, 18–19.

26. Moa, *Mitos*, 183–89; Vidal, opinion column in *El Mundo*, November 20, 2002. Moa also argued in pages 190–94 that the Left was not progressive or the representative of the workers but a radical group seeking the abolition of religion, the state, and the family. A "good part of the real people found such medicine much worse than the disease." The Right was not a champion of the rich but of "religion, private property, the family, the state, and the unity of Spain." He defended the truth of religion and claimed that conservatives were so moderate that their actions were "next to cowardice at times, until the threat made it a question of life or death."

27. Santos Juliá quoted in the *Guardian*, November 14, 2005; Pérez Garzón, in Pérez Garzón and Manzano Moreno, *Memoria histórica*, 31–32.

28. A sense of society's general attitude toward Franco's uprising can be extrapolated from survey data that asked whether Spain was better off under Franco or under the democracy. Between 1984 and 1990 the year-by-year results for Franco declined in this manner: 21 percent, 16 percent, 15 percent, 12 percent, 7 percent, 8 percent. The results for the democracy between 1984 and 1990 were 58 percent, 58 percent, 62 percent, 62 percent, 67 percent, 77 percent, 76 percent. See Aguilar and Humlebaek, "Collective Memory and National Identity," 145. See the review of Moa's book by U.S. historian Stanley Payne, http://wais.stanford.edu/Spain/spain_piomoaandthecivilwar7803.html/. Payne argues, in part, that hostility to the dictatorship and political correctness have caused many scholars to deemphasize the divisions within the Left, antidemocratic tendencies of some leftists, failures of the republic's governments, and the atrocities committed by that side. Payne argues that Moa's exaggerations are an expected part of polemical debate and may prompt revision of some stale, formulaic thinking.

29. These points and the following paragraphs are based upon Silva and Macías, *Fosas de Franco*, 66–76, 122, 96, 120–21, 21, and the essay by Natalia Junquera at the beginning of Pérez Garzón and Manzano Moreno, *Memoria histórica*, 9–13, 18–20.

Scholars and journalists agree that avoidance of ugly truths about the past is most pronounced in small settlements or villages, where families were on opposing sides in the civil war. To illustrate this point, in the 2004 movie *El 7th Día*, directed by Carlos Saura, the leading character and narrator says, "Small villages never forget. Cities do, because the old is replaced with the new. But here, everything stays the same."

30. Silva and Macías, *Fosas de Franco*, 96, 121; Natalia Junquera, "Lo que ocurre en las fosas del franquismo," in Peréz Garzón and Manzano Moreno, *Memoria histórica*, 20.

31. *La Razón*, December 2, 2006, 8.

32. Aguilar Fernández, *Política de la memoria*, chap. 4; Cuesta Bustillo, *Odisea de la memoria*, 395–401.

33. *El País*, November 21, 2002; Cuesta Bustillo, *Odisea de la memoria*, 324, 325; *El Mundo*, November 21, 2002. See also Aguilar Fernández,"*Evocación de la guerra*," 279–317.

34. "Aún quedan por abrir 1.203 fosas del franquismo," *El País*, May 6, 2011, 20.

35. *La Razón*, December 14, 2006, December 15, 2006; *ABC*, December 15, 2006, April 21, 2007, November 2, 2007, July 27, 2006, July 19, 2006; *La Razón*, December 6, 2006.

36. Rajoy, quoted in *ABC*, July 19, 2006, and in *La Razón*, December 17, 2006; *La Razón*, December 3, 2006, December 5, 2006; *ABC*, July 29, 2006.

37. *El Mundo*, December 6, 2006; *ABC*, December 15, 2006; Cierva, *113.178 caídos*.

38. The Cervantes Prize is awarded annually to a writer from a Spanish-speaking nation. It honors lifetime achievement in literature written in Spanish and thus can only be given once to any individual.

39. Emilio Lamo de Espinosa quoted in *ABC*, July 19, 2006; Nieva quoted in *La Razón*, December 28, 2006, 7, January 2, 2007; *El Mundo*, January 2, 2007; Reyes Mate in Pérez Garzón and Manzano Moreno, *Memoria histórica*, 120; Aguilar Fernández, *Políticas de la memoria*, 473.

40. For reasons of length, these questions will receive greater coverage in the final chapter.

41. *ABC*, March 24, 2005, August 23, 2008, October 10, 2010.

42. "En Poyales del Hoyo no quieren Memoria Histórica," *El País*, August 7, 2011. See also the edition of August 9, 2011.

43. *ABC*, July 30, 2006. The comments on the change in atmosphere are based on the author's visits in 2009 and 2011.

44. *ABC*, December 11, 2010; *El País*, July 3, 2010. The autonomies in Spain have given widely differing degrees of support to matters of reparation or to the projects of exhumation. In some areas little has been done, whereas other regions have been active. For an example, see "Andalucía indemnizará a las mujeres víctimas de vejaciones durante el franquismo" (Andalucia will indemnify women who were victims of humiliation during the Franco regime), *El País*, September 21, 2010.

In May 2011 the government released a map and data detailing the number and location of *fosas*, or common graves, of those executed by Franco and the Nationalist forces. From the 2,232 graves located by the government with the aid of victims' organizations and autonomies not under PP control, 5,407 bodies have been recovered in recent years. 1,203 of these *fosas* have never been opened. Every autonomous community in Spain has some unmarked graves from the civil war, with the greatest number in Aragón and Andalucía. A commission of experts investigated the possibility of identifying and separating Nationalist and Republican remains interred together in El Valle de los Caídos but determined that this was impossible. The government's map can be found at http://www.memoriahistorica.gob.es/. See also *El País*, May 6, 2011, 20.

45. *El País*, February 5, 2010, September 29, 2010, and many other dates; Junquera, "Lo que ocurre en las fosas," 18–20; for the reprinted text of Garzón's decision, see Cierva, *113,178 caídos*, 25–37.

46. *El País*, January 27, 2011, February 5, 2011, February 23, 2011, 17; March 6, 2011, 2–9; June 18, 2011. On December 26, 2012, *El País* reported that the office of the state prosecutor recommended that all such cases be investigated as cases of forced disappearance, a step that will allow DNA tests and exhumations, if needed.

47. Interview with Bishop Xavier Novell in *El País Semanal*, 26, from the spring of 2011, article in possession of author.

48. "Mil sacerdotes españoles rompen el silencio"; Callahan, *Catholic Church in Spain*, 603, 502, 576; "Los obispos desautorizan a su presidente y dan marcha atrás," *Público*, November 23, 2007.

49. Callahan, *Catholic Church in Spain*, chap. 29.

50. *El País*, July 8, 2010, March 31, 2011 ("Los españoles dicen no al Gobierno y a la oposición," a report on the survey "Pulse of Spain," which was based on five thousand interviews), and August 1, 2011. By 2011 the percentage of heterosexual couples who were not married had grown to 19.3 percent, and the number of new marriages per 1,000 inhabitants had fallen from 5.8 percent in 1980 to 3.8 percent. *El País*, "Familias a la medida," June 18, 2011, 38–39.

51. *El País*, March 31, 2011.

52. *ABC*, March 9, 2001, January 6, 2002, March 19, 2002, March 22, 2002.

53. The incident involving Lieutenant General José Mena Aguado was as revealing in a negative way as it was surprising. During the Christmas season, the general, a respected and high-ranking army commander, was the speaker at ceremonies in Sevilla. His appearance, a few months before he was scheduled to go into the reserves, took place amid growing demands by some Catalan politicians for independence. (The question of the peripheral nationalisms in Spain is an important one that stems, in large part, from resistance to the efforts of General Franco to suppress non-Castilian languages or cultures. This issue will be discussed more thoroughly in a later chapter.)

After acknowledging that political issues were out of bounds for the military, General Mena proceeded to criticize a proposal to expand Catalonia's autonomy. He observed that the constitution protected Spain's nationality by putting limits on the powers of the autonomies but he then went on to remark that if the "impassable limits" of the constitution ever were ignored, "it would oblige the Armed Forces to regulate the destinies of that autonomy in the same way that currently destinies in foreign parts are regulated." He then cited Article 8 of the Spanish constitution and said that it gave the armed forces the "mission to guarantee the sovereignty and independence of Spain, to defend its integrity, and the constitutional order."

La Razón reported that Mena's words "fell as an authentic 'bomb' among the Spanish political class, which reacted practically as a bloc against them." Most parties promptly asked for his resignation. Only the PP stopped short of outright condemnation of Mena, using the event to blame the government for creating this unsettling controversy. The head of the General Staff waited only six hours before proposing to José Bono, the minister of defense, that Mena be removed from his post. Bono summoned Mena to his office the very next day, met with him "barely fifteen minutes," and imposed house arrest as a "preventative measure" due to Mena's failure to observe the "duty of neutrality" and the resulting "loss of confidence" in him. A few days later the government put Mena into the reserves and named a successor for his command.

Some conservative newspaper columnists and editorials used the incident to condemn talk of independence, and forty-two retired military officers quickly published a letter defending Mena. They stressed that "many of the commanders and subordinates of the units under his orders" were troubled by the issue of the autonomies. They suggested that Mena was trying to reassure those officers, and they argued that rather than engaging in any clandestine plot, he had chosen a very public occasion to voice his concerns out of a sense of duty. These officers, clearly of or influenced by dangerous, older schools of thought, closed their letter by expressing regret that Spanish society had arrived at the "deplorable situation" in which the armed forces were marginalized from major political issues, were expected to look the other way, and "do not have a formed opinion to respect."

As troubling as this event might seem to an outside observer, it quickly passed from the scene in Spain. Some normally well-informed citizens with whom this author spoke did not even remember it. The outcome seemed to reveal, in a negative way, that the new conception of an army that was faithful and subordinate to the democratic constitution had triumphed. The retired officers, whom General Mena promptly joined, may have represented the last gasp of the old military order that had a desire or temptation to dictate to politicians. If such officers remained in the military, they undoubtedly saw from the reactions to the event that they would have no supporters in the political world and even fewer, if possible, in society at large. Concerns about military interference in politics are absent from Spain today, and there is a greater willingness to discuss and condemn past military interference.

In pages devoted to the attempted coup of February 23, 1981 (known as 23-F), *El País* reported on polling data from 1991 and 2011 that revealed the public's changing attitudes. The percentage of Spaniards who believe that the outcome of the failed 1981 coup strengthened their democracy has increased from 51 to 60 percent, and only a miniscule number believe it weakened the democratic system. When asked if 23-F should be forgotten, or remembered so that such an event never could occur again, the polls' results showed an increasing willingness to remember. In 1991 the same large percentage, 48 percent, had responded in favor of forgetting as in support of remembering. But in 2011, 73 percent favored remembering the event so that it would never again occur. When asked if it seemed probable that such an attempted coup could be repeated now, 88 percent of Spaniards replied "no" and only 8 percent replied "yes." *El País*, February 23, 2011. See *La Razón*, January 7, 8, 9, 10, 2006, and *El País*, January 6, 11, and 13, 2006.

54. See David Blight's fine book, *Race and Reunion*.

55. For example, see Thomas J. Brown, "The Confederate Battle Flag and the Desertion of the Lost Cause Tradition," in Brown, *Remixing the Civil War*.

56. See Lincoln's Annual Message to Congress in December 1863, in Basler, *Collected Works* 7:48–49.

57. For treatment of these issues, see Escott, "What Shall We Do with the Negro?"

58. *New York Times*, December 1, 1864, November 24, 1864, December 25, 1864, January 6, 1865, January 16, 1865. See also November 27, 1864.

59. David Blight has pointed out the importance of this image of family in *Race and Reunion*.

60. Neff, *Honoring the Civil War Dead*, 113, 126, 127, 133–25.

61. McPherson, *Ordeal by Fire*, 486.

62. Carter, *When the War Was Over*.

63. Blaine is quoted in the *North American Review*, volume 128, number 268 (March 1879): 277–28; *Atlantic Monthly*, volume 23, number 135 (January 1869): 124–25.

64. White opponents of Reconstruction quoted in Franklin, *Reconstruction*, 105; "The Political Condition of South Carolina," *Atlantic Monthly*, volume 39, number 232 (February 1877): 179; "The Southern Question," *North American Review*, volume 123, number 253 (October 1876): 259.

65. Quotation from the Slaughterhouse Cases, in which the Court also said that it refused to be "a perpetual censor upon all legislation of the States, on the civil rights of their own citizens." *The Butchers' Benevolent Association of New Orleans v. The Crescent City Live-Stock Landing and Slaughter-House Company*.

66. William Henry Trescot in "The Southern Question," *North American Review*, volume 123, number 253 (October 1876): 258.

67. Speeches of Rutherford B. Hayes, September 19, 1877 (in Gallatin and Nashville), September 20, 1877 (in Decherd), September 22, 1877 (in Atlanta).

68. See Connelly, *Marble Man*; Connelly and Bellows, *God and General Longstreet*; Piston, *Lee's Tarnished Lieutenant*; Escott, "Uses of Gallantry," 47–74.

69. Thomas Wolfe in a passage from O Lost (the restored edition of *Look Homeward, Angel*), quoted in Madden, *Thomas Wolfe's Civil War*, 75; Faulkner, *Intruder in the Dust*, 194–95.

70. Some of these points were developed by Kirk Strawbidge in his paper, "A Genteel Reunion: Thomas 'Stonewall' Jackson, Robert E. Lee, and the Making of the Model American Man," given at the annual meeting of the Southern Historical Association in Baltimore, October 28, 2011.

71. See the works cited above in note 68 by Connolly, Connolly and Bellows, and Walter Piston; also John S. Wise, "The End of an Era: The Last of Lee's Army," *Atlantic Monthly*, volume 83, number 498, 507. There are many exaggerations or

debatable elements of the Lee legend. For an introduction to that issue, see Nolan, *Lee Considered*.

72. Janney, *Burying the Dead*, 4, 5, 7–9.

73. Ibid., 1–12; W. Fitzhugh Brundage's essay in Mills and Simpson, *Monuments to the Lost Cause*, 68–72.

74. Thomas Nelson Page, "Marse Chan," in Page, *In Ole Virginia*.

75. Thomas Nelson Page, "The Burial of the Guns," in Page, *Novels, Stories, Sketches and Poems* (story copyrighted in 1894).

76. Cooke, *Surry of Eagle's Nest*; Bagby, *Old Virginia Gentleman*; Smedes, *Memorials of a Southern Planter*; *Atlantic Monthly*, volume 61, number 368 (June 1888): 835–41.

77. Alexander H. Stephens's "Cornerstone" speech of March 21, 1861, may be found in many places, including Durden, *Gray and the Black*, 7–8.

78. Page, *Negro*, 208.

79. Ibid., 207.

80. This sampling of southern quotations comes from the *Atlantic Monthly*, volume 39, number 232 (February 1877): 177; *North American Review*, volume 123, number 253, 273, and volume 128, number 266 (January 1879): 54 and 56.

81. In the *North American Review*: Brooks Adams, "The Platform of the New Party," volume 119, number 244 (July 1874): 44; William Graham Sumner, "Politics in America, 1776–1876," volume 122, number 250 (January 1876): 86; Francis Parkman, "The Failure of Universal Suffrage," volume 127, number 263 (July–August 1878): 2, 5, 4, 10, 12; James Parton, "Antipathy to the Negro," volume 127, number 265 (November–December 1878): 488–90; Henry Cabot Lodge, "The Restriction of Immigration," volume 152, number 410 (January 1891): 36. These examples could be multiplied many times.

82. Alexander Winchell, "The Experiment of Universal Suffrage," *North American Review*, volume 136, number 315 (February 1883): 120; H. B. Anthony, "Limited Suffrage in Rhode Island," *North American Review*, volume 137, number 324 (November 1883): 418–21; William L. Scruggs, *North American Review*, volume 139, number 336 (November 1884): 492–502; H. H. Chalmers, "The Effects of Negro Suffrage," *North American Review*, volume 132, number 393, 239–40; Goldwin Smith, "Is Universal Suffrage a Failure?" *Atlantic Monthly*, volume 43, number 255 (January 1879): 74.

83. "Presidential Elections" *Atlantic Monthly*, volume 42, number 253 (November 1878): 543–55, quotation on 544; "The Political Attitude of the South," *Atlantic Monthly*, volume 45, number 272 (June 1880): 823; "Equality," *Atlantic Monthly*, volume 45, number 267 (January 1880): 30; N.S. Shaler, "The Negro Problem," *Atlantic Monthly*, volume 54, number 325 (November 1884): 699–703; "The United

States and the Anglo Saxon Future," *Atlantic Monthly*, volume 78, number 465 (July 1896): 35–37.

There was a racial element, also, in Franco's view of Spanish history, as he sought to negate the presence of Arabs and Jews in the Iberian past and recognize only the influence of Gothic peoples.

84. Wendell Phillips in "Ought the Negro to Be Disfranchised? Ought He to Have Been Enfranchised?" *North American Review*, volume 128, number 268 (March 1879): 258; D. H. Chamberlain, "Reconstruction and the Negro," *North American Review*, volume 128, number 267 (February 1879): 169 and 167; T. Thomas Fortune, "The Afro-American," *Arena*, volume 3, number 13 (December 1890): 118; Robert Smalls, "Election Methods in the South," *North American Review*, volume 151, number 408 (November 1890): 593–600; Douglass, speech in Louisville, Kentucky, on September 24, 1883, in *Three Addresses*, 20–21, 61, 68; Frederick Douglass, in "The Future of the Negro," *North American Review*, volume 139, number 332 (July 1884): 85. Unfortunately, by the end of the nineteenth century, Chamberlain would change his views and write critically about Reconstruction.

85. Richard T. Greener, "The Future of the Negro," *North American Review*, volume 138, number 332 (July 1884): 92; Gaines, *Negro and the White Man*, 200, 175, 97; Bruce, *New Man*, 143; Reverend J. C. Price, "The Negro in the Last Decade of the Century; What He Can Do For Himself," *Independent*, January 1, 1891, 5; Professor W. S. Scarborough, "The Race Problem," *Arena*, volume 2, number 11 (October 1890): 563. See also Meier and Rudwick, *Negro Thought in America*.

86. Laps D. McCord, "The Negro Problem," *Independent*, December 4, 1890, 4; Senator John T. Morgan, "The Race Question in the United States," *Arena*, volume 2, number 10 (September 1890): 389; Senator Wade Hampton, "The Race Problem," *Arena*, volume 2, number 8 (July 1890), 133; W. H. Page, "The Last Hold of the Southern Bully," *Forum*, volume 16 (November 1893): 303; McClure, *South*, 209, 214, 206, 216.

87. Professor James Bryce, "Thoughts on the Negro Problem," *North American Review*, volume 153, number 421 (December 1891): 647, 656, 657.

88. Rayford Logan used the term "nadir" and emphasized the last years of the nineteenth century in *The Negro in American Life and Thought*; Elkins, *Slavery*, 13.

89. General James Rusling, interview with President William McKinley, *Christian Advocate*, January 22, 1903; Taft's words are quoted in Miller, *Benevolent Assimilation*, 134.

90. Theodore Roosevelt, "Lincoln and the Race Problem," a speech at the Republican Club of New York City, February 13, 1905, http://www.sojust.net/speeches/theodore_roosevelt_lincoln.html/ and "The New Nationalism," speech in Osawatomie, Kansas, August 31, 1910, http://teachingamericanhistory.org/library/index.asp?document=501/.

91. Woodrow Wilson, "The Reconstruction of the Southern States, in Current, *Reconstruction in Retrospect*, 12; "Wilson's Racism," from the website of the World Future Fund, http://www.worldfuturefund.org/wffmaster/Reading/war.crimes/US/Wilson.htm#WILSONS RACISM/.

92. This point was memorably made by V. O. Key in his classic book *Southern Politics*.

93. Cox, *Dixie's Daughters*, 161–62.

94. Ibid., 26, 98–100, 103–4,108, 125; Bailey, "Free Speech and the 'Lost Cause,'" in Texas," 459.

95. Cox, *Dixie's Daughters*, 120, 124, 141–42, 158; Bailey, "Free Speech and the 'Lost Cause,' in Texas," 463.

96. Bailey, "Free Speech and the 'Lost Cause,' in Texas," 463–64, 465; Bailey, "Free Speech at the University of Florida," 2; Bailey, "Free Speech and the 'Lost Cause' in the Old Dominion," 242–43. Another famous case was that of John Spencer Bassett at Trinity College, which later became Duke University.

97. Quoted by John David Smith in his introduction to Phillips, *Life and Labor*, xix, and Phillips, *American Negro Slavery*, 343; Phillips, *Life and Labor*, 201.

98. Bowers, *Tragic Era*; Beale, *Critical Year*.

99. Silver, *Mississippi*; Cox, *Dixie's Daughters*, 161–62.

100. Loewen and Sebesta, *Confederate and Neo-Confederate Reader*, 16.

101. Booker T. Washington argued that "it is not best" for Negroes or southern whites that the Negro "surrender any of his constitutional rights" in an 1899 article in the *Atlantic Monthly*. See "The Case of the Negro," *Atlantic Monthly*, volume 84, number 505 (November 1899): 577–87.

102. For more information on these cases, see chapter 3.

103. Letter from Birmingham Jail in Escott and Goldfield, *Major Problems*, 555. It is noteworthy how much both Douglass and King emphasized the importance of freedom as an American value from which African Americans could not be permanently excluded.

104. "Radio and Television Report to the American People on Civil Rights, June 11, 1963," http://www.jfklibrary.org/Research/Ready-Reference/JFK-Speeches/Radio-and-Television/.

105. Quoted in Goldfield, *Still Fighting the Civil War*, 74.

106. Max Planck, quoted in Novick, *That Noble Dream*, 348.

107. Loewen and Sebesta, *Confederate and Neo-Confederate Reader*, 331.

108. Ibid., 332, 18.

109. Thomas J. Brown, "The Confederate Battle Flag and the Desertion of the Lost Cause Tradition," in Brown, *Remixing the Civil War*, 40.

110. Some claim that the UDC has twenty thousand members, but its influence on school texts has evaporated (to be replaced on occasion by ad hoc groups that favor creationism over Darwinian evolution). Loewen and Sebesta, *Confederate and Neo-Confederate Reader*, 320. At every one of the service academies of the United States, including for the Merchant Marine, and at the Citadel and Virginia Military Institute (VMI), honors named after Confederate leaders go to outstanding cadets or graduates. There are eight awards in all, such as the Robert E. Lee Sabre given at West Point, the Commodore Matthew Fontaine Maury Award at the Naval Academy, or the Stonewall Jackson Award at VMI. A protest movement began a few years ago that calls on President Obama to halt the distribution of these awards and to end the practice of sending a wreath to the Arlington Confederate Monument on Memorial Day. This protest is based on the fact that the UDC "has a long history of opposition to the values of a multiracial democratic United States of America" and has not revised its positions. To date, President Obama has taken no action on this protest. See Arlington Confederate Monument Report.

111. Core Beliefs Statement.

112. Southern Poverty Law Center, intelligence files.

113. The exact wording of the website has changed from the summer to the fall of 2011. As of November 2011, the phrase "true history" seems to have disappeared, to be replaced by an appeal to readers to resist distortions "by some in an attempt to alter history." See http://www.scv.org/whatis.php/.

114. Horwitz, *Confederates in the Attic*.

115. Even today, the Lost Cause narrative continues to cloud the minds of elementary or secondary school teachers in many parts of the nation. James Loewen, a scholar who has worked with secondary school teachers in many regions, has found that a large majority identify states' rights as the cause of the Civil War. Less than 20 percent—an even smaller percentage than he encounters among general adult audiences—attribute the war to conflict over slavery. Loewen and Sebesta, *Confederate and Neo-Confederate Reader*, 7.

116. Some months before Lincoln had privately and confidentially expressed this preference to the governor of his small, newly organized, loyalist regime in occupied Louisiana. When that idea was ignored, Lincoln did nothing and instead gave his strong support to a government that the majority in Congress scorned as unrepresentative.

117. James McPherson, in a review in the *New York Times*, August 27, 2000, and in the *New York Review of Books*, March 29, 2007.

118. For a more detailed examination of these issues and Lincoln's policies, shaped in and limited by a racist North, see Escott, "What Shall We Do with the Negro?" See also Magness and Page, *Colonization after Emancipation*.

Chapter 3. The Past and Political Evolution

1. It should also be noted that the rules of the electoral system in Spain have favored the dominance of two major parties. Unless a party gains a sizable percentage of the total vote, its representation in the Congress turns out to be inferior to the level of its support at the polls.

2. The Republican Party polled less than 40 percent of the votes in the 1860 presidential election; its victory came in the Electoral College.

3. *Macon (Ga.) Telegraph*, January 6, 1865.

4. For example, legal experts have noted and commented upon a trend of recent Supreme Court decisions empowering the states, and more than two dozen state attorneys general filed suits challenging the constitutionality of President Obama's health-care reform.

5. Sebastian Balfour, "The Reinvention of Spanish Conservatism: The Popular Party since 1989," in Balfour, *Politics of Contemporary Spain*, 147. Indeed, Balfour, writing in 2005, used "the majority" rather than "many."

6. Marañón, *Conversaciones*, 175–85.

7. Aznar, *España*, 20–25; Aznar, "Discurso de investidura," 1996. See also Balfour, "Reinvention of Spanish Conservatism," 150.

8. Constitución Española, Articulo 2, http://www.lamoncloa.gob.es/NR/rdonlyres/79FF2885-8DFA-4348-8450-04610A9267F0/0/constitucion_ES.pdf/.

9. Aznar, *España*, chap. 2, especially 29–30, 35, and 38.

10. Aznar, "Discurso de investidura." Spanish governments give great importance to foreign policy in the Mediterranean and Latin America and try to promote ties of language and culture. For Aznar's tendency toward neoconservatism, see Tusell, *Aznarato*, chap. 4.

11. "Las cesiones del Gobierno" and "Ante todo, no molestar al Papa," *El País*, August 14, 2011.

12. "El PSOE dice que . . . ," *El País*, November 8, 2010. Whenever a dissenting bishop has criticized the church's role in the 1930s or under Franco, his colleagues and superiors have rejected his statements. In addition to the surprising, or shocking, apology of the bishop of Balboa, Ricardo Blázquez, in 2007, the bishop of Vitoria, Miguel Asurmendi, celebrated a memorial service in a Basque capital in 2009 in which he condemned the church's "silence" about the execution of Republican priests as "not only a wrong omission, but a lack of truth and an act against justice and charity, for which we ask pardon." It was not accidental that these two statements came from the Basque Country, where opposition to Franco and his regime was very strong. But Bishop Blázquez received no support, and an official, approved statement by the conference of bishops in Spain condemning the church's stance with Franco has never been made.

13. "Las cesiones del Gobierno"; "Ante todo, no molestar al Papa"; "Ocho detenidos y 11 heridos en los incidentes tras la marcha laica en Madrid," *El País*, August 18, 2011. Various opinion polls show that there is support for euthanasia from between 60 and 77 percent of the population.

14. *La Razón*, October 8, 1999. This article followed the court's decision by a few months, but the article showed that the paper hoped to stimulate a debate.

15. *El País*, October 16, November 1, November 5, and December 21, 2012.

16. Balfour, "Reinvention of Spanish Conservatism," 158.

17. Ibid.; "La enseñanza de catolicismo cae ocho puntos en un lustro," March 24, 2011; *El Mundo*, November 1, 2002, and November 22, 2002, 4; *La Razón*, December 6, 2006 and December 9, 2006.

18. "La Iglesia no puede prescindir de docentes por 'pecar' *fuera* de clase," El País, April 20, 2011.

19. Two articles in *El País*, March 17, 2011, 38.

20. *El País*, November 6, 2012.

21. *ABC*, November 30, 2002; *La Razón*, January 2, 2007, 41; "Rajoy lanza su discurso más liberal," *El País*, March 6, 2011; televised statement, March 8, 2011, on the news broadcast of TVE.

22. Alicia Fraerman, "Gender Equality Law Triumphs," January 30, 2008, Inter Press Service News Agency, http://ipsnews.net/; "El líder de PP busca el voto de la mujeres," *El País*, May 6, 2011; opinion by Christina Alberdi, *La Razón*, January 2, 2007.

23. *El Mundo*, June 1, 2007; *La Razón*, January 9, 2006; *El Mundo*, December 20, 2002; Rajoy quoted in *El País*, March 6, 2011.

24. Balfour, "Reinvention of Spanish Conservatism," 160.

25. *El País*, May 13, 2011, and following days; Aznar's address to Congress, February 4, 2004, http://beersand politics.com/; BBC News, April 18, 2004, available at http://news.bbc.co.uk/.

26. Xosé-Manoel Núñez Seixas, "From National-Catholic Nostalgia to Constitutional Patriotism: Conservative Spanish Nationalism since the Early 1990s," in Balfour, *Politics of Contemporary Spain*, 133–34.

27. *La Razón*, October 7, 15, and 24, 1999, December 3, 2006; for the PP's successful challenge in the *Tribunal Constitucional*, see *El País*, June 28, 2010.

28. On July 17, 2010, *El País* reported survey results in an article titled "Independentismo catalán." These results showed that 23.6 percent of respondents in Cataluña felt that the state should allow communities to be independent if they wished. In the Basque Country the figure was 21.9 percent, and in Galicia it was only 1.7 percent. See also Laura Freixas, "La batalla por la identidad," *El País*, April 20, 2011, 23.

29. "El contenido de la botella," *El País*, April 20, 2011, 14.

30. *La Razón*, October 14, 1999; *El Mundo*, October 13, 1999; *El Mundo*, November 5, 6, and 7, 2002.
31. González, "Discurso de investidura," 1982.
32. Ibid.
33. Rodríguez Zapatero, "Avance en políticas sociales 2004–2011."
34. "Zapatero llama a defender la marca PSOE . . . ," March 6, 2011.
35. Vice president Maria Teresa Fernández de la Vega quoted in *El País*, July 11, 2006; "Constitución, laicidad y Educación para la Ciudadanía," 2006, http://www.psoe.es/.
36. *La Razón*, December 6 and 11, 2006; column by Rafael Navarro-Valls, *El Mundo*, January 3, 2007; Dolores Cospedal on television news, during April or May 2011, viewed by the author. It was already clear that the PP intended, should it gain a majority in the national government, to annul or revise the PSOE's law on education for citizenship. In Valencia in the recent past, the PP-controlled government sought to frustrate that law by mandating that it would be taught in English, but the courts intervened.
37. "Los obispos y Wert negociaron con sigilo," *El País*, December 8, 2012, and "Andalucía recupera los contenidos eliminados per Wert de Ciudadanía," *El País*, September 12, 2012. Wert is the PP government's education minister. The PSOE education law was called Educación para la Ciudadanía. See also "El Supremo cierra la última puerta a los 'objectores' a Educación para la *Ciudadanía*," *El País*, December 13, 2012.
38. Political needs played an important role in initiating this process. Zapatero and PSOE needed to form a coalition with Catalan parties in order to have a governing majority, and the Catalans demanded consideration in return.
39. Opinion piece by Antonio Elorza, *El País*, July 30, 2010, and opinion piece by José Montilla (president of Catalonia's Generalitat and former Socialist minister), *El País*, July 17, 2010. The government objected on constitutional grounds to this consultative referendum, which was politically significant as an indication of Catalan public opinion. On June 17, 2011, the Tribunal Constitucional ruled that Cataluña could hold such consultative referenda but subject to two restrictive conditions: the referendum had to be limited to the competencies of the Generalitat and the central government first had to give, or refuse, permission for such a consultation. *El País*, June 18, 2011, 17.
40. José Montilla, "Cataluña y España en la encrucijada," *El País*, July 17, 2010; Antonio Elorza in *El País*, July 30, 2010; Joan B. Culla I Clará, "Inconstitucionalidad preventiva," *El País*, July 2, 2010; *El País*, August 20 and 21, 2010, and September 6, 2010; *El País*, August 22, 2010.
41. "Apuntes sobre Cataluña y España," *El País*, July 26, 2010.

42. *El País*, October 6, 2010. Local interests play a role as well, because if Cataluña or some other autonomy gains more authority and more revenue from the central government, that can affect the funding of the other autonomies.

43. *La Razón*, October 13, 10, and 15, 1999; *El Mundo*, November 2, 2002; *La Razón*, December 1 and 3, 2006.

44. *ABC*, March 3, 2008; "Proposal of the PP for a Pact for the Reform and Bettering of Education in Spain," January 18, 2010, from the official website of the Partido Popular, http://www.pp.es/; *El País*, November 19, 2010.

45. Aleix Vidal-Quadras, "La nación traslúcida," *Política Exterior*, volume 57 (May–June 1997): 130–40 and 143–51.

46. Vidal-Quadras in Marañón, *Conversaciones*, 236–27; J. Ramón Parada, "España: ¿una o trina?" *Política Exterior*, volume 53 (September–October 1996): 119–38.

47. "La líder catalana del PP pide más clases en castellano para su hijo," *El País*, June 18, 2011, 17.

48. "Bildu impone el euskera como única lengua en sus apariciones públicas," *El País*, July 2, 2011, 14. According to this article and a recent survey conducted by the Basque government, 37 percent of Basques speak Euskera well or fairly well, but only 20 percent use it regularly. In social relations only 13 percent use the language as their means of communication. In the family and the workplace the figures increase slightly, to 17 and 19 percent respectively.

49. Miguel Herrero de Miñón, "Nacionalismos y estado plurinacional en España," *Política Exterior*, volume 51 (May–June 1996): 7–20 and "La España Grande (Respuesta a algunos exabruptos)," *Política Exterior*, volume 54 (November–December 1996): 163–65.

50. Joxe Joan Gonzáles de Txabarri, "El nacionalismo democrático vasco," *Política Exterior*, volume 57 (May–June 1997): 111–22, 125–29, especially 113 and 128.

51. Freixas, "Batalla por la identidad," 23.

52. "Independentismo catalán," *El País*, July 17, 2010. A survey from 2011 found that 24.5 percent of Catalans favored an independent Catalan state, and 19.4 percent defined themselves only as Catalans. See "El contenido de la botella," *El País*, April 20, 2011, 14.

53. "El contenido de la botella," *El País*, April 20, 2011, 14.

54. See articles in *El País*, December 17, 19, 2012.

55. Goldfield, *Still Fighting the Civil War*, 281, 316. The answer, he suggests, is a common, accurate, and shared understanding of the facts of the nation's history.

56. Abbott, *Republican Party and the South*, 236–37.

57. Ibid., x, xi, 226–27. The Southern Claims Commission moved tardily to examine the more than twenty-two thousand claims for compensation of more than $60 million. In 1877 half of the cases were still unresolved, and when the

commission completed its work in 1880, only $4.6 million had been awarded, less than 10 percent of the amount claimed.

58. Thompson, *Reconstruction of Southern Debtors*.

59. Ibid., 239–40, 236.

60. Ibid., 228, 231. See also Durden, *James Shepherd Pike*; and John Sproat, *Best Men*.

61. Tindall, *Disruption of the Solid South*, 9–15; Budiansky, *Bloody Shirt*, 2; *Republican Campaign Text Book for 1880*, http://www.archive.org/details/republican-campa03commgoog/; Norton et al., *People and a Nation*, 2nd ed., 564.

62. *Republican Campaign Text Book for 1880*, table of contents and its facing page, also 4, 3, 9, 37, 102, 125.

63. Norton et al., *People and a Nation*, 4th ed., 609, 2nd ed., 564. Today $157 million would be about $4.5 billion.

64. The quotations are from David Goldfield and Richard M. Weaver, in Goldfield, *Still Fighting the Civil War*, 19 and 43.

65. Ibid., 27.

66. Escott and Goldfield, *Major Problems in the History of the American South*, 1st ed., 2:45, 39, 41.

67. Escott, *Many Excellent People*, 243; 1892 Populist Party Platform, available on line at various sites, including http://www.presidency.ucsb.edu/ws/index.php?pid=29616#axzz1dyINtS1g/; Tom Watson, "The Negro Question in the South, *Arena*, volume 6 (October 1892): 540–50.

68. Goldfield, *Still Fighting the Civil War*, 196–97. See also Kousser, *Shaping of Southern Politics*; and Woodward, *Tom Watson*.

69. Certainly by this point, if not before, a self-reinforcing sequence had been established. See Mahoney, "Path Dependence in Historical Sociology," 508.

70. Goldfield, *Still Fighting the Civil War*, 33–34.

71. Quoted in ibid., 34, 35.

72. Quoted in ibid., 56, 58–61.

73. Ibid., 209, 207.

74. Quoted in ibid., 199.

75. Simkins, *Pitchfork Ben Tillman*, 402–3.

76. Tindall, *Persistent Tradition*, 68; McGill quoted in Tindall, *Disruption of the Solid South*, 30–31.

77. Tindall, *Persistent Tradition*, 69

78. Bart Dredge, "Defending White Supremacy: David Clark and the *Southern Textile Bulletin*, 1911–1955," *North Carolina Historical Review*, volume 89, number 1 (January 2012): 59–91, quotation from page 61.

79. Mowry, *Another Look*, 81, 75.

80. Ibid., 75–76.

81. Ibid., 67, 71.

82. Ibid., 37, 87.

83. Ibid., 64–67; "Charleston Navy Base History," North Charleston website, http://www.northcharleston.org/visitors/attractions/museumsandart/navalbasehistory.aspx/. Eventually the Charleston navy base was closed in the 1990s.

84. Mowry, *Another Look*, 67–71, 78–81.

85. Ibid., 71; Goldfield, *Still Fighting the Civil War*, 197; Tindall, *Disruption of the Solid South*, 31–32.

86. Cobb, *South and America*, 62–63. See also Morton Sosna, "More Important than the Civil War? The Impact of World War II on the South," in Cobb and Wilson, *Perspectives on the American South*, 145–58.

87. Roland, *Improbable Era*, 24, 174.

88. Ibid., 99, 116–17.

89. Ibid., 183, 119, 122. Woodward described a "colonial economy" in *Origins of the New South*. These distinctive aspects would continue. A national survey in the mid-1970s showed that "southerners were more than three times as likely as non-southerners to be Baptists. . . . Church attendance was higher among southerners, at least monthly for 85 percent of the blacks and 67 percent of the whites, compared with only 55 percent of the non-southerners." See Bass and DeVries, *Transformation of Southern Politics*, 16.

90. Smith, *Congressman from Mississippi*, vii–viii, 312, 117, 106, 120.

91. These cases, respectively, overturned coerced confessions by black defendants, ruled that Texas's Democratic Party was not a private club and therefore blacks were allowed to vote in its primaries, ruled that segregation on interstate buses was illegal, and overturned real estate covenants that were racially discriminatory.

92. Kluger, *Simple Justice*; Franklin, *From Slavery to Freedom*, chaps. 27 and 29.

93. Smith, *Congressman from Mississippi*, 99; Tindall, *Disruption of the Solid South*, 36.

94. Among the many places where these documents may be found is Escott and Goldfield, *Major Problems* 2:541–43. Lyndon Johnson did not sign the Southern Manifesto.

95. See Bartley, *Rise of Massive Resistance*; Loewen and Sebesta, *Confederate and Neo-Confederate Reader*, 331.

96. Walker, *Ghost of Jim Crow*, 87, 89, 4, 95–96, 121–22.

97. Ibid., 4, 88–89, 101, 103–4.

98. Kennedy, "Radio and Television Report to the American People."

99. According to Professor Kent B. Germany, "Most accounts, particularly by Bill Moyers, claim that the president made this statement to him following the signing of the Civil Rights Act. Lady Bird Johnson and Harry McPherson

trace the statement to a conversation after the signing of the Voting Rights Act in 1965." See Bill Moyers, "Second Thoughts: Reflections on the Great Society," *New Perspectives Quarterly*, volume 4 (Winter 1987); Jan Jarboe, "Lady Bird Looks Back: In Her Own Words, a Texas Icon Reflects on the Lessons of a Lifetime," *Texas Monthly* (December 1994): 117; "Achilles in the White House: A Discussion with Harry McPherson and Jack Valenti," *Wilson Quarterly*, volume 24 (Spring 2000): 92.

100. *Time*, "The South: New Language on Inauguration Day," February 1, 1971.

101. Goldfield, *Still Fighting the Civil War*, 256–57; Cobb, *South and America*, 189. In 2007 there were only forty-three blacks in statewide office throughout the United States.

102. Goldfield, *Still Fighting the Civil War*, 268. In the era of segregation, especially in rural areas, buses often had to travel long distances in order to avoid placing students in mixed-race, local schools.

103. Reed, *One South*, especially chapter 8, "Blacks and Southerners," written with Merle Black; Goldfield, *Still Fighting the Civil War*, 286–87; Benjamin Griffith's review of V. S. Naipaul's *A Turn in the South*, *Hudson Review*, volume 42, number 3 (Autumn 1989): 525.

104. Cobb, *South and America*, 166–67.

105. Ibid., 204.

106. Goldfield, *Still Fighting the Civil War*, 183–84, 85.

107. Black and Black, *Politics and Society in the South*, 313–14; Goldfield, *Still Fighting the Civil War*, 261.

108. Cobb, *South and America*, 185; Dennis, *New Economy*, 6

109. Black and Black, *Politics and Society in the South*, 313.

Chapter 4. Reconciliation

1. Ian Buruma, "The Twisted Art of Documentary," *New York Review of Books*, volume 57, number 18 (November 25, 2010): 44.

2. Ángela Vallvey, in *La Razón*, January 19, 2011, 14; see Paloma Aguilar Fernández, "La evocación de la guerra y del franquismo en la política, la cultura y la sociedad españolas," in Juliá, *Memoria de la guerra*, and her essay "Justice, Politics and Memory in the Spanish Transition," in Barahona De Brito, González-Enriquez, and Aguilar, *Politics of Memory*, 114–18.

3. *El País*, Sunday, May 29, 2011, in section Domingo on Rajoy as "el sobreviviente"; Javier Tusell offers a similar judgment in his book, *El Aznarato*, 367. There he describes two axes in Spanish politics, the Left versus the Right, and the greater or lesser acceptance of pluralism in culture or group identity within Spain. Tusell comments that the Partido Popular is able to gain support among social and

intellectual groups, through the second axis—support that perhaps would be unattainable in relation to values of Left vs. Right.

4. Constitution of 1978, Article 3, subsections 1, 2, and 3, http://www.lamoncloa.gob.es/NR/rdonlyres/79FF2885-8DFA-4348-8450-04610A9267F0/0/constitucion_ES.pdf/.

5. In addition to independence movements, which will be discussed later in this chapter, many of the autonomies ran up large debts that require assistance by the financially strapped national government.

6. As will be discussed later, an additional charge was brought against Garzón—a charge that he violated the rights of accused terrorists by ordering audio surveillance of their conversations in prison with their lawyers. Ultimately Garzón was found guilty of this matter rather than on the charge of *prevaricación*.

7. President Grant's inaugural addresses are available on line at http://www.bartleby.com/. On that website search for "Presidential Inaugurals."

8. Emphases added to President Wilson's address.

9. David Blight, "The Civil War Sesquicentennial," *Chronicle of Higher Education*, June 2, 2009, http://www.davidwblight.com/sesq.htm/.

10. Cuesta Bustillo, *Odisea de la memoria*, 388–92. Américo Castro, a historian and cultural critic, and Indalecio Prieto, an important politician in the 1930s, were Republicans, whereas Gil Robles was a major leader of conservative, pro-Catholic rightists or, as many scholars would say, of those of Fascist ideals during the Second Republic.

11. Aguilar and Humlebaek, "Collective Memory and National Identity," 121–64.

12. Ibid.

13. Roniger and Sznajder, *Legacy of Human Rights Violations*, 220, 210, 212.

14. Junquera, "Lo que ocurre en las fosas," 13–14.

15. Aguilar Fernández, *Políticas de la memoria*, 456–70; Junquera, "Lo que ocurre en las fosas," 14.

16. Aguilar Fernández, *Políticas de la memoria*, 456–70.

17. "El Supremo de Brasil rechaza la revisión de la ley de amnistía," *El País*, April 30, 2010. On the question of revising the law, opinion was divided in Brazil. Even some of those who had been tortured did not want to reopen the question. However, in the wake of the court's decision, all sectors of opinion seemed to be in agreement that the archives of the military dictatorship (which lasted from 1964 to 1985) ought to be opened so that families could learn where victims now described as "disappeared" were buried.

18. Associated Press, "Uruguay Senate likely to overturn amnesty for dictatorship crimes, despite voters' approval," *Washington Post*, April 12, 2011; "Uruguay ratifica la ley de amnestía para la dictatura," *El País*, May 21, 2011.

19. As of 2010, the covenant had 72 signatories and 167 parties.

20. Sadat, "Exile, Amnesty and International Law," 44; see the webpage for the UN Human Rights Committee with links to the International Covenant on Civil and Political Rights at http://www2.ohchr.org/english/bodies/hrc/; Napoleoni, *Garzón*.

21. "Especial Pinochet," El País, http://www.elpais.com/especiales/2001/pinochet/portada.html/.

22. Quoted in Sadat, "Exile, Amnesty and International Law," 43.

23. Auto of Judge Garzón, October 16, 2008, as reprinted in Cierva, *113.178 caídos*, 28–37. (Page 33 of Garzón's auto.)

24. Napoleoni, *Garzón*, 24–25.

25. Coixet, *Garzón*, 125–28; 110–12.

26. On an important procedural matter, La Sala Especial of the Tribunal Supremo, by a vote of thirteen to two, prohibited five magistrates from participating in the decision against Garzón on the grounds that their objectivity was compromised. This was the first time such an action was taken. (See *El País*, June 14, 2011.) For the decision against Garzón, see newspapers for February 9, 2012. Additional articles on Garzón's case may be found in the issues for January 19, February 27, and May 9, 2012. In March 2012, the Tribunal Supremo formally barred any further criminal investigation of killings by Franco's forces as crimes against humanity and upheld the authority of the law of amnesty. The court did say that families whose ancestors had disappeared could bring actions in local courts to open graves and identify the victims.

27. "Charges against Spanish Investigative Judge Must Be Dropped," April 22, 2010, Amnesty International website, http://www.amnesty.org/en/news-and-updates/charges-against-spanish-investigative-judge-must-be-dropped-2010-04-22/. An official of Amnesty International added, "The 1977 Amnesty Law barring prosecutions of crimes under international law violates Spain's obligations under international law and it is a duty of the Judiciary, sooner or later, to state that such a piece of legislation is simply null and void."

28. *New York Times*, September 23, 2011.

29. Two of the most informative and thoughtful articles about the TRC are Minow, "Between Vengeance and Forgiveness," 319–55, and Allen, "Balancing Justice and Social Unity, 315–53.

30. Minow, "Between Vengeance and Forgiveness," 341.

31. Ibid., especially 325–32.

32. Ibid., especially 340, 341, 342.

33. Ibid., 324, 325, 337.

34. Allen, "Balancing Justice and Social Unity," 317, 349, 352.

35. O'Connor, "Fostering Forgiveness," 177, 165–82; Minow, "Between Vengeance and Forgiveness," 338.

36. Aguilar Fernández, *Políticas de la memoria*, 468"; Cuesta Bustillo, *Odisea de la memoria*, 326. Similarly, in the United States, museums and historical organizations often shy away from in-depth depictions of the years of Reconstruction, since the events of that era collide with powerful myths propagated by old elites. See the article in the *New York Times*, December 5, 2011, by Edward Rothstein, "The South Reinterprets its 'Lost Cause.'"

37. "No he leído la biografía de Franco," *El País*, June 4, 2011.

38. Ibid.

39. "¿Qué esperar de un país que no llama dictador a Franco?," *El País*, July 2, 2011, 56; "Acto de Darío Rivas con las víctimas de franquismo," *nuevatribunaes*, June 29, 2011.

40. *San Cristóbal/Ezkaba: Muros derribados para amurallar la memoria: Informe pericial sobre los derribos realizados por el Ministerio de Defensa en el Fuerte-Penal de San Cristóbal/Ezkaba*, Navarra (Iruñea/Pamplona, February 2001), Iniciativa Autobús de la Memoria/Oroimenaren Autobusa, http://www.autobusdelamemoria.org/.

41. *El Mundo*, November 22, 2002; *La Razón*, December 28, 2006; *ABC*, November 2, 2008.

42. Obama's Philadelphia speech, March 18, 2008, http://www.wnd.com/?pageId=59257/, among other sites.

43. Pérez Garzón and Manzano Moreno, *Memoria histórica*, 117–20, 140.

44. Ibid., 130–32, 121–22, 127.

45. The phrase is Santiago Carrillo's.

Chapter 5. Economic Change and the Transformation of Cultural Landscapes

1. David J. Rutledge, quoted in the *Washington Post*, December 22, 2010.

2. Álvarez-Nogal and Prados de la Escosura, "Decline of Spain," 319–66, especially Table 8 on 338, which shows that 23.2 percent of the nation's population was "urban" in 1857; Harrison, *Economic History*, 5, 25–39.

3. Harrison, *Economic History*, chap. 4 and 91–102, 131–41; Harrison, *Spanish Economy*, 7.

4. Harrison, *Economic History*, 146–49; Harrison, *Spanish Economy*, 8; Harrison and Corkill, *Spain*, 51–52.

5. Harrison, *Economic History*, 152–54; Harrison, *Spanish Economy*, 8.

6. Harrison, *Economic History*, 154–56; Harrison, *Spanish Economy*, 8; Harrison and Corkill, *Spain*, 99–101.

7. Harrison, *Spanish Economy*, 145.

8. Harrison, *Economic History*, 155; Harrison, *Spanish Economy*, 156, 160–61.

9. Harrison, *Economic History*, 154–63, 160; Harrison, *Spanish Economy*, 158, 159, 8.

10. Harrison and Corkill, *Spain*, 43–44; Harrison, *Spanish Economy*, 156.

11. Harrison and Corkill, *Spain*, 19, 88–89, 125–26; ISTA Population in Spain, http://www.irantour.org/spai/spainpopulation.html/.

12. Harrison and Corkill, *Spain*, 19, 125–26, 127–29, 135–36.

13. Economists differ as to explanations of Spain's generally higher levels of unemployment. One group of economists attributes the problem to laws and practices that make it difficult to fire workers and thus make employers reluctant to hire them. Other economists point out that there are other European countries that have the same types of laws and practices without the same levels of unemployment. A contributing factor seems to be the relative lack of competitiveness of Spain's small companies and enterprises. Many of the large firms are advanced and competitive.

14. See Wright, *Political Economy of the Cotton South*, 89, 91, 94–97, 158–59.

15. Wright, *Old South, New South*, 76.

16. Ibid., 107.

17. Ibid., 124–25.

18. Ibid., 159–62.

19. Ibid., 162, 165–71, 164.

20. Ibid., 68, 162, 70. Many of the first textile mills were located in the countryside in order to be close to sources of waterpower. After steam and electricity became the major sources of power for the mills, there was no longer a need to locate in rural areas, but leaders of the industry, such as D. A Tompkins, then recommended locating outside city limits in order to avoid lawyers and law suits.

21. Ibid., 14, 78–79, 123.

22. Ibid., 78.

23. Ibid., 198–201, 205.

24. Ibid., 213–16.

25. Ibid., 216–19.

26. Ibid., 233–34, 236, 242–43, 245; Bass and De Vries, *Transformation of Southern Politics*, 503.

27. Wright, *Old South, New South*, 245.

28. Ibid., 245, 247, 238; Bass and DeVries, *Transformation of Southern Politics*, 500–501.

29. Cobb, *South and America*, 62–63. See also Morton Sosna, "More Important than the Civil War?" 145–58.

30. Ronald H. Bayor, "Race, Ethnicity, and political change in the Urban Sunbelt South," 127–39, quote on 139, in Miller and Pozzetta, *Shades of the Sunbelt*; Leach, "Progress under Pressure."

31. Numan V. Bartley, "In Search of the New South: Southern Politics After Reconstruction," in Kutler and Katz, *Promise of American History*, 160.

32. Roland, *Improbable Era*, 16; Cobb, *Selling of the South*; Wright, *Old South, New South*, 257–58, 261–62.

33. Figure 6 in Clay and Stuart, *Charlotte Metro Region*, 6; Goldfield, *Still Fighting the Civil War*, 273. The statistics from the Charlotte Metro Region come from the U.S. Department of Commerce, Bureau of the Census, 1985 and 1988, and from the U.S. Department of Agriculture, Agricultural Statistics, 1980, 1984, and 1988.

34. Cobb, *South and America*, 204–7.

35. Dennis, *New Economy*, 3.

36. Wright, *Old South, New South*, 239, 270.

37. Ibid., 239, 263; Bass and DeVries, *Transformation of Southern Politics*, 21; Bureau of the Census, *Per Capita Personal Income by State, 1990 to 2010*, Statistical Abstract of the United States, http://www.census.gov/compendia/statab/past_years.html/.

38. Bass and DeVries, *Transformation of Southern Politics*, 498–500, 22; Black and Black, *Politics and Society*, 17.

39. Frey, "New Great Migration." See the cover page and page 11 of the attached report (in pdf form).

40. Blair-Rockefeller Poll.

41. See, for example, Reed, *My Tears Spoiled my Aim*; quoted in Goldfield, *Still Fighting the Civil War*, 8.

Bibliography

Primary Sources

Arlington Confederate Monument Report website. http://www.arlingtonconfederatemonument.blogspot.com/.

Aznar, José María. "Discurso de investidura." 1996. On line at http://beersandpolitics.com/.

———. *España: La segúnda transición.* Madrid: Espasa Calpe, 1994.

Bagby, George William. *The Old Virginia Gentleman, and Other Sketches.* New York: Scribner, 1910.

Basler, Roy P., editor. *The Collected Works of Abraham Lincoln.* 9 volumes. New Brunswick, NJ: Rutgers University Press, 1953.

Blair-Rockefeller Poll. University of Arkansas. On line at http://blaircenter.uark.edu/.

Bruce, H. C. *The New Man: Twenty-nine Years a Slave, Twenty-nine Years a Free Man.* York, PA: P. Anstadt & Sons, 1895.

Carrillo, Santiago. *La difícil reconciliación de los españoles: De la dictadura a la democracia.* Barcelona: Editorial Planeta, 2011.

Cooke, John Esten. *Surry of Eagle's Nest; or, The Memoirs of a staff-officer serving in Virginia.* New York: Bunce and Huntington, 1866.

Core Beliefs Statement. League of the South website. http://dixienet.org/New%20Site/corebeliefs.shtml/.

Dilectissima Nobis. By Pope Pius XI. Papal Encyclicals Online. http://www.papalencyclicals.net/Pius11/P11NOBIS.HTM/.

Documentos colectivos del episcopado Español, 1870–1974. Edited by Jesús Iribarren. Madrid: Biblioteca de Autores Cristianos, 1974.

Douglass, Frederick. *Three Addresses on the Relations Subsisting between the White and Colored People of the United States.* Washington, DC: Gibson Bros., 1886.

Gaines, Bishop W. J. *The Negro and the White Man.* Philadelphia: AME Publishing House, 1897.

González, Felipe. "Discurso de investidura." 1982. On line at http://beersandpolitics.com/.
Grant, Ulysses S. Inaugural Addresses. Bartleby.com website. http://www.bartleby.com/.
Harris, Joel Chandler. *Life of Henry Grady, including His Writings and Speeches*. New York: Haskell House Publishers, 1972.
"Iniciativa Autobús de la Memoria/Oroimenaren Autobusa." On line at http://www.autobusdelamemoria.org/.
Iribarren, Jesús, editor. *Del episcopado español, 1870–1974*. Madrid: Biblioteca Documentos colectivos de autores cristianos, 1974.
Kennedy, John Fitzgerald. "Radio and Television Report to the American People on Civil Rights." June 11, 1963. On line at http://www.jfklibrary.org/Research/Ready-Reference/JFK-Speeches/Radio-and-Television/.
Ley 46/1977, de 15 de octubre, de Amnistia. On line at http://noticias.juridicas.com/base_datos/Penal/l46-1977.html/.
Mahoney, James. "Path Dependence in Historical Sociology." *Theory and Society*. Volume 29, Number 4, 507–48.
Marañón, Tom Burns, editor. *Conversaciones sobre la derecha*. Barcelona: Plaza Janés, 1997.
McClure, Alexander Kelly. *The South: Its Industrial, Financial, and Political Condition*. Philadelphia: J. B. Lippincott, 1886.
Merry y Colón, Manuel, and Antonio Merry y Villalba. *Compendio de historia de España: Redactado para server de texto en los seminaries y colegios católicos*. Sevilla: Imp y Lit. de José María Ariza, 1889.
"Mil sacerdotes españoles rompen el silencio contra las omisiones y complicidades en el campo católico." On line at http://www.pliniocorreadeoliveira.info/ES_197611_Milsacerdotesespanolesrompenelsilencio.htm/.
Page, Thomas Nelson. *In Ole Virginia: or, Marse Chan and Other Stories*. New York: Charles Scribner's Sons, 1887.
———. *The Negro: The Southerner's Problem*. New York: Charles Scribner's Sons, 1904.
———. *The Novels, Stories, Sketches and Poems of Thomas Nelson Page*. New York: Charles Scribner's Sons, 1906.
Plá y Deniel, Enrique. *Las dos ciudades: Carta pastoral que dirige a sus diocesanos el Excmo. Y Rvdmo. El 30 de septiembre de 1936*. Salamanca: Establecimiento Tipográfico de Calatrava, 1936.
Populist Party Platform, 1892. On line at http://www.presidency.ucsb.edu/ws/index.php?pid=29616#axzz1dyINtS1g/.
Republican Campaign Text Book for 1880. Washington, DC: Republican Congres-

sional Campaign Committee, 1880. On line at http://www.archive.org/details/republicancampao3commgoog/.

Rodríguez, Teodore. *El problema social y las derechas*. Madrid: El Escorial, 1935.

Rodríguez Zapatero, José Luis. "El avance en políticas sociales, 2004–2011." February 24, 2011. PowerPoint summary obtained from the PSOE website. http://www.psoe.es/.

San Cristóba/Ezkaba: Muros derribados para amurallar la memoria: Informe pericial sobre Los derribos realizados por el Ministerio de Defensa en el Fuerte-Penal de San Cristóba/Ezkaba, Navarra. Iruñea/Pamplona, February 2001. Iniciativa Autobús de la Memoria/Oroimenaren Autobusa.

Smedes, Susan Dabney. *Memorials of a Southern Planter*. Baltimore: Cushings and Bailey, 1887.

Smith, Frank E. *Congressman from Mississippi*. New York: Pantheon Books, 1964.

South Carolina Resolutions on Abolitionist Propaganda, 1835. In *Documents of American History*. Volume 1, 9th ed., edited by Henry Steele Commager. New York: Appleton-Century-Crofts, 1973.

Southern Poverty Law Center. Intelligence files. On line at http://www.splcenter.org/get-informed/intelligence-files/.

Speeches of Rutherford B. Hayes. Rutherford B. Hayes Presidential Center website. http://www.rbhayes.org/.

Suarez, Adolfo. "Discurso de dimisión." January 29, 1981. On line at http://www.retoricas.com/.

Syllabus of Errors Condemned by Pope Pius IX. Papal Encyclicals. On line at http://www.papalencyclicals.net/Pius09/p9syll.htm/.

Unamuno, Miguel de. *Obras completes*. Madrid: Escelicer, 1966.

Secondary Sources

Abbott, Richard H. *The Republican Party and the South, 1855–1877: The First Southern Strategy*. Baton Rouge: Louisiana State University Press, 2002.

Aguilar, Paloma, and Carsten Humlebaek. "Collective Memory and National Identity in the Spanish Democracy: The Legacies of Francoism and the Civil War." *History and Memory*. Volume 14, Issues 1 and 2 (combined) (Spring–Winter 2002): 121–64.

Aguilar Fernández, Paloma. *Políticas de la memoria y memorias de la política: El caso español en perspectiva comparada*. Madrid: Alianza Editorial, 2008.

Allen, Jonathan. "Balancing Justice and Social Unity: Political Theory and the idea of a Truth and Reconciliation Commission." *University of Toronto Law Journal*. Volume 49, Number 3 (Summer 1999): 315–55.

Alonso, Gregorio, and Diego Muro. *The Politics and Memory of Democratic Transition: The Spanish Model*. New York: Routledge, 2011.

Alvarez-Nogal, Carlos, and Leandro Prados de la Escosura. "The Decline of Spain (1500–1850): Conjectural Estimates." *European Review of Economic History*. Volume 2 (2007): 319–66.

Bailey, Fred Arthur. "Free Speech and the 'Lost Cause' in Texas: A Study of Social Control in the New South." *Southwestern Historical Quarterly* (January 1994): 452–77.

———. "Free Speech and the 'Lost Cause' in the Old Dominion." *Virginia Magazine of History and Biography*. April 1995, 237–66.

———. "Free Speech at the University of Florida." *Florida Historical Quarterly*, July 1992, 1–17.

Balfour, Sebastian, editor. *The Politics of Contemporary Spain*. New York: Routledge, 2005.

Balfour, Sebastian, and Alejandro Quiroga. *España Reinventada: Nación e identidad desde la transición*. Barcelona: Península, 2007.

Barahona De Brito, Alexandra, Carmen González-Enriquez, and Paloma Aguilar, editors. *The Politics of Memory: Transitional Justice in Democratizing Societies*. Oxford: Oxford University Press, 2001.

Bartley, Numan. *The Rise of Massive Resistance: Race and Politics in the South during the 1950s*. Baton Rouge: Louisiana State University Press, 1969.

Bass, Jack, and Walter DeVries. *The Transformation of Southern Politics: Social Change and Political Consequence Since 1945*. New York: Basic Books, 1976.

Beale, Howard K. *The Critical Year: A Study of Andrew Johnson and Reconstruction*. New York: Harcourt Brace, 1930.

Benedict, Michael Les. *The Fruits of Victory: Alternatives in Restoring the Union, 1865–1877*. Philadelphia: J. B. Lippincott, 1975.

Black, Earl, and Merle Black. *Politics and Society in the South*. Cambridge: Harvard University Press, 1987.

Blanco, Juan. *23-F: Crónica fiel de un golpe anunciado*. Madrid: Fuerza Nueva, 1995.

Blight, David. "The Civil War Sesquicentennial." *Chronicle of Higher Education*, June 2, 2009. On line at http://www.davidwblight.com/sesq.htm/.

———. *Race and Reunion*. Cambridge: Belknap Press of Harvard University Press, 2001.

Blum, Edward J. *Reforging the White Republic: Race Religion, and American Nationalism, 1865–1898*. Baton Rouge: Louisiana State University Press, 2005.

Bowers, Claude. *The Tragic Era: The Revolution after Lincoln*. Cambridge, MA: Houghton Mifflin, 1929.

Branch, Taylor. *At Canaan's Edge: America in the King Years, 1965–1968*. New York: Simon and Schuster, 2006.

———. *Parting the Waters: America in the King Years, 1954–1963*. New York: Simon and Schuster, 1988.

———. *Pillar of Fire: America in the King Years, 1963–1965*. New York: Simon and Schuster, 1998.
Brown, Thomas J. *Remixing the Civil War*. Baltimore: Johns Hopkins University Press, 2011.
Budiansky, Stephen. *The Bloody Shirt: Terror after Appomattox*. New York: Viking, 2008.
Callahan, William J. *The Catholic Church in Spain, 1875–1998*. Washington, DC: Catholic University Press, 2000.
Carr, Raymond. *Modern Spain, 1875–1980*. New York: Oxford University Press, 2000.
———, editor. *Spain: A History*. New York: Oxford University Press, 2000.
Carter, Dan. *When the War Was Over: The Failure of Self-Reconstruction in the South, 1865–1867*. Baton Rouge: Louisiana State University Press, 1985.
Cercas, Javier. *Anatomía de un instante*. Barcelona: Mondadori, 2009.
Cierva, Ricardo de la. *113.178 caídos por Dios y por España*. Madrid: Editorial Fénix, 2009.
Clay, James W., and Alfred W. Stuart, editors. *Charlotte Metro Region: Hub of the Carolinas*. Charlotte: University of North Carolina Department of Geography and Earth Sciences, n.d. (approximately 1989).
Cobb, James C. *The Selling of the South: The Southern Crusade for Industrial Development, 1936–1980*. Baton Rouge: Louisiana State University Press, 1982.
———. *The South and America since World War II*. New York: Oxford University Press, 2011.
Cobb, James C., and Charles R. Wilson, editors. *Perspectives on the American South: An Annual Review of Society, Politics and Culture*. Volume 4. New York: Routledge, 1987.
Coixet, Isabel. *Garzón: La fuerza de la razón*. Barcelona: Random House Mondadori, SA, 2011.
Coixet, Isabel, and Barbara Bellows. *God and General Longstreet*. Baton Rouge: Louisiana State University Press, 1982.
Connelly, Thomas L. *The Marble Man: Robert E. Lee and His Image in American Society*. New York: Knopf, 1977.
Cox, Karen L. *Dixie's Daughters: The United Daughters of the Confederacy and the Preservation of Confederate Culture*. Gainesville: University Press of Florida, 2003.
Cuenca Toribio, José Manuel. *Relaciones Iglesia-Estado en la España contemporánea (1833–1985)*. Madrid: Editorial Alhambra, 1985.
Cuesta Bustillo, Josefina. *La odisea de la memoria: Historia de la memoria en España, siglo XX*. Madrid: Alianza Editorial, 2008.

Current, Richard N., editor. *Reconstruction in Retrospect: Views from the Turn of the Century*. Baton Rouge: Louisiana State University Press, 1969.

Dallek, Robert. *Flawed Giant: Lyndon B. Johnson and His Times, 1961–1973*. New York: Oxford University Press, 1998.

Davis, David Brion. *The Slave Power Conspiracy and the Paranoid Style*. Baton Rouge: Louisiana State University Press, 1970.

Dennis, Michael. *The New Economy of the Modern South*. Gainesville: University Press of Florida, 2009.

Doyle, Don. *Nations Divided: America, Italy, and the Southern Question*. Athens: University of Georgia Press, 2002.

Durden, Robert F. *The Gray and the Black: The Confederate Debate on Emancipation*. Baton Rouge: Louisiana State University Press, 1972.

———. *James Shepherd Pike: Republicanism and the American Negro, 1850–1882*. Durham, NC: Duke University Press, 1957.

Elkins, Stanley. *Slavery: A Problem in American Institutional and Intellectual Life*. 3rd ed. Chicago: University of Chicago Press, 1976.

Escott, Paul D. *The Confederacy: The Slaveholders' Failed Venture*. Santa Barbara, CA: Praeger, 2010.

———. *Many Excellent People: Power and Privilege in North Carolina, 1850–1900*. Chapel Hill: University of North Carolina Press, 1985.

———. "The Uses of Gallantry: Virginians and the Origins of J. E. B. Stuart's Historical Image." *Virginia Magazine of History and Biography*. Volume 103, Number 1 (January 1995): 47–74.

———. *"What Shall We Do with the Negro?": Lincoln, White Racism, and Civil War America*. Charlottesville: University of Virginia Press, 2009.

Escott, Paul D., and David Goldfield, editors. *Major Problems in the History of the American South*. Volume 2. Lexington, MA: D. C. Heath, 1990.

Faulkner, William. *Intruder in the Dust*. New York: Random House, 1948.

Fehrenbacher, Don E. *Slavery, Law, and Politics: The Dred Scott Case in Historical Perspective*. New York: Oxford University Press, 1981.

Foner, Eric. *Free Soil, Free Labor, Free Men: The Ideology of the Republican Party before the Civil War*. New York: Oxford University Press, 1970.

———. *Reconstruction: America's Unfinished Revolution, 1863–1877*. New York: Harper and Row, 1988.

Franklin, John Hope. *From Slavery to Freedom: A History of Negro Americans*. 3rd ed. New York: Alfred A. Knopf, 1967.

———. *Reconstruction: After the Civil War*. Chicago: University of Chicago Press, 1961.

Freehling, William W. *The Road to Disunion*. 2 volumes. New York: Oxford University Press, 1990 and 2007.

———. *The South vs. the South: How Anti-Confederate Southerners Shaped the Course of the Civil War*. New York: Oxford University Press, 2001.

Frey, William H. "The New Great Migration: Black Americans' Return to the South, 1965–2000." Brookings Institution Report. Online at http://www.brookings.edu/reports/2004/05demographics_frey.aspx/.

Gies, David T., editor. *The Cambridge Companion to Modern Spanish Culture*. New York: Cambridge University Press, 1999.

Gillette, William. *Retreat from Reconstruction, 1869–1879*. Baton Rouge: Louisiana State University Press, 1979.

Goldfield, David R. *America Aflame: How the Civil War Created a Nation*. New York: Bloomsbury Press, 2011.

———. *Still Fighting the Civil War*. Baton Rouge: Louisiana State University Press, 2002.

Goodwyn, Lawrence. *Democratic Promise: The Populist Moment in America*. New York: Oxford University Press, 1976.

Griffin, Clifford S. *The Ferment of Reform, 1830–1860*. Arlington Heights, IL: Harlan Davidson, 1968.

Hammond, John Craig, and Matthew Mason, editors. *Contesting Slavery: The Politics of Bondage and Freedom in the New American Nation*. Charlottesville: University of Virginia Press, 2011.

Harrison, Joseph. *An Economic History of Modern Spain*. New York: Holmes & Meier, 1978.

———. *The Spanish Economy in the Twentieth Century*. New York: St. Martin's Press, 1985.

Harrison, Joseph, and David Corkill. *Spain: A Modern European Economy*. Aldershot, UK: Ashgate Publishing, 2004.

Hayes, Samuel P. *The Response to Industrialism, 1885–1914*. Chicago: University of Chicago Press, 1957.

Horwitz, Tony. *Confederates in the Attic: Dispatches from the Unfinished Civil War*. New York: Pantheon Books, 1998.

Howe, Daniel Walker. *What Hath God Wrought: The Transformation of America, 1815–1848*. New York: Oxford University Press, 1009.

Janney, Caroline E. *Burying the Dead but Not the Past*. Chapel Hill: University of North Carolina Press, 2008.

Jenkins, William Sumner. *Pro-slavery Thought in the Old South*. Chapel Hill: University of North Carolina Press, 1935.

Juliá, Santos. *Hoy no es ayer*. Barcelona: RBA-Libros, 2009.

———, director. *Memoria de la guerra y del franquismo*. Madrid: Santillana Ediciones Generales, 2006.

Juliá, Santos, José Luis García Delgado, Juan Carlos Jiménez, and Juan Pablo Fusi. *La España del siglo XX*. Madrid: Marcial Pons, Ediciones de Historia, SA, 2007.
Key, V. O. *Southern Politics in State and Nation*. New York: Vintage Books, 1949.
Kluger, Richard. *Simple Justice: The History of Brown v. Board of Education and Black America's Struggle for Equality*. New York: Alfred A. Knopf, 1976.
Kousser, J. Morgan. *The Shaping of Southern Politics: Suffrage Restriction and the Establishment of the One-party South, 1880–1910*. New Haven: Yale University Press, 1974.
Kutler, Stanley T., and Stanley N. Katz, editors. *The Promise of American History*. Baltimore: Johns Hopkins University Press, 1982.
Lazo, Alfonso. *Una familia mal avenida: Falange, iglesia y ejército*. Madrid: Editorial Sintesis, 2008.
Leach, Damonia Etta Brown. "Progress under Pressure: Change in Charlotte Race Relations, 1955–1965." Master's thesis, University of North Carolina at Chapel Hill, 1976.
Lewis, David L. *King: A Biography*. Urbana: University of Illinois Press, 1978.
Link, Arthur S. *Progressivism*. Arlington Heights, IL: Harlan Davidson, 1983.
———. *Woodrow Wilson and the Progressive Era, 1910–1917*. New York: Harper, 1954.
Linz, Juan J., and Alfred Stepan. *Problems of Democratic Transition and Consolidation: Southern Europe, South America, and Post-Communist Europe*. Baltimore: Johns Hopkins University Press, 1996.
Litwack, Leon. *North of Slavery: The Negro in the Free States, 1790–1860*. Chicago: University of Chicago Press, 1961.
Loewen, James, and Edward H. Sebesta, editors. *The Confederate and Neo-Confederate Reader*. Jackson: University Press of Mississippi, 2010.
Logan, Rayford W. *The Negro in American Life and Thought: The Nadir, 1877–1901*. New York: Dial Press, 1954.
Madden, David, editor. *Thomas Wolfe's Civil War*. Tuscaloosa: University of Alabama Press, 2004.
Magness, Phillip W., and Sebastian N. Page. *Colonization after Emancipation: Lincoln and the Movement for Black Resettlement*. Columbia: University of Missouri Press, 2011.
McDonald, Forrest, and Grady McWhiney. "The Antebellum Southern Herdsman: A Re-interpretation." *Journal of Southern History*. Volume 41, Number 2 (May 1975): 147–66.
McPherson, James M. *Battle Cry of Freedom: The Civil War Era*. New York: Oxford University Press, 1988.
———. *Ordeal by Fire: The Civil War and Reconstruction*. New York: Alfred A. Knopf, 1982.

Meier, August, and Elliot Rudwick. *Negro Thought in America, 1880–1915: Racial Ideologies in the Age of Booker T. Washington*. Ann Arbor: University of Michigan Press, 1966.

Merino, Julio. *Tejero: 25 años después*. Madrid: Espejo de Tinta, 2006.

Miller, Randall M., and George E. Pozzetta. *Shades of the Sunbelt: Essays on Ethnicity, Race, and the Urban South*. Westport, CT: Greenwood Press, 1988.

Miller, Stuart C. *Benevolent Assimilation: The American Conquest of the Philippines, 1899–1903*. New Haven: Yale University Press, 1984.

Mills, Cynthia, and Pamela H. Simpson, editors. *Monuments to the Lost Cause: Women, Art, and the Landscapes of Southern History*. Knoxville: University of Tennessee Press, 2003.

Minow, Martha. "Between Vengeance and Forgiveness: South Africa's Truth and Reconciliation Commission." *Negotiation Journal*. Volume 14, Number 4 (1998): 319–55.

Moa, Pio. *Los mitos de la Guerra Civil*. Madrid: Esferalibros, 2003.

Moradiellos, Enrique. *1936: Los mitos de la Guerra Civil*. Barcelona: Ediciones Península, 2004.

Morodo, Raúl. *Los orígines ideológicos de franquismo: Acción Española*. Madrid: Alianza Editorial, 1985.

Mowry, George E. *Another Look at the Twentieth-Century South*. Baton Rouge: Louisiana State University Press, 1973.

———. *The Era of Theodore Roosevelt, 1900–1912*. New York: Harper, 1959.

———. *The Progressive Era, 1900–1920: The Reform Persuasion*. Washington, DC: American Historical Association, 1972.

———. *Theodore Roosevelt and the Progressive Movement*. Madison: University of Wisconsin Press, 1946.

Napoleoni, Loretta. *Garzón: La hora de la verdad*. Barcelona: Principal de los Libros, 2001.

Neff, John. *Honoring the Civil War Dead: Commemoration and the Problem of Reconciliation*. Lawrence: University Press of Kansas, 2005.

Nietzsche, Friedrich. *Unmodern Observations*. Edited by William Arrowsmith. New Haven: Yale University Press, 1990.

Nolan, Alan. *Lee Considered: General Robert E. Lee and Civil War History*. Chapel Hill: University of North Carolina Press, 1991.

Norton, Mary Beth, David Katzman, Paul Escott, Howard Chudacoff, Thomas Paterson, and William Tuttle. *A People and a Nation*. Boston: Houghton Mifflin, 1994.

Novick, Peter. *That Noble Dream: The "Objectivity Question" and the American Historical Profession*. Cambridge: Cambridge University Press, 1988.

O'Connor, June E. "Fostering Forgiveness in the Public Square: How Realistic a Goal?" *Journal of the Society of Christian Ethics*. Volume 22 (Fall 2002): 165–82.

Pérez Garzón, Juan Sisinio, and Eduardo Manzano Moreno. *Memoria histórica*. Serie Debates Científicos de SCIC. Madrid: Los Libros de la Catarata, 2010.

Perote, Juan Alberto. *23-F: Ni Milans ne Tejero: El informe que se ocultó*. Madrid: Foca, 2001.

Phillips, Ulrich B. *American Negro Slavery*. New York: D. Appleton, 1918.

———. *Life and Labor in the Old South*. New introduction by John David Smith. Columbia: University of South Carolina Press, 2007.

Piston, William Garrett. *Lee's Tarnished Lieutenant: James Longstreet and His Place in Southern History*. Athens: University of Georgia Press, 1987.

Potter, David M. *The Impending Crisis, 1848–1861*. New York: Harper & Row, 1976.

Preston, Paul. *El holocausto español: Odio y exterminio en la Guerra Civil y después*. Barcelona: Random House Mondadori, SA, 2011.

Reed, John Shelton. *My Tears Spoiled My Aim, and Other Reflections on Southern Culture*. Columbia: University of Missouri Press, 1993.

———. *One South: An Ethnic Approach to Regional Culture*. Baton Rouge: Louisiana State University Press, 1982.

Richards, Michael. "From War Culture to Civil Society: Francoism, Social Change, and Memories of the Spanish Civil War." *History and Memory*. Volume 14, Numbers 1 and 2 (combined) (Spring–Winter 2002): 93–120.

Roland, Charles P. *The Improbable Era: The South since World War II*. Lexington: University Press of Kentucky, 1975.

Roniger, Luis, and Mario Sznajder. *The Legacy of Human Rights Violations in the Southern Cone*. New York: Oxford University Press, 1999.

Rubio, Manuel. *23-F: El proceso: Del sumario a la sentencia*. Barcelona: Libros Ceres, 1982.

Sadat, Leila N. "Exile, Amnesty and International Law." Washington University School of Law Working Paper No. 05-04-03. On line at http://papers.ssrn.com/sol3/papers.cfm?abstract_id=712621/.

Segura, Santiago, and Julio Merion. *Jaque al Rey*. Barcelona: Planeta, 1983.

Shubert, Adrian. *A Social History of Modern Spain*. London: Unwin Hyman, 1990.

Silva, Emilio, and Santiago Macías. *Las fosas de Franco: Los republicanos que el dictator dejó en las cunetas*. Madrid: Ediciones Temas de Hoy, 2003.

Silver, James. *Mississippi: The Closed Society*. New York: Harcourt, Brace and World, 1964.

Simkins, Francis Butler. *Pitchfork Ben Tillman: South Carolinian*. Baton Rouge: Louisiana State University Press, 1944, 1967.

Sproat, John. *The Best Men: Liberal Reformers in the Gilded Age*. New York: Oxford University Press, 1968.

Stout, Harry. Beecher Lectures, 2005. On line at http://www.yale.edu/divinity/convocation/lectures.htm/.

Taylor, George Rogers. *The Transportation Revolution, 1815–1860*. New York: Harper Torchbooks, 1958.

Thompson, Elizabeth Lee. *The Reconstruction of Southern Debtors*. Athens: University of Georgia Press, 2004.

Tindall, George Brown. *The Disruption of the Solid South*. Athens: University of Georgia Press, 1972.

———. *The Persistent Tradition in New South Politics*. Baton Rouge: Louisiana State University Press, 1975.

Tise, Larry E. *Proslavery: A History of the Defense of Slavery in America, 1701–1848*. Athens: University of Georgia Press.

Tusell, Javier. *El Aznarato: El gobierno del Partido Popular, 1996–2003*. Madrid: Santillana Ediciones Generales, SL, 2004.

Villada, Zacharías García. *El destino de España en la historia universal*. Madrid: Edition Cultura Española, 1936.

Viñas, Ángel, editor. *En el combate por la historia: La República, la guerra civil, el franquismo*. Barcelona: Pasado & Presente, 2012.

Walker, Anders. *The Ghost of Jim Crow: How Southern Moderates Used Brown v. Board of Education to Stall Civil Rights*. New York: Oxford University Press, 2009.

Watts, Sarah L. *Rough Rider in the White House: Theodore Roosevelt and the Politics of Desire*. Chicago: University of Chicago Press, 2003.

Wiebe, Robert H. *The Search for Order, 1877–1914*. New York: Hill & Wang, 1967.

Woodward, C. Vann. *Origins of the New South*. Baton Rouge: Louisiana State University Press, 1951, 1971.

———. *Tom Watson: Agrarian Rebel*. New York: Macmillan, 1938.

Wright, Gavin. *Old South, New South: Revolutions in the Southern Economy since the Civil War*. New York: Basic Books, 1986.

———. *The Political Economy of the Cotton South: Households, Markets, and Wealth in the Nineteenth Century*. New York: Norton, 1978.

Zilversmit, Arthur. *The First Emancipation; the Abolition of Slavery in the North*. Chicago: University of Chicago Press, 1967.

Index

ABC, 49, 66, 67, 68, 69, 70, 73, 115, 119, 189
Abolitionism, 28
Adams, Brooks, 87
African Americans, 31, 33, 35, 36, 39, 40,
    41, 42, 60, 76, 81, 88–89, 91–92, 96–97,
    102–3, 138, 142, 143, 145, 149, 150, 152, 155,
    157–58, 168, 190, 208–9, 212
African National Congress, 179
Agriculture: in Spain, 196, 197, 200, 201,
    202; in the United States, 203–5, 206,
    207, 208–10, 212
Aguilar Fernández, Paloma, 4, 185
Alabama, 41, 83, 99, 100, 151, 157, 158, 206,
    212, 214
Alianza Popular, 108, 113, 132
Allen, Jonathan, 182
Al Qaeda, 24
Álzaga, Oscar, 17
Amnesty: discussed, 69, 171, 172, 173–75,
    179–80, 181; mentioned, 4, 170; in Spain,
    19, 57–58, 64, 65, 71, 167, 177, 184, 187–88
Amnesty International, 71
Anarchists, 9, 50, 62
Andalucia, 9
Anson, Luis María, 68
Anticlericalism, 10
Anticommunism, 15, 16
Anti-Semitism, 62
Apartheid, 179, 181
Argentina, 172–73, 176, 189
Arkansas, 155, 157, 211
Armada, General Alfonso, 186

Army: improved image of, in Spain, 73–74;
    mentioned, 170; in Spanish politics, 11,
    12, 18, 19, 22, 48–49, 56, 65, 72
Askew, Reubin, 157
Asmal, Kader, 183
Association for the Recovery of Historical
    Memory, 63, 64, 67, 70, 177, 178
Asturias, 12
Atheism, 3, 50, 51, 52, 116
Atlantic Monthly, 80, 83, 86, 88, 91
Atrocities in war, 14
Atwater, Lee, 99
Audiencia Nacional, 63, 176
Autonomías, 19, 22–23, 110, 167
Azaña Díaz, Manuel, 11–12
Aznar, José María, 23–24, 113–14, 117,
    120–21, 126, 129, 189

Bagby, George William, 85
Bailey, Fred, 94
Banks, Enoch Marvin, 94
Baptists, 136, 151, 160–61
Barcelona, 9, 10, 127, 130, 134
Bardem, Juan Antonio, 58
Barnett, Ross, 155
Bartley, Numan, 211
Basque country, 9, 12, 15, 17, 19, 22, 24, 110,
    113, 126, 129, 131–32, 133
Basques, 62
Beale, Howard K., 95
Becker, Carl, 191
Belgium, 176, 178

Bildu, 24, 120, 131–32
Birge, Mrs. M. M., 94
Bishop Plá y Deniel, 49, 50
Bishop Xavier Novell, 49
Bitterness: causes of, 2–3, 14–15, 31–33, 35; nurturing of in South, 42–43
Black, Earl, 161, 162
Black, Merle, 162
Black codes, 33
Blaine, James G., 80, 139, 140
Blight, David, 169
"Bloody shirt," 140–41
Bolshevism, 11, 13, 45, 50, 51, 144
Bowers, Claude, 95
Brazil, 173–74, 179
Brown vs. Board of Education, 96, 152, 154, 169
Bruce, H. C., 89
Bryce, James, 89–90
Bumpers, Dale, 157
Burgos, Antonio, 189
Buruma, Ian, 163
Busbee, George, 136
Butler, Benjamin, 32
Byrnes, James, 149

Calhoun, John C., 29
Calvo Sotelo, Leopoldo, 20
Cánovas del Castillo, Antonio, 113
Carabaña, Julio, 192
Cardinal Antonio María Rouco Varela, 72, 115
Cardinal Isidro Gomá, 50
Cardinal Segura y Sáenz, 12, 15
Cardinal Vicente Enrique y Tarancón, 56, 72
Carrero Blanco, Admiral Luis, 17, 56
Carrillo, Santiago, 57
Carter, Jimmy, 99, 157
Cash, W. J., 144
Castilian language, 51, 110, 127, 128, 129, 131, 166
Castro, Américo, 170
Catalan language, 122, 127, 130, 131

Catalonia: mentioned, 9, 11, 12, 13, 15, 17, 19, 22, 113; nationalism or secessionism in, 17, 52, 110, 121, 122, 126–28, 129, 130–35
Catholic Church: in Chile, 173; ideology of, in Spain, 9–10, 13, 49–53, 72, 115, 125; image of, 72–73; mentioned, 8, 70; power of, in Spain, 9, 10, 12, 23, 48–49, 67, 108, 110, 113–18, 166, 185; support of, for Franco, 13, 15, 16, 166; and Vatican II, 15
Catholicism: character of in Franco's Spain, 12–13, 15, 50–53, 166; mentioned, 8, 170
Cemeteries: for Union soldiers, 79; for Confederate soldiers, 83–84
Censorship: in Spain, 15, 52, 68; in the U.S. South, 53, 94, 95, 141, 144, 152
Century Magazine, 168
Chacón, Carme, 128, 135
Chamberlain, Daniel, 88
Chile, 172–73, 176
Cierva, Ricardo de la, 54, 68
Cinema: in Spain, 58
Cisneros, Gabriel, 18
Citizens Councils, 154
Civil Rights Act of 1964, 41, 98, 156
Civil Rights Movement, 41, 77, 97, 104, 106, 137, 169; economic impact of, 210–11
Civil war: costs of, in Spain, 2, 14; costs of, in the U.S., 2, 31–32
Civil War re-enactors, 102
Clean Hands (organization), 71, 118
Clinton, Bill: 162
Cobb, James, 160, 210
Cold War, 15, 40, 97, 169, 198
Coleman, James P., 154
Collins, LeRoy, 154
Commemorations, 3, 5, 46, 65; of Franco after his death, 59–60; role of Catholic Church in, 51; under Franco, 51, 55
Communism, 3, 10, 11, 12, 28, 50, 51, 52, 72
Communist Party: of Spain, 16, 19, 55–56, 62, 112
Concentration camps, 3, 14
Confederates, 47

Confederate States of America, 2, 29, 31, 187
Connor, Bull, 97
Constitutionalism, 8, 11, 20
Constitution of 1978, 18, 20, 73, 113, 166–67
Convergència i Unió, 121, 131, 132, 134, 135
Cooke, John Esten, 85
Cortes, 18, 19, 21
Cospedal, Dolores, 135
Counter-Reformation, 8
Cox, Karen, 95
Crimes against humanity, 71
Crusade: as description of Franco's uprising, 50, 72
Cuba, 10, 38, 90
Cuesta Bustillo, Josefina, 60
Culture: discussed, 5, 45, 101, 110, 136, 137, 144, 151, 159, 165–66, 195–96, 202, 214–15; in North and South of antebellum U.S., 27–28

Darwin, Charles, 144
Davis, Jefferson, 32–33, 82–83, 93
Declaration of Independence, 25, 26, 30, 31, 34, 76, 96, 97, 138, 164
De Klerk, Frederick, 181
Democracy, 8, 13, 22, 24, 52, 56, 57, 64, 68, 87, 97, 107, 174, 178, 183, 203
Democratic Party, 36–37, 40, 78, 92, 95, 108–9, 126, 137, 140, 143, 146, 149; change of ideology of, 110–11, 137, 155–57; regional schizophrenia of, 111, 147–50, 156
De Priest, Oscar Stanton, 39, 152
Disfranchisement, 37, 90, 92, 137, 142, 149, 206
Dixon, Amazi Clarence, 144
Dixon, Thomas, 92
Douglass, Frederick, 88–89
Du Bois, W. E. B., 96
Dueñas, María, 58

Early, Jubal, 84
Economic change: impact of, in Spain, 16, 192–93, 195, 197–202; impact of, in the U.S., 27, 28, 37–38, 39, 192–93; mentioned, 3, 192; in the South, 35–36, 41–42, 150–51, 158, 195, 207–8, 209–11, 214–15
Eisenhower, Dwight, 15, 40
Elites, 196, 198, 202, 203, 207; persistence in power of, 184–87
Elkins, Stanley, 90
El Mundo, 59, 67, 119, 120, 121, 122, 125–26, 129, 189
El País, 21, 63, 64, 73, 128, 166, 172, 186
El Salvador, 172
Emancipation, 3, 30–31, 32, 34, 86
Emancipation cause, 76, 81, 96, 98, 106
Emigration from Spain, 199, 200
Engels, Friedrich, 194, 202
Enlightenment, 8, 9, 44
Episcopal Conference of Spain, 50–51, 72, 117
Erasmus, 44
ETA (Euskadi Ta Askatasuna), 17, 18, 19, 23, 24, 25, 57, 70, 114, 120, 126, 166, 167
European Community, 21–23, 195
European Tribunal of Human Rights, 178
European Union, 201
Euskera language, 131–32
Evangelicals, 111
Executions: in Morocco, 172; in Spain, 2, 14, 51, 165;
Exiles, 2, 14, 47, 52, 60, 165, 170

Falange, 15, 52, 54, 69, 71, 177
Fascism, 11, 12, 13, 14, 45, 51, 52, 54, 62, 65, 109
Faulkner, William, 44, 82
Felipe II, 8, 54
Fernández de la Vega, María Teresa, 125
Fifteenth Amendment, 34, 92, 145, 165
Florida, 94, 151, 154, 157, 210
Forgiveness, 171, 180, 181, 182, 183
Fortune, T. Thomas, 88
Fourteenth Amendment, 34, 80–81, 90, 96, 165, 185
Fosas (common graves), 2, 14, 63, 65, 66, 69

Fraga Iribarne, Manuel, 16, 17, 112–13, 170, 188
France, 176
Franco, Francisco: as dictator, 14–17, 34, 107–8, 113, 135, 165, 170, 171, 177, 197–98; burial site of, 54; ideology of, 15–16, 51–53, 142, 149; as leader of military uprising, 13–14, 109; mentioned, 2, 11, 18, 47, 48, 49, 51, 59, 65, 70, 115, 119, 121, 148, 186, 188; statues of, 69
Freixas, Laura, 121, 133

Gaines, Bishop W. J., 89
GAL (Grupos Antiterroristas de Liberación), 23
Galicia, 12, 22, 69, 133–34, 196
Garcia-Cárcel, Ricardo, 67
García Lorca, Federico, 14, 177
García Vallada, Zacharías, 50
Garzón, Baltasar, 70, 71, 167, 175–78, 188
Gender roles: in Spain, 15, 53, 119, 120, 124, 125, 187; in the U.S., 83–84, 93–94, 100, 101, 149, 160–61
Georgia, 26, 32, 83, 95, 99, 100, 140, 143, 154, 157, 158, 160, 211
Germany, 13, 14, 172, 189
Gironella, José María, 58
Goldfield, David, 138, 144, 159
Goldwater, Barry, 99
González, Felipe, 20–23, 57, 112, 123, 128, 129
González de Txabarri, Joxe Joan, 132–33
Governmental structures: in Spain and U.S., 48
Graham, Billy, 151
Grant, Ulysses S., 94, 140, 168
Greeley, Horace, 139
Greener, Richard T., 89
Griffith, D. W., 92
Guardia Civil, 15, 20, 70, 122
Guatemala, 172

Hampton, Wade: quoted, 135
Harrison, Benjamin, 141

Harrison, Pat, 148
Hayes, Rutherford B., 35, 81, 168
Haygood, Atticus G., 145
Hellman, Lillian, 145
Herrero de Miñón, Miguel, 132, 135
Hill, Samuel S., Jr., 151
Historical memory: and changes in culture, 105–6; defined, 4; and generations, 46, 58–61; mentioned, 5, 6, 46; and Spanish politics, 64; and terms of debate, 61–62, 67
Hodges, Luther, 154
Hollings, Ernest "Fritz," 98–99, 159
Homosexuality, 115, 122, 124
Hope, John, 96
Hornero Méndez, César, 189–90
Human rights, 173–80, 189
Humphrey, Hubert, 153
Huyssen, Andreas, 60

Ideologies: clash of, 11, 13, 45, 51
Ideology: of African Americans in the U.S., 76; of Catholic Church in Spain, 10, 12; and family loyalties, 61, 63, 64, 103; and Franco's National Catholicism, 47, 49, 50–53, 55, 90; and generational change, 46, 47, 53–54, 59–60, 76–77, 84, 92–94, 100–104, 106, 111, 202–3; and memory, 3, 5, 45; mentioned, 7; of Nationalists in Spain, 3, 47; of North in U.S., 2, 76, 77–78, 103–5; of Republicans in Spain, 3, 47, 55; of South in U.S., 2, 25, 28, 47, 75–76, 79–80, 81, 82–83, 84, 86–87, 92, 141–42
Imperialism: in the U.S., 38–39, 90–91
Industrialization: in Spain, 8, 9, 197, 199, 200, 201; in the U.S., 27, 36, 37–38, 81, 136, 143, 150, 158, 164, 184, 205–6
Industrial recruitment: in South, 211–12
Inquisition, Holy Office of, 8, 9
Inter-American Court of Human Rights, 178
International brigades, 65
International law, 167, 175–80

International Monetary Fund, 199
Investment: foreign direct, in Spain, 201; by international organizations in Spain, 199; military, by U.S. in Spain, 198; military, in South, 210, 213

Jackson, Thomas "Stonewall," 82
Jefferson, Thomas, 86
Jesuits, 11
Jews, 3, 8, 50
Jim Crow laws, 37, 40, 99, 206
Jiménez de Parga, Manuel, 130
Jiménez Lozano, José, 68
Johnson, Andrew, 33, 34, 79, 80
Johnson, Lyndon, 25, 41, 42, 98, 111, 156, 161
Jones, Sam, 144
Judaism, 52
Juliá, Santos, 60
Junquera, Natalia, 63, 64, 172
Justice, 4, 167, 171, 172, 179, 181, 182, 183, 188, 189, 190, 191

Kennedy, John F., 41, 97–98, 155–56
Key, V. O., 146
King, Martin Luther, Jr., 41, 75, 97, 99, 156, 188
King Alfonso XIII, 11, 17
King Juan Carlos de Borbón: political role of, 17–18, 20, 131, 170; quoted, 8
King Mohamed VI, 172
Krog, Antjie, 182
Ku Klux Klan, 35, 80, 104, 140, 142, 187

Ladies Memorial Association, 83, 168
Laicism, 12, 115, 124, 125
La Razón, 66, 115, 119, 120, 122, 125, 129, 166
La Vanguardia, 115
Law of Historical Memory, 66, 69, 70, 203
Lazaga, Pedro, 58
League of the South, 101
Lee, Robert E., 81, 82–83, 93

Liberalism, 8, 52
Liberal Republican revolt, 139
Lincoln, Abraham, 26, 29, 30, 32, 47, 77–78, 79, 98, 104–5, 139, 164
Literature: in Spain, 58, 61; in the U.S., 84–87, 142
Lodge, Henry Cabot, 87
Loewen, James, 192
Longstreet, James, 82
López Facal, Ramón, 192
Lost Cause: as ideology of Southern elite, 75–76, 84, 85, 91, 93–94, 100, 141–42, 169, 184, 185, 187, 192, 195, 206; as modified over time, 77, 86–87; as support for racism, 75; 77, 85; triumph of, 81, 87–88, 89, 106, 137; waning of influence of, 100–103, 157, 162, 165, 195, 209, 210–11, 214–15
Louisiana, 99, 158, 212, 214
Low wages: in U.S. South, 205, 206, 207–9
Lula da Silva, Luiz Inácio, 173

Macías, Santiago, 49, 63
Madariaga, Salvador de, 170
Maddox, Lester, 157
Mandela, Nelson, 163, 183
Mandela, Winnie, 181
Manufacturer's Record, 146
Manzano, Eduardo, 191, 192
Marx, Karl, 1, 50, 202
Marxism, 20–21, 50, 52
Mas, Artur, 122, 127, 134
Masons, 3, 50, 52
Massachusetts, 36
Massive Resistance, 40, 154, 169
Mate, Reyes, 191
Mayor Oreja, Jaime, 116
McClure, Alexander Kelley, 89
McGill, Ralph, 145
McKinley, William, 90–91
McPherson, James, 104, 105
Memory. *See* Historical memory
Menem, Carlos, 172–73
Meredith, James, 155

Mexico, 176
Migration: in U.S. South, 208–9, 212, 214
Minow, Martha, 181
Mississippi, 83, 98, 99, 100, 140, 148, 151, 154, 155, 157, 158, 159, 160, 209, 210, 214
Mitchell, Margaret, 142
Moa, Pio, 61–62, 102
Mola Vidal, General Emilio, 15
Monseignor Olaechea, 50
Morocco, 10, 109, 170, 172
Morodo, Raúl, 7
Mowry, George, 136, 147
Mujica, José, 174–75
Mxenge, Churchill, 163, 181

NAACP, 39, 96, 102, 152
National Association of those Affected by Irregular Adoption, 71
National Catholicism: 51, 110, 53. *See also* Catholic Church; Catholicism; Franco, Francisco; Ideology
Nationalism, 44, 45; and problem of regional nationalisms in Spain, 113–14, 126–35
NATO, 15, 22
Navarre, 22, 110, 189
Navarro, Eduardo, 17
Neff, John, 79
New Deal, 208, 209
New York Times, 74, 78
Ngewu, Cynthia, 180
Nietos (grandchildren), 47, 60, 61, 63, 202
Nietzsche, Friedrich, 4
Nieva, Francisco, 44, 68, 189
Nixon, Richard, 99
North: goals of in Civil War, 30–31, 33, 35
North Carolina, 83, 150, 151, 154, 160, 206, 211, 212

O'Connor, June, 183
Obama, Barack, 100, 190
Olvido (forgetting), 42, 56, 58, 167
Omar, Dullah, 182

Opus Dei, 15, 16, 200
Oreja, Marcelino, 19
Organization for European Economic Cooperation, 199
Ortega y Gasset, José, 53, 130
Osorio, Alfonso, 18

Page, Thomas Nelson, 75, 84–85, 87
Parkman, Francis, 87
Parks, Rosa, 40
Parton, James, 87
Pemartín Sanjuán, José, 7
Pérez Rubalcaba, Alfredo, 21, 134–35
Philippines, 10, 38, 90
Phillips, Ulrich B., 95
Phillips, Wendell, 88
Pickett's Charge, 82
Pike, James Shepherd, 139
Pinochet, Augusto, 70, 173, 175–76, 188
Planck, Max, 99
Pope Benedict XVI, 112, 115–16
Pope John XXIII, 54, 115
Pope John Paul II, 72
Pope Pius IX, 10
Pope Pius XI, 13, 49
Popular Front, 12, 51
Populist Party, 36–37, 38, 143
PP (Partido Popular), 23–24, 60, 61, 64, 65, 66, 67, 69, 70, 108, 109, 110, 113; ideology of, 111, 114–15, 117–20, 125, 126; on regional nationalisms, 113–14, 121–22, 127, 129, 130–31, 135
Price, Reverend J. C., 89
Prieto, Indalecio, 170
Primo de Rivera, José Antonio, 54, 55, 59, 69, 70, 121, 170
Primo de Rivera, Miguel, 10–11, 197
Prisons, 2, 33, 51, 54, 65, 165, 189
Progressivism, 38–39, 91–92
Protestantism: and evangelicals in North and South, 48; in South, 144–45, 151, 160–61; mentioned, 8, 10, 52
PSOE (Partido Socialista Obrero

Español), or Socialists, 20–24, 57, 64, 66, 67, 108, 109, 110, 112, 113, 115–16, 118, 120; ideology of, 123–26; on regional nationalisms, 127–30
Public opinion: in Spain, 58, 88
Puerto Rico, 10, 38, 90
Pujol, Jordi, 121
Purges: in Spain, 3, 14

Racism: in Confederacy, 33; in North, 31, 38, 48, 77, 78, 80, 87–88, 136–39, 141, 153–54, 183–84; in South, 37, 75–76, 89, 97, 100, 108, 143–45, 159, 161, 185, 187, 214; in U.S., 27, 29; 30–31, 33, 38–39, 60, 79, 80, 87, 89, 90–92, 95–96, 110, 111, 147, 149, 165, 168, 210
Rajoy, Mariano, 24, 67, 112, 117, 119, 120, 121, 126, 129–30, 166
Randall, James G., 104
Reagan, Ronald: 99–100, 161
Reconciliation: limited terms of, 164–71; mentioned, 3, 5, 164, 196; in South Africa, 180, 182; in Spain, 54, 56, 57, 67, 114, 184–85; in the U.S., 164, 183–84; uneven terms of, 183–85
Reconquest, 8
Reconstruction, 3, 33–35, 47, 79–81, 88, 89, 106, 138, 139, 142, 165, 168, 183–84, 185, 187
Reformation, 8
Refugees, 2
Reparations, 173, 188
Republican Party (U.S.), 34, 108–9, 126; and absence of dedication to equality, 30–31, 34–35, 138–39; changing ideology and growth of in South, 42, 99–100, 110–11, 156, 161–62
Republicans: in Spain, 3, 47, 48, 52, 55, 58, 60, 61, 66, 67, 68, 69, 71, 108, 177, 202; in the U.S., 80, 99, 138, 139, 140, 141
Richards, Michael, 60, 163
Ridruejo, Dionisio, 53
Rivas, Darío, 188–89

Rivers, L. Mendel, 148
Robles, Gil, 170
Rodriguez, Teodoro, 49–50
Rodríguez Ibarra, Juan Carlos, 128–29
Roniger, Luis, 171
Roosevelt, Franklin, 111, 148, 149, 208
Roosevelt, Theodore, 91
Rose, Laura Martin, 93
Rousso, Henry, 60
Ruiz-Gallardón, Alberto, 117
Rutherford, Mildred, 94
Rutledge, David J., 194

Salgado, Elena, 119
Sánchez-Camacho, Alicia, 131
Scarborough, W. S., 89
Schurz, Carl, 139
Secession, 29–30, 136, 194
Second Republic of Spain, 11, 49, 55, 61–62, 109, 123, 197, 202
Secularism, 10–12, 115–16, 166. *See also* Laicism
Segregation, 37, 41, 76, 92, 96, 98, 99, 104, 137, 142, 145, 149, 151, 152, 154–55, 158, 187, 195, 207, 209, 210, 214
Service sector of economy, 198–99, 212
Shaler, Nathan, 88
Sherman, William Tecumseh, 2, 32, 47, 78
Silva, Emilio, 49, 63
Slave-holders: claims of, about paternalism, 91; defensiveness of, 18–19; power of, 27–28; pride of, after defeat, 79; rehabilitation of, image of, 84–86; role of, in sectional crisis, 49
Slavery: and religion, 30; defenses of, 28, 84–86, 101; discussed, 26–30, 47, 86, 110
Smalls, Robert, 88
Smedes, Susan Dabney, 85–86
Smith, Ellison "Cotton Ed," 148, 149, 209
Smith, Frank, 151–52
Social Darwinism, 88
Socialism, 10, 13, 52, 72

Sons of Confederate Veterans, 92, 95, 102, 144
South (U.S.): economic character of, 26–27, 143, 145–48, 150; economic elite in, 145–49, 159–60; political character of, 25, 27
South Africa, 179–83, 189
South Carolina, 26, 28, 31, 83, 88, 98, 99, 139, 142, 145, 148, 151, 153, 154, 157, 158, 159, 161, 194, 209, 212, 214
Southern Claims Commission, 139
Southern Historical Society, 81–83
Southern Manifesto, 153–54
Southern Poverty Law Center, 101
Southern Textile Bulletin, 146
Soviet Union, 40, 97
Spanish-American War, 10, 38, 90
States' rights, 34, 110, 194
Stephens, Alexander, 25, 31, 33, 79, 86, 164
Stone, Cornelia Branch, 93
Stout, Harry, 2
Stuart, J.E.B., 82
Suárez, Adolfo, 18–19, 108, 112
Sumner, William Graham, 87
Sunbelt, 100, 211, 213
Supreme Court (U.S.), 35, 37, 40, 81, 90, 98, 152, 154, 158
Switzerland, 176, 199
Syllabus of Errors, 10
Sznajder, Mario, 171

Taft, William Howard, 91
Tejero, Lieutenant Colonel Antonio, 20
Tennessee, 212
Territorial issue, 288–29
Terrorism: in Spain, 17, 19, 24; in the United States, 164. *See also* ETA
Texas, 94, 151, 210, 212, 213
Theft of infants and children, 71–72, 173, 178
Thirteenth Amendment, 165
Thurmond, Strom, 111, 153, 158
Tillman, Ben, 145

Tindall, George, 146
Tourism, 16, 198–99, 201–2
Transition, the, 17–19, 42, 47, 56–58, 60, 64, 67, 68, 69, 72, 107–8, 109, 112, 129, 130, 166, 170, 177, 185, 188, 192, 201, 202
Tribunal Constitucional, 117, 118, 119, 127, 130, 131, 134, 177
Tribunal Supremo, 71, 118, 131
Trotter, William Monroe, 96
Truman, Harry, 97, 153
Truth and reconciliation commissions, 171–72, 179–83
Tutu, Bishop Desmond, 180–81
"Two Cities," 50
"Two Spains," 8, 9, 11, 52, 136
"Two United States," 25, 36, 37, 43, 136, 142, 143–44, 147, 162, 208

UDC (Unión del Centro Democratico), 19, 108, 112
Unamuno, Miguel de, 7
Unemployment (or *paro*), 23
Union cause, 76, 77, 81, 106
United Confederate Veterans, 92, 95
United Daughters of the Confederacy, 84, 92–94, 95, 100, 144, 187
United Nations Committee Against Torture, 178, 179
United Nations Human Rights Committee, 175, 178, 179
Urbanization, 184, 197, 200, 202, 214
Urban League, 39
Uruguay, 173–75
U.S. Import-Export Bank, 199

Valley of the Fallen (Valle de los caídos), 49, 54, 70
Vallvey, Ángel, 166
Varela Ortega, José, 67
Vatican II, 15, 56
Vázquez, Tabaré, 174
Veterans' reunions, 168–69
Vidal, César, 61–62

Vidal-Quadros, Aleix, 107, 130–31
Virginia, 26, 30, 84, 85, 210, 213, 214
Voting Rights Act of 1965, 41, 98, 156

Wallace, George, 157, 158
Washington, Booker T., 91, 96
Watson, Tom, 143
Weber, Max, 67, 68
West, John C., 157
Whitney, Eli, 26
Whitten, Jamie, 159
Wilson, Woodrow, 39, 91–92, 148, 169
Wise, John S., 83

Wolfe, Thomas, 82
Women, southern, 83–84, 93–94
World Bank, 199
World War I, 39, 68, 208
World War II, 13, 39, 40, 52, 96–97, 150, 152–53, 197, 208, 209
Wright, Gavin, 207, 213

Young, Andrew, 158

Zapatero, José Luis Rodríguez, 24, 64, 66, 67, 112, 115–16, 118, 120, 123–25, 126, 129, 166

Paul D. Escott is Reynolds Professor of History Emeritus at Wake Forest University and the author of numerous books, including *Slavery Remembered: A Record of Twentieth-Century Slave Narratives*; *Many Excellent People: Power and Privilege in North Carolina, 1850–1900*; *"What Shall We Do with the Negro?": Lincoln, White Racism, and Civil War America*; and *The Confederacy: The Slaveholders' Failed Venture*.

* * *

The University Press of Florida is the scholarly publishing agency for the State University System of Florida, comprising Florida A&M University, Florida Atlantic University, Florida Gulf Coast University, Florida International University, Florida State University, New College of Florida, University of Central Florida, University of Florida, University of North Florida, University of South Florida, and University of West Florida.

www.ingramcontent.com/pod-product-compliance
Lightning Source LLC
Chambersburg PA
CBHW031432160426
43195CB00010BB/702